1984

Clinical Social Work in the Eco-Systems Perspective

SOCIAL WORK AND SOCIAL ISSUES
COLUMBIA UNIVERSITY SCHOOL OF SOCIAL WORK

CLINICAL SOCIAL WORK IN THE ECO-SYSTEMS PERSPECTIVE

Carol H. Meyer, Editor

COLUMBIA UNIVERSITY PRESS   NEW YORK   1983

Library of Congress Cataloging in Publication Data
Main entry under title:

Clinical social work in the eco-systems perspective.

(Social work and social issues)
Includes bibliographies and index.
Partial contents: The search for coherence / Carol H.
Meyer—The eco-systems perspective / Geoffrey L.
Greif and Arthur A. Lynch—Casework, a psycho-
social therapy / Richard D. Woodrow—[etc.]
1. Social case work—Addresses, essays, lectures.
I. Meyer, Carol H.   II. Series.
HV43.C534   1983   361.3′2   83-2124
ISBN 0-231-05194-8

COLUMBIA UNIVERSITY PRESS
NEW YORK AND GUILDFORD, SURREY

*Clothbound editions of Columbia University Press books are Smyth-sewn
and printed on permanent and durable acid-free paper.*

Contents

Part Three

The Contributors

Sandra Abrams, Social Worker, Columbia Presbyterian Hospital, New York, N.Y.

Geoffrey L. Greif, Adjunct Professor of Social Work, Widner University, Chester, Pa.

Rosemary Grieve, Clinical Instructor, Yale School of Nursing, New Haven, Conn.; clinical social worker in private practice.

Meredith Hanson, Clinical Instructor, Downstate Medical Center, Brooklyn, N.Y.

Arthur A. Lynch, clinical social worker in private practice, New York, N.Y.

Carol H. Meyer, Professor, Columbia University School of Social Work, New York, N.Y.

Barry Panzer, Mental Health Consultant, New York City Program for Sudden Infant Death, Brooklyn, N.Y.; clinical social worker in private practice.

Richard D. Woodrow, Lecturer, Columbia University School of Social Work, New York, N.Y.

Preface

The advance of professional thinking in clinical practice takes place in a number of ways. Some ideas march forward inexorably, without reference to external events and without regard for validation criteria. Like cats with nine lives, these ideas survive no matter the exigencies. They do so perhaps because the ideas are so powerful, because clinicians find them so useful or become habituated to them, or because there is no comparable substitute idea. Freudian psychoanalytic theory is an example.

Other ideas have opposite characteristics. They move forward modestly, almost with hesitation, for they rely upon empirical evidence to support their credibility. These ideas usually reflect scholarly work in circumscribed areas; they are communicated after long periods of inquiry, and their value is often recognized only incrementally, that is, until they evolve into identifiable practice models. Reid and Epstein's *Task-Centered Casework* (1972) is an example.

Then there are ideas that derive from professional/clinical experience, supported by a selected compilation of theories, and developed out of the minds of strong thinkers, good writers, effective teachers, and articulate practitioners. Professional people like these become leaders of schools of thought when they formulate what are commonly called "practice models." Such ideas are reflected in some of the social work practice approaches discussed in this book.

Of course there are also practice ideas that are fads, that may color the work of a generation of practitioners but then fade away. They are ideas to be reckoned with at the time they appear, but they do not seem to move professional thinking forward. Encounter groups of the 1960s are examples.

Finally, there are ideas that seem to have appeared from nowhere. At first they are viewed with suspicion and alarm, and then with dismay, for they offer a disjuncture with existing formulations of practice. True to Kuhn's view (1970) of changing paradigms being a response to a crisis in professional confidence, practices that have earned their legitimacy through their ideological power, empiricism, familiarity, or popularity can be seriously challenged by new paradigms which redefine problems or propose alternative perspectives. Such an idea is the developing ecological/general systems theory, or eco-systems perspective.

This book is about the use of the eco-systems perspective as a conceptual overhang, under which selected familiar, clinical (casework) approaches to social work practice are analyzed. We seek to illustrate the effect on these practice approaches or "models" of the use of the eco-systems perspective, and along the way, to clarify the current confusion of meanings regarding perspectives and models.

The professional task always is to make ideas and knowledge applicable to practice. Ideas in a profession cannot luxuriate in libraries and become goals in themselves. It is no simple task to accomplish the transition of thought to action. Practitioners are impatient, of course; they are eager to get to the "bottom line" that tells them what to do; they are not like academicians, who want to test the logic of the ideas and to know their origin. In the best of all professional worlds there should be less separation between practice and academic social workers and between theory and practice. Practitioners are always under real pressure to hurry and get things done effectively, and yet they are obligated as professionals to think things over critically before they accept ideas, just as academicians are obligated to consider the applicability and practicality of ideas.

Textbooks, manuals, and the like are often written to straddle the worlds of theory and practice that all social workers agree should not be separated. Casebooks are written to illustrate theory in action, while books about skills deemphasize theory and its logic and compile lists of guiding principles for action. The mode of this book is to present it all—theory, principles, and case illustrations—in such an exciting way that the book will be more compelling than a piece of shoptalk, or professional exchange among some theoretically oriented clinical social work practitioners.

In view of the complexity of the material, the book is addressed to professionally trained social workers and to graduate social work students. We have assumed that the reader will have a background in social work practice theory, beginning competence in the use of at least one direct practice approach in the social work repertoire, and awareness that social work is in need of "putting things together."

The choice of authors to carry the burden of this exploration was not arbitrary. Six of the authors were doctoral students at the Columbia University School of Social Work when the idea of this book was generated. They were talented and eager to take up the challenge of writing this book with me, and those were sufficient criteria to apply in choosing them. The seventh author was a practicing clinician in a psychiatric outpatient clinic. It was immediately after hearing her presentation of her work in a continuing education seminar the idea occurred to me that a book should be written about this kind of practice. It is not often that an approach to practice and two cases can be seen as having such heuristic value.

As scholars of practice the authors were able to analyze particular practice approaches without viewing themselves as "salespeople" or advocates. Throughout the writing process it was evident that we were all independent thinkers, determined in our search for coherence in practice. Not surprisingly, we, as well as the practice approaches presented here, were brought together by the eco-systems perspective.

This is totally a Columbia University School of Social Work book. It is written by Columbia students and a professor and it is part of the *Social Work and Social Issues* series in the Columbia University Press offerings. Despite its family-like characteristics, it is intended to be a book that will be useful in other places.

Thus prepared, the journey can begin.

CAROL H. MEYER
Columbia University School of Social Work

REFERENCES

Kuhn, Thomas. 1970. *The Structure of Scientific Revolutions.* 2d ed. Chicago: University of Chicago Press.

Reid, William J. and Laura Epstein. 1972. *Task-Centered Casework.* New York: Columbia University Press.

Acknowledgments

In keeping with the systemic orientation of this book, the search for its roots and its influences has turned up multiple sources. The past, present, and near future join, and people in a steady stream come to mind. Who is at the core of it all? How did it start? Where will it end? Of course there are no final answers; there is only salience.

It is time for me to express affectionate thanks to my teachers who cluster in the past. Gordon Hamilton, Lucille Austin, Florence Hollis, and Philip Klein are prominent among those who raised such startling questions as to have pushed me to seek coherence in social work practice even now. The present influences are quite naturally my Columbia colleagues, whose persistence and independence of mind cause me to keep trying to explain what I mean. The near future rests, of course, with students, and to those who have joined me in this endeavor and who have influenced me beyond repair, I offer thanks for closing the circle.

Clinical Social Work in the Eco-Systems Perspective

PART ONE

INTRODUCTION

Carol H. Meyer

Part One has two essays. My introductory paper explains the rationale of the enterprise and deals with some current issues in social
work practice that appear to be central to its future conduct. The
essay by Geoffrey L. Greif and Arthur A. Lynch is an exposition of
the eco-systems perspective, including its theoretical roots, the difference between ecology and general systems theory, and the potential impact of the use of the perspective upon traditional practice
approaches.

I

THE SEARCH FOR COHERENCE

Carol H. Meyer

There are two purposes that we hope will be served by this book. First, we want to clarify the often confusing professional debates about perspectives and practice approaches in social work. Through the sorting out of terminology, modes of thought, and theoretical commitments we seek to transform ideologically tinged debate into more rational dialogue. The related second purpose is to contribute to a desirable consensus among social work practitioners. Adherents to clinical practice in their use of psychosocial orientations, behavioral, and problem-solving methods, often seem to pursue individual ends, making it very difficult to affirm that there is a coherent social work practice. Lessening of internal professional dissension should help social workers to turn their collective attention to other matters of concern. Believing that the route to coherence is not through integration of practice approaches that are inherently different in a number of dimensions, but rather is through the use of an integrating perspective, we offer the eco-systems construct as the conceptual umbrella beneath which all clinical practitioners can practice with an eclectic repertoire to carry out a common purpose.

The Roots of Fragmented Practice Purposes

Social work may have been the most complex endeavor to develop into a profession. Unlike other professions, it did not originate with a coherent purpose as in medicine or law. Casework, from which the preponderant social work methodology derived, evolved from voluntarism, philanthropy, and agency-based apprenticeship. Its ideological roots were in religious, charitable, and essentially sentimental views of services, expectations of client behavior, and problem definitions. The profession has been shaped by these early lay interpretations for almost one hundred years. Indeed, one can find in practices in child welfare, for example, remnants of the nineteenth-century ideology that persist even into the 1980s. The singular coherent purpose that existed before Mary Richmond codified social casework could be described as something like moral uplift. As social work struggled to become a profession, it sought a purpose that would govern all its activities. Lacking such a common bond, caseworkers before 1929 pursued purposes that were defined by the settings in which they practiced—hospitals, clinics, family and child welfare agencies and so forth. In the last fifty years, tentative *methodological* purposes were attempted in casework, group work, and family treatment. Naturally, these could not serve as unifying professional social work purposes.

The reform movement in social work had different roots from those of social casework and the other methods. These roots were essentially located in the settlement house movement. As a sociopolitical endeavor it was not concerned with the development of methodology; its purpose was social reform, a goal that was hardly subject to the influence of a particular practice approach. Group work as a method began in settlement houses but matured in the same kinds of settings as those in which caseworkers functioned, thereupon developing its own methodology that separated it from the reform movement.

The reform impulse in social work has been translated over time into environmental interventions which have been highlighted in community organization and some current generalist practice approaches. This development has the capacity to introduce still different practice purposes that are larger than either traditional casework or group work purposes.

Family treatment as a modality in social work has its own defined purposes that are related to interventions in internal family processes. Thus, it becomes quite obvious that when traditional case-work, group work, community organization, and family treatment methods and social reform efforts are placed alongside each other, each with methodology derived from different knowledge bases and purposes evolving out of different contexts and perspectives, any effort to join them at their foundation would be futile. An alternative approach noted in the newer generalist practice models has been to "begin again" and to redefine the practice enterprise, crossing over the methods boundaries and emphasizing common processes.

As social work gradually and painfully evolved into a profession, many individual and group efforts have been made to define over-arching professional purposes. The Milford Conference (1929) and the O'Hare Conference on conceptual frameworks (1979) cited in *Social Work* (January 1981) are examples of such efforts. Within these fifty years when practice approaches proliferated, not only among methods and modalities but also within the framework of each modality, social work practitioners developed ideological commitments to various models. In 1983 there are major schools of thought associated with a host of different approaches within casework, group work, family treatment, and the so-called generalist models that include cross-method approaches. It has become increasingly difficult to claim a unitary practice approach in social work.

An Emerging Consensus about Social Work Purpose

Whether or not the profession at large accepts the proposed definition of social work purpose, social workers are aware that this or some reasonable adaptation of it will be necessary so as to ensure professional (as opposed to methodological) survival. The most widely accepted definition of social work purpose that was developed at the O'Hare Conference on conceptual frameworks is: "To promote or restore a mutually beneficial interaction between individuals and society in order to improve the quality of life for everyone" (*Social Work* [January 1981:6]).

The alternative to acceptance of some such definition of purpose is continuing reliance upon individual ideas supported by belief, ideology, and group interest, as to what social work should be about. As far as practice is concerned, that is precisely its status now. There are dozens of approaches, some empirically based, but no less free than other approaches of theoretical value biases and ideology. Ideology has been defined as a representation of "the manner in which human beings meet their needs in the context of society through symbolic models of reality which legitimate individual and group interests through reductive abstractions" (Kinloch 1981:16).

Social workers, being human and having individual and group interests, seek to support these interests just as do other groups in society seek to support theirs. In a sense, the very choice of knowledge used, or unit of attention addressed, or methodology applied in the construction of practice models is political and determined by value commitments to some degree. Then, when multiple groups express their multiple group interests, confusion, contradictions, and conflicts over theoretical turf become prevalent. That is why it is usually best, in the interests of higher professional (self-) interests, for these separate group interests to seek common purposes. However, method by method and approach by approach, it is not possible through additive means to achieve a unifying professional purpose; a linkage between method and purpose needs to be established.

This book seeks to offer a stepping-stone toward agreement with social work's current definition of professional purpose, or some modification in its wording. It is our judgment that the intervening of a common perspective for practice is needed, because the leap from the present status of proliferating models to the status of universal professional agreement is too large, both conceptually and politically. Since 1970 several generalist social work practice models have been created exactly for the purpose of bringing together multiple methods, processes, and units of attention (Pincus and Minahan 1973; Goldstein 1973; Germain and Gitterman 1980). These generalist social work models have reached toward the goal of commonality in social work practice, but they have not been able to achieve consensus for some large sectors of the professional community who remain committed to traditional practice models.

Further, the issue of "clinical social work" remains unresolved, perhaps because clinical practitioners have been unable to find a perspective compatible with the newer generalist models. Some clinical practitioners might feel that no single practice model can account in depth for all case situations, or that the newer models contain too broad a focus for the depth in which some individual cases need to be treated. Many clinical practitioners have attempted to "stretch" their casework models to account for family, group, and environmental interventions. Others have attempted to develop true eclectic repertoires to enable them in practice with client groups to deal with problems and organizational constraints that had not been addressed by the traditional casework models. It is in support of this latter approach to the proliferating models that this book is written. Its intention is to show that an eco-systems perspective requires an eclectic use of practice models, that this perspective is syntonic with the emerging purposes of social work as a profession, and that it is not dystonic with the practice interests of clinical practitioners.

Clinical Social Work Practice

Clinical practice has become one of those rubrics (ideas? approaches? titles?) that is definable through the eyes of the beholder. Despite our awareness that official definitions do not always serve underlying purposes and activities, it is evident that the NASW definition of clinical social work is the place to begin to understand the phenomenon.

The Board of the NASW *Register of Clinical Social Workers* (April 1976) set forth the following definition:

> A Clinical Social Worker is, by education and experience, professionally qualified at the autonomous practice level to provide direct, diagnostic preventive, developmental, supportive and rehabilitative services to individuals, families, and/or groups whose functioning is threatened or affected by social and psychological stress or health impairment.
>
> Clinical Social Work is practiced under the auspices of public, voluntary or proprietory agencies and institutions which address familial, economic, health, recreational, religious, correctional, judicial and/or educational concerns, or within a private office.

The Register goes further to identify exactly what the NASW views as a clinical practitioner by stating:

> This involves direct practice with a client/patient on a one to one, one to family, or one to group basis. Except for those applying under [certain] provisions, methods of social work practice NOT acceptable for the purpose of this Register include Administration, Community Organization, Social Planning, Supervision and Consultation, Teaching, Research or Research Interviewing.

A cursory review of the curricula of schools of social work, as well as a review of social work agencies and institutions and all practice models in social work, would show clearly that the NASW definition of clinical social work practice is identical with what is universally understood to be direct social work practice. In effect, those social work activities that are not eligible for listing in the *Register*, according to the guidelines, underline the point that clinical social work is direct, "hands-on" social work practice. The definition does not suggest *a* model of clinical practice, nor does it specify any personality theory.

Given the authority of the NASW to define the terms of its membership's professional identity, little more would have to be said about clinical social work practice. Yet, there remain issues to be clarified, code-word implications to be illuminated, and theoretical differences to be aired.

An historical explanation would be helpful to the understanding of the persistence in social work of a two-track system of direct social work practice, even despite the commendable effort of the NASW to combine the interests of practitioners in both of these "tracks." The "tracks" might be defined as "clinical" and "direct practice." The story begins in the 1960s, although its roots go further back, perhaps to 1917. In the 1960s the civil rights and peace movements had significant effects upon professions, education, and all "establishment" institutions. An important consequence of that social unrest which was taken to the streets and into once private and autonomous educational and professional sites was that the entire system of help was opened up. In social agencies, hospitals, and clinics populations like minority groups, very poor people, and others who had felt left out of social work services as well as health services demanded entrance into the systems of help and care. This political reality challenged social work practitioners in hitherto unthought of ways. They were times of crisis for all professionals who had to rethink their purposes and their practices.

At the time of this emerging social change, social casework was the predominant social work practice modality, and although there were quite different practice approaches or models being used, such as psychosocial casework, psychosocial therapy, behavior modification, functional casework, problem-solving casework, and crisis intervention, among others (Roberts and Nee 1970) casework was mistakenly understood to be a kind of unilateral approach to social work practice. For reasons that will be best understood in the reading of essays 3, 4, 5, and 6, social casework, addressed to selective clientele or types of problems and not to the general population, was viewed as dysfunctional for its times. Further on in this paper some of the characteristics of the casework models that made them vulnerable to the charges of having been "irrelevant" will be discussed.

There was a series of social work responses to the social upheaval. There was a strong political response among many social workers who assumed radical positions in regard to service delivery and modes of help, and there also were social workers who withdrew from the fray and pursued their familiar goals. Hindsight indicates that social workers were like everyone else, they reacted in individual ways to the events of the 1960s. But there was also a serious response in the efforts of some to redefine practice so that it would become more appropriate for the times. As new practice approaches developed they naturally sprang from the practice orientations of the theoreticians involved (Meyer 1970, 1976; Pincus and Minahan 1973; Goldstein 1973; Siporin 1975). In keeping with internal philosophic and theoretical changes taking place within social work (Bartlett 1970, William Gordon 1965, Gordon Hearn 1958) and reflecting new knowledge (von Bertalantfy 1965; Hartmann 1958; White 1963) these new practice approaches all defined themselves as social work practice. Having found it impossible to "stretch" traditional practice models—be they in casework, group work, or community organization—the newer practice approaches all sought to enlarge the scope and purposes of practice so as to respond more effectively to the demands of the times and new knowledge. The movement from casework to social work was more than semantic; it meant ultimately that family, group, community, and organizational interventive approaches were to be included under the heading of social work practice, and that new efforts were to be made to intervene in the client's environment.

The early development of these practice orientations—some were understood to be new approaches while others were understood to be new ways of defining practice—indicated right away that issues like the gain in scope of intervention, coverage of client problems, span of professional attention, practice repertoire, and skills to be expected of new graduates, were going to mean a change in the identity, role, and function of the caseworker, group worker, and community organizer. The practitioner came to be defined as *social worker,* but in the ensuing ten years, from the early 1970s to the early 1980s, three interesting phenomena occurred. A group work conference was held in Cleveland in 1980 to revive interest in group work, and a community organization conference was held in Louisville in 1981 to revive interest in community organization. As for casework, it is our view that the interest in revival of the casework role began much earlier, in the early 1970s when the Association of Clinical Social Workers was formed. In 1979 a conference on clinical social work was held in Denver (Ewalt 1980). It would seem, from the historical perspective, that clinical social work actually might be the re-emergence of social casework.

But one must contemplate the reason for using the term clinical rather than casework, a transposition that has obscured an explanation of the confusion. Once again, an historical review would be illuminating. In the 1960s, not only was the system of help challenged so as to include more potential clients, the professional membership itself was challenged to include those who had not hitherto been included. For this and other reasons, the NASW and the Council on Social Work Education worked to create an undergraduate level of social work education. Social workers with the degree of Bachelor of Social Work (BSW) were perceived to be a previously excluded population, now eligible for professional status, and the BSW cadre was expected to staff the public agencies where broader population groups were to be the potential clients in need of services. Once the BSW social worker was included in the professional social work family, the title of social worker, and its subsystem companion title of caseworker, was no longer confined to a professional with the degree of Master of Social Work (MSW). It should be noted that the term "caseworker," which has been used in public welfare since the depression, always troubled professional social workers when public welfare caseworkers were not professionally trained. The BSW level of entry apparently highlights this problem, institutionalizing the long-time interests of MSW's to distinguish their status from non-MSW's; be they non-professional or BSW.

This might have been reason enough for the shift of title from caseworker to clinical social worker, but there were other events taking place in the field, namely, a burgeoning private practice movement and the development of third-party payments in the mental health field. These developments indicated to qualified MSW social workers that there was need for a differentiation in professional status. In the nursing profession it has always been recognized that a registered nurse has different qualifications than a practical nurse. Today, in the nursing profession there are, of course, nurse clinicians.

The first NASW Register of Clinical Social Workers supports this historical interpretation through its statement of goals and objectives among which are:

> To encourage the acceptance of the NASW Register standards as criteria for key clinical social service positions . . . assist third party payment vendors to improve service standards . . . through professional recognition and contract inclusion of clinical social workers.

The Register's definition of eligibility as a clinical social worker includes "a master's or doctoral degree in social work." Thus, through educational qualifications, the clinical social work title and professional status are protected, and the distinction between MSW and BSW ensured. Our interpretation of the meaning of clinical social work practice is political and not theoretical. This interpretation and the NASW definition make possible the view that direct social work practice and clinical social work practice possibly are identical. The direct practice/casework/clinical practice approaches that follow in this book are applicable to the direct/clinical practitioner in social work, whether that practitioner be called clinician, caseworker, or social worker.

Social Casework Approaches to Practice*

Social casework, like clinical social work, has many definitions. It has been viewed as an individualizing process (Cannon 1954; Meyer 1970) wherein no particular model is suggested, but merely the notion that individuals, families, and groups can be sorted out from the mass. More commonly, it has also been defined theoretically as a particular knowledge base and methodology articulated so that it can be taught and practiced as an integral model. The casework theoreticians of note, only a few of whom are represented in this book, are well known in social work and each had different views of people and emphasized different kinds of intervention. Among the major original theorists were: Mary Richmond (1917) who originated the idea of social (as opposed to medical) diagnosis of human problems; Gordon Hamilton (1940) who developed the psychosocial orientation of casework that predicted the broad knowledge base and the dual focus of interventions with the person and environment; Virginia Robinson (1930) and Jessie Taft (1937), who developed the idea of problems defined by agency function, and elaborated on the processes involved in casework practice; and Bertha Reynolds, who emphasized the impact of the social/political environment upon people's lives.

Helen Harris Perlman, whose casework approach is discussed in detail in paper 4 defined casework as problem-solving, and Florence

*The reader will note alternate use of *approach* and *model* (model sometimes enclosed in quotes). I have questioned before the use of the term "model" (Meyer 1973a) as being too pretentious and prescriptive for the state of the art of practice approaches. However, the term is in current usage, so we will use it—with some ambivalence.

Hollis, whose work is discussed in paper 3 defined it as psychosocial therapy. The sociobehaviorists, discussed in paper 5 introduced an empirical base to the casework process, relying heavily upon environmental reinforcement of observable behaviors. Howard Parad (1965) and Lydia Rapoport (1970) defined crisis intervention as a smaller system of psychosocial casework. As discussed in paper 6 this approach is in a state of radical theoretical change.

In current casework thinking, there has been progress in developing empirical models in casework. Joel Fischer's *Effective Casework Practice* (1978) and William Reid and Laura Epstein's *Task-Centered Casework* (1972) are prime examples of this development. In these approaches, methodology is addressed to determining what works for clients, with heavy emphasis upon an empirical, step-by-step feedback process between worker and client. While other casework approaches, both traditional and in process of development, are available, those that have been mentioned should be sufficient to support our observation that casework is not a unitary practice model; it is an approach in social work practice that deals with people's psychosocial problems, but in different modes depending upon the knowledge base used, the unit of attention addressed, the goals of the approach in question, and the methodology involved.

In the course of identifying the elusive "clinical" component in casework, works such as Herbert Strean's *Clinical Social Work* (1978) have brought to the forefront some important issues relevant to the psychotherapeutic theme that may well be the latent characteristic of clinical social work. The psychotherapeutic motif, drawn from psychoanalytic theory, has had both beneficial and mischievous effects upon the casework process. Psychotherapy as a goal of casework would not meet the requirements of the person-situation purposes of social work, if only because of the "person" emphasis in the term *psycho*therapy. Hollis sought to bring the concept into the purview of social work through her idea of psycho*social* therapy, but some question remains as to whether or not her approach could be "stretched" to account sufficiently for environmental interventions (see essay 3).

The psychoanalytic knowledge base of psychotherapy, *Clinical Social Work* (Strean), relying as it does upon work with unconscious intrapsychic conflict and ego as defense mechanism, requires a methodology that includes working through transference manifestations, for example. This practice approach has a rich tradition and is appropriate for particular kinds of people with particular kinds of problems. As such, it might well have been included in this book as an example of a casework approach. However, we have chosen to include Hollis' psychosocial therapy interpretation instead because her approach is screened through social work knowledge, values, and purpose, and is not derived directly and solely from psychoanalytic theory, as is psychotherapy. We view psychotherapy as a generic practice across disciplines. Having its own validity, it is not totally syntonic with the professional social work definition of purpose, but it is a subsystem of psychosocial therapy.

Casework Overtaken by Events

We have discussed the fact that casework has many faces, and yet the criticisms heaped upon it from within the profession have been undifferentiated. The linear methods of social casework were designed to improve people's lives in selected ways, but they came to be viewed as grand theories, and thus were criticized for not addressing grander problems. In the heat of the 1960s and early 1970s some of the criticisms bordered upon hyperbole, and we shall consider some of these now as pejorative due to the heightened political sensitivity of those times. The fact that casework could not deal with macro problems of poverty, racism, and other social problems was evident, for broad social change could never have been its purpose. The purpose of social casework was always narrower than the purposes of social work, in view of its boundaries that did not include community work, social policy, or social planning. At best, it worked in a situational context (Siporin 1972) or with a transactional focus. The misunderstanding of its purview and potential utility created negative attacks that seemed to some unfair, but events overtook the practice of casework nevertheless.

Casework and the Medical Model

One of the nonsubstantive arguments that derived from this period had to do with the "medical model," a term which was overused as a code word for blaming the victim. "Medical" was associated with a "disease" view of client situations, in that if something in a case was dysfunctional, the cause was viewed as resting in the client's psychopathological problem. Analysis of the casework approaches represented in this book suggests that this was not entirely so. In all the models the psycho*social* event was a given, but the choice and location of interventions seemed to occur predominantly with the client as the source of the problem and resource for change. The client's environment, or the social side of his or her situation, was often neglected. No casework approach has ever stated explicitly that this interventive choice necessarily indicated a treatment focus on psychopathology, but the structural limitations of the approaches made for a preoccupation with the person over the environment.

The medical model criticism also had to do with assumptions of "cure" of problems, as if psychosocial problems were the same as physical problems, especially those that were subject to germ contagion. Emotional problems, having been associated in psychoanalytic theory with intrapsychic conflict and psychological development, were also viewed as curable, following the practice of psychoanalysis. Psychoanalytic theory is part of the knowledge base of several casework models, but a psychoanalytic theory of personality (as knowledge, not as psychoanalytic practice) is insufficient as an explanatory base for psychosocial practice that has the purpose of intervening at the intersection of person and environment, in the psychosocial event. Furthermore, psychoanalytic practice techniques, always leaning toward cure of an imbalanced intrapsychic system, are limited in their usefulness both in the immediate current functioning of a person and in the environmental side of the psychosocial equation. Social work clinical practice strategies are governed by the person-environment professional purpose, and even when they are tilted toward intervention with the person, these techniques are not the same thing as psychoanalytic techniques.

So many issues were exploited through the arguments about the medical model that it could fairly be said that the criticism was overdetermined and colored by the realities and political circumstances of the times. The term itself suggests inaccurate generalities. Medicine has been moving away from the pursuit of germs as the primary cause of illness and has become more interested in multiple causation, noxious environments, and preventive medicine. Even in medicine, the goal of cure has been exchanged for the more achievable goal of (relative) health. Casework was associated with medicine from the beginning, when Mary Richmond's reference group was doctors (Germain 1971) and she incorporated some of their medical characteristics into her conception of *Social Diagnosis*. It has occurred to me that had Mary Richmond been associated with dentists, caseworkers instead of pursuing the medical model might well have adopted the preventive model of seeing their clients twice a year.

The later concerns of the developing mainstream of practice in social work that became interested in environmental intervention, transaction, coping, adaptation, and competence, lead to an extreme rejection of such psychoanalytic notions as psychopathology and the underlying psychoanalytic conceptions of intrapsychic conflict which were considered to be too deterministic. While it is beyond the scope of this article to expand further upon this area of knowledge, it should be noted that the 1980s have offered evidence in psychiatry as well, of a shift in the focus of problem definitions that once derived from solely intrapsychic causation.

The Psychiatric Classification System: Diagnostic Manual III (DSM III) and the interest in *Eco-Psychiatry* (APA 1979) are but two examples, although debate continues as to the definitions and causes of pathological behaviors and psychological stress. Yet, the criticism of casework remained; the reaction against psychoanalytic theory being extended, through erroneous logic, to a rejection of social casework, when they were never the same thing in the first instance. This reaction to social casework in the late 1960s and the 1970s by many in social work may have contributed to its own antithesis in the emerging of clinical social work. However, as noted above, we seek to differentiate any particular practice model of psychoanalytically based clinical social work from the clinical social work definition being promoted by the NASW, which does not specify the knowledge base or the depth of interventive directions to be taken by the clinical social worker. In our view, there are multiple practice models that qualify as "hands-on" clinical practice (Meyer 1982).

Structural Limitations in Social Casework

Historically, there have been continuing efforts in social casework to bring together conceptually the psychosocial aspects of the social work "case." Notable among these efforts were those of Bertha Reynolds and Gordon Hamilton. Selections from their writings cannot do justice to their significance, but a few sentences will remind us of the long-time professional struggle to bring together the notion of psychosocial, albeit in a linear way. (It should not be overlooked that both these theorists were psychoanalytically oriented, although not preoccupied with psychoanalytic interpretations of psychosocial events.)

Bertha Reynolds said:

> Social Casework helps people to test and understand their reality, physical, social and emotional, and to mobilize resources within themselves and in their physical and social environment to meet their reality or to change it (1951:131).

Gordon Hamilton said:

> The strength of social work lies in its ability to operate at both ends of the psychosocial event, in its refusal to limit itself either to the manipulation of external factors alone, even though this is one of its traditional and proper concerns, or to the treatment of the inner factors alone, even though the latter has been vastly tempting (1952:318).

These observations could not more clearly define the domain of social casework as being that of the person-in-environment or the psychosocial event. Even though these great thinkers predated the development of systems ideas and transactional concepts, they were able to think in comprehensive terms and to avoid narrow preoccupations. Whether their ability to take intellectual risks and achieve a kind of brilliance in their thoughts and writing was due to their backgrounds and experiences, or whether social work simply was accidentally graced by their presence, they surely were precursors of the professional purposes as they are currently defined. Yet, even though they attempted to span person and environment, they were limited by the knowledge and language available to them in the 1930s, 1940s, and 1950s. In a world that might have appeared to be more stable, linear relationships were sufficient for these caseworkers; they still were able to transcend the boundaries of person and environment in their practice conceptualizations.

The dictionary defines *linear* as meaning "the relationship between two variables such that a change in one is accompanied by a proportional change in the other." Linear as a concept can be visualized as a line on a graph connecting two points. The concept can be understood as transactional in the sense that "a change in one is accompanied by a proportional change in the other." So the original practice theorists in social casework pursued the connection between psychological and social variables within a linear formulation available to them before the 1960s. This formulation permits only a dual focus and cannot allow for multiple events (causation) occurring at the same time; as the term linear implies, it is confined to viewing point A to point B or A to C and thus defines case situations in a narrow perspective.

Examples of linear, psychosocial practice approaches, or models as they have come to be called, proliferated in the 1950s and early 1960s, but among the most well-known are those devised by Florence Hollis, *Psychosocial Therapy* 1964; Helen Harris Perlman, *Casework: A Problem-Solving Process* (1957); Edwin J. Thomas et al., *Socio-Behavioral Approaches* (1967); and Howard Parad, ed., *Crisis Intervention* (1965). These models have remained, with only minor modifications, to the present as the approaches most often used in direct social work practice.

Despite the commitment of these approaches to interventions that address psychosocial problems, there has been a persistent structural problem in their conceptualization that has made it difficult for any of these approaches to account for phenomena beyond the scope of their defined interventions. None of them can serve as "grand theories" of practice, although many practitioners have used them as if they could. There is no challenge intended to their validity or utility when they are used appropriately, in the right case situation at the right time and in the right place. The challenge is to their use on all occasions, as if they were intended to explain the multidimensional variables in all case phenomena (Meyer 1973a). No linear perspective can explain systemic events, although systemic perspectives can allow for linear interventions.

Imbalance of Cause and Effect

A line connecting two psychosocial points requires that an equation be defined in order for one event to affect a proportional change in the other. This equation has been difficult to define and prove, because human life, as opposed to controlled laboratory experiments, is full of intervening variables. It is not possible to hold two events constant so as to determine precisely the effect of one upon the other. For example, in the case of a problem of truancy, one might treat a child and help him to remain in school, or intervene with a schoolteacher to improve the school environment. It is possible that either one of those interventions will eventuate in the child returning to school, and even more possible that both interventions will guarantee success if the child returns problem-free to an improved school environment. However, other multiple intervening events would always affect the outcome of either intervention in unpredictable ways. In such a case, one might consider the family's concerns and behavior, the responses of the child's school friends, the culture and safety of the neighborhood, and the support systems in the school, as variables that could combine to chart the course of the case, and even explain its outcome.

The linear, one-to-one relationship between cause and effect, or child and schoolteacher, is difficult to establish. At the least, a practitioner would need a clear picture of the complex, interrelated components in the case before determining which methodological intervention to use. In the example just described, multiple interventions might be more appropriate. Depending upon the needs and resources, one could envision casework methods with the child, family treatment with the family, group work with the child and his friends, and/or organizational intervention with the school bureaucracy.

To approach this case with any method at the outset, would be to miss alternate and perhaps more effective interventions. As no method is applicable to all the possibilities, a comprehensive, systemic assessment is required first. The decision as to what to do, and what practical approach to use, once having recognized the relatedness of the variables, will depend upon considerations of salience, accessibility of various actors, potential for improvement, available resources in the client and in the environment, and the practitioner's competence.

Imbalance of Knowledge and Skill

For an equation to be established between two psychosocial points in a case, there has to be some degree of parity in knowledge and skills related to both arenas of intervention. Psychological, personality, or behavioral theory is, as is well known, integrated and coherent in its own right. There are dozens of such theories, each commanding its own major theorists, schools of thought, literature, and indications for practice in multiple disciplines. Whether a social caseworker uses behavioral, psychoanalytic, or ego theory, it is possible to become learned in that theory and adept in utilizing it in some social work practice approach. (It is understood that social work practitioners do not practice personality theories undiluted, and that they are governed by social work purposes, values, and knowledge, and thus work through the medium of social work approaches.)

Environmental knowledge is not coherent or comprehensive in the same way as is knowledge about human growth and development, behavior, coping and adaptation, or psychopathology. The practitioner has to accumulate a kind of package of theories drawn from many theoretical sources in order to develop a knowledge base to inform practice interventions in the environment. So as to practice within the parameters set forth by social work's professional purposes, a clinical practitioner must call upon theory that is outside the boundaries of social casework approaches; these approaches cannot "stretch" because they are defined at the outset to deal with narrower events. However environment is defined, it would surely, in individual cases, call upon knowledge of family theory, organizational theory, theories about support networks, theories of the physical environment, and so on. Beyond knowledge there are, of course, practice skills to be mastered, and environments do not present themselves for interventions as readily as do people.

It becomes clearer why it has been so tempting for caseworkers to become preoccupied with the person side of the equation. As long as the linear equation exists, linear, either/or choices have to be made. In the balance between person and environment theories person-oriented skills are the easiest to develop and master because they are derived from clear and concise theoretical implications. I have mentioned elsewhere that as in a jigsaw puzzle, the figured pieces are the ones to be put together first; the vast blue sky has so little definition, it is hard to work with and since it is viewed as background the pieces of blue sky are usually put in place last. Personality theories have offered definition to practice skills, while the "vast blue sky" of the environment, not yet clearly subject to direct interventions, is left to chance attention. This has all occurred because of the structural limitations of linear methods; it has not been necessarily due to mischievousness on the part of caseworkers, nor a bias against environmental concerns. The bias may be in the structure of the models, not in the intentions or value commitments.

New developments in psychological theory have eased the constraints of the dichotomous knowledge areas, although they have not resolved the either-or issues. Modern ego psychology has certainly expanded the boundaries of psychoanalytic personality theory, for example. The notions of object-relatedness, adaptation, coping, mastery, and competence have brought psychological dynamics out from intrapsychic emphasis toward relatedness to the environment. None of these functions can be effective without some response from the environment; they are all transactional phenomena. Clinicians who work with a client's ego development and functioning soon discover that concomitant work with the client's environment is necessary so as to make it possible for the person to relate, to cope, and to achieve mastery and competence in his or her life.

Clinicians who are effective in this kind of practice also become aware that successful functioning of autonomous ego inevitably affects the state of unconscious conflict within the client through changes in self-image, self-confidence, and mature responses to the environment. Thus, there is rich reward to be obtained from the use of ego psychology as the knowledge base in personality theory.

Yet, the problem of polarization between psychosocial events is still not resolved through the use of ego theory. Adaptativeness for example, is not a one-time event, nor can it be achieved through mastering a single life task or coping with a particular problem. Adaptation is a process by which the ego deals with reality; it is ongoing, multidirectional, and somewhat unpredictable. We are still faced with having to provide a wider conceptual context for practice, one that will permit the clinician to see the array of possibilities in case situations for adaptation through mastery and coping. And, of course, since adaptation must be directed at impinging environments so that some reciprocal adaptation occurs, there is still the environmental knowledge, splintered as it is, that has to be included in the clinician's repertoire. That is, if the psychosocial paradigm is to continue to serve the purpose of social work, social work clinicians will have to develop skills to intervene in people's impinging environments.

In the matter of interventive skills, there are structural imbalances in this area as well. A linear perspective of psychosocial problems requires that not only knowledge, but also interventions occur in one or another side of the equation. To the extent that the security of knowledge tends to direct clinicians to choose psychological interventions, the case is not always served in the most appropriate way when environmental interventions are called for. This difficulty is ameliorated somewhat when case situations are understood in a transactional perspective, but it still is not resolved. The conceptualization of a case situation can be holistic, viewed as integrative of person and environment and be neutral as to the source or cause of dysfunction, yet interventions do have to take place either directly with the person or with forces in the environment. The transactional view is conceptual, not practical; one can recognize and be directed in one's practice by the reciprocal impact of person and environment, but concrete skills are applicable only in one or the other arena.

Cases can be defined transactionally; one can think about transactions, visualize the reciprocity of the person and environment, know bridging concepts such as are found in modern ego theory, communications theory, and general systems theory, but in the end, interventions have to be directed to the person or environment—there are, after all, boundary considerations involved. What is the difference, then, if one uses a linear or a systemic perspective for viewing the dynamics in a case? If in the concrete sense, skills cannot transcend the person-environment boundaries, what is the use of broadening the conceptualization of person-environment? The purpose (which is elaborated in the following article) has to do with understanding the case situation in its true complexity, so as to proffer broader interventive options. The assessment tells all so far as where and how to intervene. Without a contextual framework, with reliance only upon a linear equation between person and environment that does not in fact exist, the temptation for clinicians is to draw upon a narrow skills repertoire, biased in the choice by the power of existing knowledge. A professional practice cannot be defined by the skills it uses, but only by the way it conceptualizes its purposes and domain and demonstrates its effectiveness. Out of such a framework skills are derived and utilized in the service of those professional purposes. It does not work in the reverse way. Thus, recognizing that there are skills applicable to person *or* environment, it is a repertoire of both kinds of skills based in systemic assessments that is necessary in a practice that is directed toward the transactional purposes of working with person(s) and environment.

The Search for Wholeness

The need to seek synthesis must be innate, for we can observe so many human examples in physical, affective, and cognitive behavior. We seek relatedness, putting things together, arranging, integrating, creating order, systematizing knowledge, and making sense of disarray in our thoughts, our behavior, and our environment. It is understood that one of the most important functions of the ego is the capacity to synthesize. Professions and education continually strive for coherence, unitary purposes, guiding principles, and overarching concepts. In such a disorderly world, this search for wholeness undoubtedly will continue.

In social work practice in the last decade there have been serious efforts to achieve a holistic view of practice. Beginning with Bartlett (1970), a shift in perspective from a methods and skills orientation to a knowledge base as the central concern of social workers meant that practitioners could view the phenomena with which they worked, determine the necessary interventive tasks that seemed indicated, and choose appropriate methods to meet the requirements of the case. This shift required a cognitive restructuring on the part of practitioners, recognition that prior to Bartlett's formulation there was a "cart-before-the horse" approach to practice. Social workers were committed to particular methods and skills almost routinely, without first assessing the phenomena and determining what, from a repertoire of methods and skills, was appropriate to use in any situation. This conceptual change was further developed by Nelsen (1975), who pointed out that an a priori use of methods and skills defined the case problem in accordance with the method being used. This approach, traditional in casework practice, meant that the practitioner could miss aspects of the case that were not attended to by the method in use. "What you see is what you get" suggests that it is more professionally accountable to see cases in their true complexity, and *then* to select the appropriate method and skills. "Wholeness" is achieved through our capacity to visualize and understand phenomena; no single interventive method can be stretched to encompass complex problems. That is what this book is about.

The underlying assumption that drives us is that an all-encompassing perspective is needed to account for the real-life person and environment complexity in social work situations. Such a perspective cannot prescribe interventions, it can only focus our vision and lead us to notice the presence and interrelatedness of the features of a case. Once having accomplished this comprehension of the phenom-

ena at hand—and only then—differential models, modalities, methods, and skills can be called upon for individualized use where appropriate. The book presents a perspective for this purpose, and illustrative methodological approaches to indicate how they go together. Both perspective and methods are needed to achieve coherence, accountability and effectiveness. There is no competition between perspective and method; they are complementary to each other in clinical practice.

As will be shown in the ensuing essays, the choice of interventive (treatment? clinical?) approaches will remain guided by idiosyncratic circumstances including: the practitioner's skills, values, and predilections; available resources in the environment and in the person; the extent of useful knowledge to support the skills chosen; and the client's interests and concerns. But commitment by practitioners to the transactional professional purposes previously described will require a comprehensive perspective that will allow the practitioner to *see* the interrelatedness of the case phenomena, and to recognize that some interventions may, under particular circumstances, serve to promote or restore transactions between the person and environment, and others will not. The operationalizing of agreed-upon purposes will require a relevant perspective for practice.

Social Work Approaches

The early 1970s brought a new conceptualization of social work practice that addressed the criticisms about linear practice models. The awareness of rapid social change, the new and multiple demands on the profession, and the availability of new knowledge of general systems theory, ego psychology, and ecology all joined to begin a new era in social work practice. In the early 1970s Meyer (1970, 1976), Siporin (1972), Goldstein (1973), and Pincus and Minahan (1973), using different sources of knowledge, different practice orientations, and different names for their approaches, all sought a situational context for practice, broader application of social work skills, and systems-type concepts that would connect multiple psychosocial variables in cases. The reaffirmation of direct practice occurred, after almost a decade of efforts at social change, but this time the reoccurrence carried with it remnants of the interest in environment as well as person seen as cause, resource, and object of intervention. Of course, following this development in thinking, there were reactions from the profession that this new conceptualization had gone too far from the person, or not far enough toward social change. As the 1970s progressed, the use of the term social work practice rather than casework or group work became commonplace; systems thinking, development of environmental interventions, and use of ego concepts such as coping, adaptation, and mastery found their way into curricula of schools of social work, and gradually into the practice repertoire of social workers.

The 1980s began with what will probably be a new set of practice models seeking to replace the linear approaches of the previous forty years. The *Life Model of Social Work Practice* (Germain and Gitterman 1980) is one such example. This model seeks a unified process that would serve practice with individuals, families, and groups, much as William Schwartz (1971) sought in order to bring together fragmented practice in his systems model of practice. The model also has referents in Perlman's *Social Casework: A Problem-Solving Process* (1957), which attempted to join person and situation through a generic process, albeit in a linear manner.

Here it is necessary to differentiate the approach in this book that follows from the ecological *Life Model of Social Work Practice* (Germain and Gitterman 1980), particularly because of the term "ecology" that is held in common between the life model which is a practice model and the ecological-systems perspective that is used in this book

1. The life model, using ecology as a metaphor, focuses upon problems in living defined as life transitions, environmental obstacles, and interpersonal processes. The eco-systems perspective merely provides a way of thinking about case phenomena, without a predefined classification of the phenomena in question.

2. The life model is a practice approach that not only defines problems in a particular fashion, but also crosses traditional methodological boundaries and develops instead a tem-

poral framework (initial, ongoing, and termination phases) as a structure for the processes of engagement, contracting, and a repertoire of practice roles and skills. The eco-systems perspective, on the contrary, has no commitment to a similar method construction, being simply an instrument of perception, assessment, and interventive planning. It allows for use of all methods of practice approaches, including the life model if the practitioner so chooses.

3. In both the life model and the eco-systems perspective, ecology is used as a metaphor (see article 2). However, the life model attempts to apply the metaphor directly, through interventions and goals, as an instrument of direct social work practice. Thus, Germain and Gitterman use ecology to define problems and to serve particular practice purposes, especially to improve the adaptive fit between people and their environments. The eco-systems perspective confines itself to use of the metaphor as context, analogously and abstractly applying it only for purposes of cognitive orientation to case problems on the presumption that adaptive fit is but one of the focuses of social work practice. The perspective invites the practitioner to be eclectic in the choice of models to employ. In brief, the life model is a model of practice and the eco-systems perspective provides a conceptual framework for multiple practice models. Siporin in a penetrating analysis of ecological systems theory in social work says:

> The ecological systems approach has enabled us to gain a larger perspective, a more unitary and comprehensive unit of attention, for a holistic and dynamic understanding of people and the socio-cultural-physical milieu (1980:16).

He comments further that eco-systems theory, as "a superstructure, enables the combined and integrative use of many different types of subtheories for different kinds of system functions" (p. 522).

This book carries out the idea that eco-systems theory is a meta-theory that offers social work practitioners/clinicians a way of thinking about and assessing the relatedness of people and their impinging environments; it does not specify the *what* (problem-definition) or the *how* (methodology) of practice. For that, it relies upon the increasingly large repertoire of available practice models, each one to make those specifications consistent with its particular theoretical orientations.

A further word about life as a model for practice needs to be mentioned. The eco-systems perspective seeks to address case problems as accurately as possible, drawing attention to the interrelated, complex reality in people's lives. While some life models of practice specify that life's processes are indeed the model of practice itself, the eco-systems perspective takes no stand on this. That life is the concern of all social work practice is not to say that there is a particular way of defining it, or even of finding agreement among practitioners that it is the "best" model of practice.

Bandler in eschewing psychoanalysis as the model of ego-supportive treatment chooses instead as the "ideal model—life itself, the natural processes of growth and development and the rich trajectory of the life span" (1963:31).

Oxley (1971) developed a life-model approach based upon the ways in which growth and positive change occur in life without therapeutic intervention. She cites maturation, interaction, action, learning, and crisis resolution as the major ways of natural change.

Strean (1972) applies the life model to casework by concentrating on those forces in the person and/or situation that interfere with or enhance psychosocial functioning.

Maluccio views competence as a key concept in the life model, "since the thrust of intervention is to promote the person's capacity to interact effectively with the environment" (1981:2). His practice focus is on competence as a way of facilitating natural adaptive processes. Elsewhere, I commented that "using life itself means knowing the client's lifestyle, where he lives and what it is like for him to cope—and what resources there are in his milieu, among his networks" (1973b:273).

Thus, we see that the use of life as a model has held interest for a number of theorists, and that in the case of Germain and Gitterman's *Life Model of Social Work Practice* there is a special focus on the ecological metaphor of adaptation. The eco-systems perspective makes no claims to derive a practice model from the ecological metaphor. As will be pointed out in essay 2, ecology is used merely to illuminate the way in which all variables are adaptively related to each other.

The Eco-Systems Perspective

Ecological ideas refer to the relationship of man to environment, and may be understood as the natural milieu for a social worker's definition of a case situation, particularly in keeping with the afore-mentioned social work purposes. Systems ideas refer specifically to GST, which has been helpful in understanding the systemic prop-erties of social work cases. The properties explained by this theory help us to recognize the relatedness of variables, order the complex-ity in cases, and direct attention to alternate points for intervention. Serving merely as a perspective (a lens) for looking at phenomena, it provides no prescription for intervention. It extends one's view of case situations; it does not tell what to do or how to define problems. It is not a theory of social systems, it is not a theory of environment or of people; it is a perspective that can help the practitioner cogni-tively, to view the real complexity of cases—*then* to choose a method most appropriate to the intervention planned. That is why it is pos-sible to draw upon practice models within the perspective.

Something has to inform the practitioner's interventions, either traditional practice models or new ones based upon empirical inves-tigation of need. The models do not contribute to the eco-systems perspective; the perspective merely raises questions about the selec-tive and eclectic use of models. Through developing a cognitive grasp of interrelated phenomena, and making a rigorous assessment of what lies before one, the social work practitioner can draw upon a repertoire of existing practice approaches and creative interventions in the service of the case at hand.

The eco-systems perspective draws attention to what is, and the decision as to how to work with the case will depend upon the task requirements thrust up from the case situation, the available re-sources in the client and the environment, and the skills and capacity of the worker which he or she is educated to understand. A distinct advantage in using an eco-systems perspective lies in its allowance for a cognitive view of substantive areas, phenomena, or categories of problems. These might be called, according to the model of prac-tice involved, tasks, crises, life transitions, mental illness, develop-mental disabilities, organizational dysfunction, and so on. We believe that use of the eco-systems perspective will induce clinical social workers to consider more seriously the *what* with which they work as well as the *how* with which they are more familiar.

REFERENCES

American Psychiatric Association. 1979. *Relating Environment to Mental Health and Illness: The Ecopsychiatric Data Base.* Task Force Report No. 16. Washington, D.C.: American Psychiatric Association.

Bandler, Bernard. 1963. "The Concept of Ego-Supportive Psychotherapy." In Howard J. Parad and Roger R. Miller, eds., *Ego-Oriented Casework: Problems and Perspectives.* New York: Family Service Association of America.

Bartlett, Harriet M. 1970. *The Common Base of Social Work Practice.* New York: NASW.

Cannon, Antoinette. 1954. "Guiding Motives in Social Work." In Cora Kasius, ed., *New Directions in Social Work.* New York: Harper.

Ewalt, Patricia L., ed. 1980. *Toward a Definition of Clinical Social Work.* New York. NASW.

Fischer, Joel. 1978. *Effective Casework Practice: An Eclectic Approach.* New York: McGraw-Hill.

Germain, Carel B. 1971. "Casework and Science." DSW dissertation, Columbia University.

Germain, Carel B. and Alex Gitterman. 1980. *The Life Model of Social Work Practice.* New York: Columbia University Press.

Goldstein Howard. 1973. *Social Work Practice: A Unitary Approach.* Columbia: University of South Carolina Press.

Gordon, William E. 1965. "Toward a Social Work Frame of Reference." *Journal of Education for Social Work* (Fall).

Hamilton, Gordon. 1940. *Theory and Practice of Social Casework.* New York: Columbia University Press.

—— 1952. "The Role of Social Casework in Social Policy." *Social Casework* (October).

Hartmann, Heinz. 1958. *Ego Psychology and the Problem of Adaptation.* New York: International Universities Press.

Hearn, Gordon. 1958. *Theory Building in Social Work.* Toronto: University of Toronto Press.

Hollis, Florence M. 1972. *Social Casework: A Psychosocial Therapy,* 2d ed. New York: Random House.

Kinloch, Graham C. 1981. *Ideology and Contemporary Sociology and Theory.* Englewood Cliffs, N.J.: Prentice-Hall.

Kuhn, Thomas. 1970. *The Structure of Scientific Revolutions,* 2d ed. Chicago: University of Chicago Press.

Maluccio, Anthony. 1981. *Promoting Competence in Clients.* New York: Free Press.

Meyer, Carol H. 1970. *Social Work Practice: The Urban Crisis.* New York: Free Press.

—— 1973a. "Practice Models: The New Ideology." *Smith College Studies in Social Work* (February).

—— 1973b. "Purposes and Boundaries: Social Casework Fifty Years Later." *Social Casework* (May).

—— 1976. *Social Work Practice: The Changing Landscape.* 2d ed. New York: Free Press.

—— 1982. "Issues in Clinical Social Work: In Search of a Consensus." In Phyllis Caroff, ed., *Treatment Formulations and Clinical Social Work.* New York: NASW.

The Milford Conference Report. 1929. New York: AASW.

NASW. 1976. *Register of Clinical Social Workers.* New York: NASW.

NASW. 1981. "Conceptual Frameworks II." *Social Work,* Special Issue (January).

Nelsen, Judith C. 1975. "Social Work's Fields of Practice, Methods and Models: The Choice to Act." *Social Service Review* (June).

Oxley, Genevieve B. 1971. "A Life-Model Approach to Change." *Social Casework* (December).

Parad, Howard, ed. 1965. *Crisis Intervention: Selected Readings.* New York: Family Service Association of America.

Perlman, Helen Harris. 1957. *Social Casework: A Problem-Solving Process.* Chicago: University of Chicago Press.

Pincus, Alan and Anne Minahan. 1973. *Social Work Practice: Methods and Models.* Itasca, Ill.: Peacock Press.

Rapoport, Lydia. 1970. "Crisis Intervention: A Mode of Brief Treatment." In Robert W. Roberts and Robert H. Nee, eds., *Theories of Social Casework.* Chicago: University of Chicago Press.

Reid, William J. and Laura Epstein. 1972. *Task-Centered Casework.* New York: Columbia University Press.

34   CAROL H. MEYER

Reynolds, Bertha C. 1951. *Social Work and Social Living.* New York: Citadel.

Richmond, Mary E. 1917. *Social Diagnosis.* New York: Russell Sage Foundation.

Roberts, Robert W. and Robert H. Nee, eds. 1970. *Theories of Social Casework.* Chicago: University of Chicago Press.

Roberts, Robert W. and Helen Northen. 1976. *Theories of Social Work with Groups.* New York: Columbia University Press.

Robinson, Virginia. 1930. *A Changing Psychology in Social Casework.* Chapel Hill: University of North Carolina Press.

Schwartz, William. 1971. "On the Use of Groups in Social Work Practice." In William Schwartz and Serapio R. Zalba, eds., *The Practice of Group Work.* New York: Columbia University Press.

Siporin, Max. 1972. "Situational Assessment and Intervention." *Social Casework* (February).

—— 1975. *Introduction to Social Work Practice.* New York: Macmillan.

—— 1980. "Ecological Systems Theory in Social Work." *Journal of Sociology and Social Welfare* (July).

Strean, Herbert. 1972. "Application of the 'Life Model' to Casework." *Social Work* (September).

—— 1978. *Clinical Social Work: Theory and Practice.* New York: Free Press.

Taft, Jessie. 1937. "The Relation of Function to Process in Social Casework." *Journal of Social Work Process* (January).

Thomas, Edwin J., ed. 1967. *The Socio-Behavioral Approach and Applications to Social Work.* New York: Council on Social Work Education.

von Bertalantfy, Ludwig. 1968. *General Systems Theory: Foundations, Development, Applications.* New York: George Braziller.

White, Robert W. 1963. *Ego and Reality in Psychoanalytic Theory.* Monograph 11. New York: International Universities Press.

II

THE ECO-SYSTEMS PERSPECTIVE

Geoffrey L. Greif and Arthur A. Lynch

The eco-systems perspective has been variously explained and understood; it has been criticized as being too abstract to be useful to clinicians or as being unnecessarily competitive with linear thinking. What seems to be needed is an analysis of its components—ecology and general systems theory (GST)—so as to clarify the perspective and its potential values, particularly as it provides a framework for clinical social work practice. The perspective is derived from the concept of ecology and the principles of GST, and when applied to practice, it focuses the social worker's vision upon the way that people and environmental forces interact. It emphasizes in as value-free a way as possible the adaptive transactions among impinging systems, and offers a way of organizing the complex variables in social work cases.

As mentioned in paper 1, a perspective for practice provides a framework from which to view, understand, and integrate what is occurring. The perspective is meant to provide a way of integrating knowledge and skills by helping the practitioner to focus more clearly on the observed situation, highlighting the action implications, and helping to arrive at interventive decisions pertaining realistically to the problem situation. The perspective offers the possibility for being a field-wide framework applicable in all situations. (The terms *unit of attention* and *client* refer to whoever initially appears in need of service. When assessed, this may change to a focus on someone or something else, depending on the defined problem. The terms can mean a community group, agency, person, family, and so forth.)

The eco-systems perspective can serve as an integrating force for social work practice models, coordinating assessment and various conceptualizations of knowledge and methods. Further, it can serve as a conceptual umbrella or organizing framework for the developing empirical data in social work. It is potentially useful for practitioners working on both macro and micro levels and within the generalist-specialist arenas. When coupled with the assessment process, it enables the practitioner to draw from a wide choice of clinical interventions and practice models so that practice can be increasingly individualized in accordance with client need.

Ecology

Ecology refers to the study of complex reciprocal and adaptive transactions among organisms and their environments. It is similar in ways to GST principles, but focuses on the junction or interface of the organism and the impinging environment. The origin of the term ecology has been traced to Ernest Haeckel who first used it in his book *Generelle Morphologie der Organisem,* published in 1866 (Stauffer 1957). He developed the concept of ecology to explain Darwin's theories of natural selection and the struggle for existence of organic beings presented in *The Origin of Species.* Haeckel further described the close-fitting relationship of the organism and its environment through processes of reciprocity and mutuality. In the nineteenth century, ecological interest and writing were focused solely on the plant family and specifically on plankton.

It was not until the twentieth century that the idea of ecology expanded to include the interplay between people and their surroundings. Dogan and Rokkan credit two sociologists, Park and Burgess, writing in 1920, with being the first to apply the concept to a human context (1969:6). Despite the early presence of the idea in such disciplines as sociology, anthropology, and architecture, it is from biology that current applications derived their source. Biologists have always been concerned with shifts among species interacting in the same area or living system.

Who survives and how they survive when a system changes either internally or due to external stimulus depend on adaptability. Boulding describes this process by using the term *niche* to refer to the immediate environment: "Niches continually change. They may shrink or they may expand, and if they shrink too much, species that are too well adapted to a particular niche will become extinct as the niche shrinks to zero" (Boulding, 1978:111). So, biologists have identified the basic model for ecological thinking, the adaptability of organism and environment—in social work terms, the familiar person-environment, inner-outer, or psychosocial focus.

Ecologists are interested in the linkages among systems and how a change in one system may affect other organisms connected to the system. As Philip Handler, a biologist, writes: "Ecologists are trained to focus on the interfaces between systems—on problems that fall between the cracks of 'basic' sciences" (Handler 1970:435). Handler sees ecology as being concerned with the connections between organisms that a specialist, supposedly interested only in his own field, would miss. To describe these ecological processes, Handler identifies three major variables: (1) the arrangement and distribution of the species in relation to time and space; (2) the manner in which the energy flows; (3) the roles of the species involved (p. 456). These variables will be discussed further since they play a major role in the assessment and intervention stages of case activities in which the social worker and the client participate.

A basic knowledge of biology would make it easier to understand the application of ecological thinking to the social sciences and social work. Yet, the concept has become popular in many disciplines, and its use can be explored in its derivative states.

In social work the unit of attention is the person-in-situation. The situation is embedded in the person's total milieu or ecological environment. Theorists have structured this ecological space in ways that are different by virtue of their own fields of knowledge.

The environment is seen by ecologists as nested levels of social organization which are interconnected through feedback structures and have accommodating relationships. These levels of social organization vary in complexity with the person as the basic building unit. The person enters each new situation with the aim of making progressive accommodations to the immediate environment in his or her niche. This accommodation is an interdependent process which is mediated by the person's internal forces and by forces from immediate or more remote ecological environments. The internal forces are composed of biological and psychological needs pressing for satisfaction. These are organized in a developmental history of experience which has been accrued through learning from interaction with the environment. The person's activities are not viewed, however, as emanating strictly from this need-reduction model. He or she is seen as participating within the total particular ecological milieu, always affecting and being affected by all the forces within it.

As a person enters each new situation, he or she usually adapts to its demands and, by his or her presence, changes the situation at least structurally. A person is constantly creating, restructuring, and adapting to the environment even as the environment affects the person. One acts dynamically in new situations based on one's identity, which is the culmination of all past interactions, the present situational demands, and what one hopes to become in the future. According to ecological theory, these complex transactions, which may or may not result in an adaptive fit between the person and situation, determine the way in which future accommodations are achieved.

While it is difficult to credit any one person with being the first to adapt ecological ideas as a metaphor for social work theory and practice, Germain, drawing upon the work of René Dubos has been quite influential in moving the field in this direction. Germain defines ecology as "the science concerned with the adaptive fit of organisms and their environments and with the means by which they achieve a dynamic equilibrium and mutuality" (Germain 1973:326). The concepts of adaptation and mutuality have been key tenets since the mid-nineteenth century and are ever present metaphorically in deciding how person and situation fit together in practice. In applying ecology to practice, Germain credits William Gordon with the notion that social work's domain is the interface between the person and the environment (Gordon 1969), thus making use of the ecological metaphor to address the "goodness of fit" between the two.

Meyer has written of the role of the social worker within this conceptualization as being "to maintain individualized services for people and to effect a better mutual adaptation between man and society, a better fit between need and service, and a better ecological balance between personality and environment" (Meyer 1973b). To do this, the worker must comprehend *how* systems interact. The writings on ecology have not fully emphasized the fact that while there is reciprocity between interacting systems, the nature of the interaction may take the form of predation, parasitism, or cooperation (Boulding 1978). Hence, the balance between an institution and a person may be woefully unequal, with the institution abusing the rights of the individual. Yet from an ecological standpoint, there would still exist reciprocity, though of an unjust or unequal nature.

The ecologically minded social worker understands the need to assess the terrain of a case, finding indirect as well as direct influence upon the client of ecological variables. These variables may range from intimate family relationships to the political atmosphere or the helping organization. The worker looks at the interface where all these variables interact, and in learning the nature of the variables, also questions the quality of their linkages to learn which need to be strengthened or modified. In any case the content range can extend from personality to cultural issues, from factors affecting the worker to legislation being enacted or to community support systems. Ecology provides the concepts helpful in recognizing the interrelatedness of the data.

Germain, in terms similar to those used by Handler, has described some of the variables that need to be considered by the ecologically oriented social worker. She writes specifically about the ecological variables of time (Germain 1976) and space (Germain 1978) and their impact on the client, the way the client organizes, uses, and responds to time, and the effect of spatial arrangements upon the individual, family or group.

Handler's identification of nonlinear, the ways in which energy flows and roles are carried out, contributes to our understanding of the function of ecological variables illustrated as follows:

A practitioner may want to understand the flow of energy in a family, to know what forms of nurturance exist for the children. From an ecological perspective, nurturance may flow from unexpected sources, perhaps not only from a parent but also from a distant relative. Or a social work consultant, seeking to understand a particular agency's role in a community, will take note of the total service structure and resources of the area, not only the internal functioning of consulting agency or its exchange with a neighboring agency.

In both examples, the ecological perspective suggests a contextual field of forces (nurturers or agency resources) that go quite beyond the confines of linear, one-to-one relationships. The perspective, then, promotes consideration of a more realistic context for practice and suggests a larger repertoire of interventions. As noted, the ecological variables of time and space contribute to an even richer understanding of "the case," as would such other ecological variables as culture, politics and economics, social policies, and organizational structures. The biological processes in ecology have been thus translated metaphorically to social processes, helping social workers to work consciously with interacting intimate and wider environments.

Ecology alone does not, however, begin to explain *how* energy flows or *why* one system or set of variables has a specific impact on another. It only says that such action takes place while emphasizing the "fit" between the two. GST, when used in association with ecological ideas, can provide concepts for understanding the hows and whys of a system's interaction with the environment. The application of this theory to social work has been considered in many places for over a decade, but in order to develop the components of the eco-systems perspective, a brief exploration and review of general systems theory is offered here.

General Systems Theory

General systems theory (GST) was designed to specify the processes of transactions within and among systems. This specification is particularly important in view of the ecological imperative. In view of the complexity of multiple, transacting-ecological variables some "ordering" is necessary. GST helps in this ordering by providing an infrastructure of abstract concepts and propositions which organize data in terms of their relatedness. As Janchill points out, "Systems Theory is not itself a body of knowledge; it is a way of thinking and of analysis that accommodates knowledge from many sciences" (Janchill 1969:77). However, there is still no universal consensus among systems theorists as to what comprises an overall definition of systems theory. Instead, various theories have emerged, the more salient concepts and propositions of which we will outline.

The historical roots of GST reach back to the 1920s and are attributed to the works of Ludwig Von Bertalantfy. Von Bertalantfy started his work while exploring the organismic view of biology in response to the prevailing concept of the "closed system," the notion that organisms existed in isolation from the environment. He believed that a concept of "open systems" where there was a mutual exchange of energy and information between an organism and the environment more clearly explained how biological systems survived (Klir 1969:97). A variety of other systems theories which paralleled his thinking were also being developed in the 1920s in the natural and social sciences and led to an increased integration of ideas. A similar concept of people as closed systems existed at that same time, it being thought that people's destinies were predetermined by genes, early experiences, physical drives, and other forces beyond the control of environmental factors.

Von Bertalantfy defines a system as "a set of elements standing in interaction" (1967:115). These sets of elements can exist within either a closed or an open system. The basic difference between the two types of system is the transaction with the environment. Where a closed system may be impinged upon by elements in the environment, it does not actively admit these elements into the system. Thus it is subject to thermodynamic equilibrium or entropy, the process of using up its own energy and expiring. In turning to the application this has for social work, if we take as an example of a closed system an institution or agency, we can predict that without new ideas, clients, or funding from which it can draw a source of energy, the agency would have to close.

In contrast to a closed system, an open system "continually gives up matter to the outer world and takes in matter from it. . . . [it] maintains itself in this continuous exchange in a steady state, or approaches a steady state in its variations in time" (Allport 1966:303). It is because of this capacity to exchange with the environment that the system survives. As no living system is ever completely open or closed (as in the agency example), the term has to be used relatively. The open system will be our main concern, and the term will be used interchangeably with system.

There are six basic concepts which help define the identity of the open system. Along with these are twelve principles which explain the way a system operates with the environment and internally.

The first of the structural concepts, *boundaries,* implies that any system that is distinct in its own right has either spatial or dynamic boundaries that in some form separate it from the rest of the environment and give it a distinct identity. The degree of boundary permeability, or the ease with which information and energy flow in and out, determines how open or closed the system is.

The second concept is the *structure* of the system. The structure refers to the set of all elements within the boundaries and the enduring patterns of their relationships. This means that while energy exchange may take place, the system maintains a recognizable sameness in its structural characteristics.

The third concept which defines the system is that of *hierarchy.* This means that systems are nested within other systems and have subsystems within themselves. There is, hence, a hierarchical relationship that exists within and among systems (Kast and Rosenzweig 1979:102).

Fourth, a system must be viewed as *transactional* since it interacts not only with other systems, but also within the hierarchy of subsystems.

The fifth concept is the *frame of reference* which specifies the identity of the system. The frame of reference tells the observer whether he or she is studying a family, person, institution; this concept is needed in establishing the nature of the system.

The sixth concept is *time.* Every system exists within a temporal dimension consisting of a past, present, and future. The future is usually viewed in terms of the system's potential; that is, it is not predictable, but is dependent upon the stasis or growth of the subsystem as it evolves interdependently with other systems.

Application of these concepts to understanding a family can further clarify their meaning. The family has *boundaries* which make it a discrete system from other families. There also can be boundaries within the family, those that represent the rules that exist between generations. For example, a child may be proscribed from disciplining a sibling. When the child does discipline, he has crossed a boundary and is performing a parental function.

The *structure* of the family system would be all the people in the family and the way in which they interact with each other. The family's *hierarchy* refers to the varying statuses of individual members or of the family subsystems. All members of the family are not equal, resulting in hierarchical relationships, which means that members can be ranked in order of importance and power on particular family issues.

The *transactional* nature of the family is observed when each of these subsystems of parents, siblings, and other family members interacts with one another and with people outside the family, like schoolmates, neighbors, colleagues, and so on.

The *frame of reference* would indicate to the viewer that the area of interest was a family, as opposed to individual members of the family.

Finally, families exist in *time* and react to evolutionary processes uniquely. Each family has its own past, made up of landmarks, dates, and reference points. The family responds to the demands of time (in the present) in an idiosyncratic way which will help determine its future course, which is largely unpredictable. These six concepts define any system and make it unlike any other system. Not defined by these concepts is the specific manner in which a system operates.

GST has developed a body of principles which explain the *way* a system operates, including its internal processing and interaction both with its subsystems and with other systems. The first five principles relate to processes and involve the structure and flow of energy external to the system. *Input* is the means by which the system takes in energy, matter, and information from the environment. Biological and psychosocial survival and growth are provided for through the input process. Once accepted into the system, the input substance is acted upon, transformed, coded, and used for the functioning of the system. This stage of the use of the input substance is called *through-put.* A person at the throughput stage acts on the environmental input not only with his/her personality, but also with awareness of the scope of the situation in his/her role in the impinging social systems, and in reference to his/her particular cultural ideology.

Once the processing begins, the system actively responds to the environment. This response, called *output,* has a direct effect on the environment and acts both as inputs for other systems and as inputs to the original system via feedback loops, the fourth principle.

The *feedback loop* consists of the return of positive and negative information which acts either to maintain system equilibrium or to disrupt the system, promoting change (Von Bertalantfy 1956:5). While positive feedback tells the system it is on a steady course to its goal, negative feedback informs the system it has deviated from its course and needs correcting. In practice, if the members of a client group were always told they were doing well, there would be no need for them to consider change.

The system that deviates too far from its course without the necessary correcting will experience *entropy,* meaning that it will have no energy input from the outside, no exchange, and will hence wind down and run itself out on its own energy (Von Bertalantfy 1956:5). Attempting to combat this entropic process, the system stores up as much energy as it can without overloading the system. This is similar to keeping a car's gas tank full to avoid a weekend search for an open station. The system then tries to maximize the input-output ratio to guard against depletion of the system's energy. The successful use of available energy resulting in a healthy maintenance of the system is called "negative entropy," the process of counteracting entropy.

Illustrative of these five principles that explain a system's internal processing of external energy would be a migrant family moving from Haiti to New York City. Such a family (a system defined by the previously stated structural features) would be exceedingly vulnerable to faulty processing of external energy, due to its sociocultural alienation from the larger society. Maintenance of its essential family structure and its potential for survival as a family, to say nothing of growth, would depend upon systems processes operating as follows:

This migrant family would need sufficient information and supports (*input*) so as to make its way in a new community. The way in which it processed this information and support (*throughput*) would depend upon the clarity of the information and the relevance of the support. A Haitian community worker who explained things in French would enhance the processing of the information. The family members, acting out of their own historical, genetic, psychological, and cultural proclivities, would consider the new information uniquely. The father might seek work on the basis of job information only, the mother might be more attuned to housing and community resources, while the children would care about school and neighborhood friends. The father, after seeking a job in vain, might bring back to his family a terrible picture of the world outside (*feedback*), while the children, having found friends, or the mother having discovered a long-lost cousin in the next street, might bring back a different kind of feedback. As a consequence of the internal processing of these mixed experiences, the family members might feel and behave differently in their next encounters with the outside world (*output*).

Negative feedback, a corrective in perception, might operate so that the father would be less depressed in his job-seeking, and the mother more cautious in seeking friends. The children, already more connected to other children than to their parents' concerns, might begin to adopt neighborhood rather than parental standards of behavior and introduce new stress into the family.

To the degree that father, mother, and children remain connected to their individually defined external environments and bring back their impressions and experiences, which will inevitably affect each of them, the family system will remain open in a state of *negative entropy*. Were this family to withdraw and bring in no new experiences, it would "wind down" as a social enterprise, suffering entropy. Entropy could occur as well through overloading of too much newness, and the family might then disintegrate into alcoholism, drugs, mental illness, or violence. The family behaviors in this example could be partially understood through application of the principles of input, throughput, feedback, output, and entropy.

The internal state of the system is also determined by five principles, the first two of which are *steady state* and *homeostasis*. The system maintains itself in a steady state characterized by a simultaneous use of energy (input) and a continual growth process (from throughput and feedback). Energy (any substance, concrete and physical or affective and ideological) is used to maintain the system while helping it to adapt to any inconsistencies in the environment. Homeostasis and equilibrium are the terms used to define the maintenance of a system at a recognizable level. They differ from a steady state, which is the ability of the system to negotiate successfully with the environment for sustenance. In order to help clarify these subtle differences, we suggest Katz and Kahn who have written that "the steady state which at the simple level is one of homeostasis over time, at more complex levels becomes one of preserving the character of the system through growth and expansion. The basic type of system does not change directly as a consequence of expansion" (Katz and Kahn 1969:98).

The third of the principles concerning the internal state of the system is *differentiation* (Von Bertalantfy 1968:211), the tendency of the system to increase in order and complexity over time. This process takes place through the system's dynamic interaction with the environment and results in greater heterogeneity and elaboration. As we age, we achieve greater knowledge, complexity, and ability to interact with the environment, thus becoming more highly differentiated.

The fourth principle occurs as a result of increased differentiation. It is called *nonsummativity* (Keeney 1979), and asserts that data obtained from isolated parts of the system cannot be added up to represent the whole system. The whole system is different from the possible multiplication of any of its parts. One of the reasons for this is the presence of these new elements that appear in the system and because of their interaction with existing elements.

As a result of this interrelatedness of elements, the final principle of *reciprocity* concerning the internal state is one of the most important and most frequently applied in clinical practice and organizational analysis. This states that a change in one part of the system has repercussions for the whole system. It is the underpinning of most personality theories and family therapy approaches and, in application, means that any change in one member of a family has some impact on all the other family members.

> The principles that explain the internal processes of a system can be observed in further analysis of the Haitian family case example.
>
> Given the continuing activity of the family with its differing environments, and given its ongoing state of negative entropy, the family may experience daily stressful upsets in equilibrium of homeostasis. This would be expected in a case where all the family members are experiencing totally new situations in job-seeking, community relationships, and friendships.
>
> If a thirteen-year-old daughter says she wants to go out with a boy alone, the Haitian cultural response as expressed within this patriarchal family might be such that the daughter is punished for even considering such an idea. Even though the child might react rebelliously in a non-Haitian way and, the family's *equilibrium* would be quite upset for a few days, the essential paternal hierarchy would be sustained, and the family, through its traditional balancing efforts would persist over time in a *steady state*.
>
> To the degree that the family continued as a self-balancing system, and as external events were assimilated by the family members, emerging qualities of differentiation would appear. The father, who might have found a job, would himself experience more Americanized ways of living from his new social contacts. Through feedback to his family, and simultaneously, through their own feedback of experiences, both mother and children would develop new interests,

adopt different models of behavior, and seek novel social experiences.

Naturally, since this diffentiation process further individualizes each family member's development, we cannot simply add one's experience to another's to explain "family behavior," for the variables to be "added" would not be of a comparable order. The father might be more outgoing and capable as a result of his job, his new friends, and his increasing self-esteem at mastering a complex urban environment. The mother might be more comfortable than when she arrived because she has found a transplanted small Haitian culture in her community, and thus she has less anxiety, and more energy to devote to her own needs and to those of her family. Finally, the children might find association with radically different social entities and become "New York City children" more rapidly than their parents could make similar adaptations.

The quality of the increasing differentiation of this system (still the same family) is *nonsummative*. However, the principle of *reciprocity* makes it possible to understand that no matter what the individual family member's responses, because they are structurally and systemically related, they remain a family, interacting and growing because they change in response to each other. The sense of urbane confidence felt by the father may affect the mother in such a way that she may feel isolated at home and thus become more tied to her "old world" structures in order to solicit reaffirmation of her Haitian ties. This shift in the parents' social attitudes and inevitable response to each other will have its effect upon the children, one of whom might choose to speak only French in school, another of whom might totally reject the mother's Haitian style of life.

All these family behaviors would have *reciprocal*, not additive, predictable consequences. When this family arrived in New York City, it was a tight unit from a rural, Caribbean culture; as we leave them at this point, they are becoming urbanized and highly differentiated but yet are still a family system experiencing reciprocity one with the other.

Two remaining principles describe the path or trajectory of a system. The first is *equifinality* and suggests that a system can reach the same final state from a variety of different paths and different initial conditions. As Von Bertalantfy wrote, the final state of an inanimate system is determined by the initial state, resulting in a linear relationship, while a living system is influenced in innumerable ways on its course toward a goal (Von Bertalantfy 1969).

Multifinality, the converse of equifinality, is the principle that similar conditions may lead to dissimilar ends; that differing final states can be reached from the same initial conditions.

> In the case of our Haitian family, social work intervention might be indicated so as to help them maintain their structure as a family and a steady state over time. The principle of *equifinality* allows the practitioner and the family to consider a range of interventive options to reach the goal of a reestablished family balance. Among the possibilities would be having the mother visit the school so as to enhance her understanding of why the children are behaving in such new ways, and/or providing English lessons. As for the father's showing evidence of drawing away from his culture and his family, one might draw upon his sense of competence and have him serve as liaison with new Haitian immigrants. The children, seeking healthy associations outside their family and yet feeling guilty about alienating their mother, might be engaged in family treatment so as to sort out the latent and mixed communications that are contributing to the family's upset balance. Given the presence of the systemic structures and processes we have described, particularly reciprocity, *equifinality* would be operative because these interventions (and others that the idiosyncratic features of the case would suggest) all derive from different locations in the system, and—given reciprocity—could each contribute to the agreed-upon goal of improved family balance.
>
> *Multifinality*, on the other hand, can be illustrated in this case, if a single event occurred such as the thirteen-year-old daughter's becoming pregnant out of wedlock. This event in this assumed culture-bound family, would have severe and multiple repercussions. For example, the father might blame himself for his own new sociability and might then retreat from his American friends and activities. The mother might call upon the supports of her Haitian network and

more assiduously attempt to close the family to external influences. A young child might perceive the environment as so threatening he would refuse to go to school. The multiple ripple effects of this or comparable unsettling events could have multiple expressions and could, if attention were not given to them, have the consequence of driving the family toward closure and entropy.

In both instances of equifinality and multifinality it is not integral to these principles that problems occur or that intervention would be necessary. The family could be seeking upward mobility, and this goal could be achieved through any number of pathways (equifinality) indicated by the features of the case. Or, an event like a job promotion could demonstrate multifinal consequences among the family members, all of which would contribute to the goal of upward mobility.

Werner Lutz is credited with being the first to apply GST to social work, with his 1956 article, "Concepts and Principles Underlying Social Casework Practice." It was not until the late 1960s, though, that the ideas began proliferating in the professional literature and in social work education.

Application to Social Work

In the past ten years, the contributions of GST to the field have been numerous with two outstanding. The first involves a shift in the view of the model of linear causality. Practitioners adopting GST as a way of analyzing case phenomena were forced to depart from previous models of causality which indicated direct cause and effect from one element to another, including the impact of a practice method upon a case problem. The new theory provided them with a transactional model of causality where all significant elements in a case act upon each other and assessments are made of: (1) the topography of a system (its boundaries, structure, hierarchy, transactions, frame of reference, and temporal dimension); (2) the nonlinear flow of energy of a system; (3) the internal state of the system. Assessments could then be based upon the system's relationship to other systems by studying the interface where systems meet and transact. This multidimensional view of systemic causality accounts for complexity and simultaneity in a way that is beyond the capacity of direct, linear cause-effect practice models.

The second contribution was the influence that systems thinking had on emphasizing holism. Due to the focus on interaction between and among systems, a wider view of the situation became necessary so as to account for everything that impinged upon the unit of attention. This view required renewed concentration on the person, and the environment, and their differential interaction as an ecological whole rather than as separate entities.

GST can provide for social work and all disciplines a framework for understanding the interaction of living organisms. Because of its widespread reach, it has been applied in such diverse fields as economics, anthropology, engineering, sociology, architecture, biology, psychiatry, psychology, mathematics, physics, speech pathology, (Lefton-Greif 1981) and social work. GST explains what happens when two or more organisms interact and offers a scientific perspective that can explain relationships and transactions among variables on an individual, family, community, and organizational level. It only provides a perspective; since unlike models of practice, it does not tell the practitioner what to do but just what is happening.

The theory tells the social worker that if a system is too closed to outside input or has boundaries that are too rigid, its consequence will be entropy. It tells the social worker, then, to look for instances of rigid boundaries and to attempt to make them more permeable, if the system needs to survive. GST applied to social work could explain how client groups use information through positive and negative feedback either to grow or to maintain the status quo. The implications for intervention flow from case data that are presented and learned about the system, based on a knowledge of the concepts and propositions underlying systems theory. It is in the practitioner's application of this information that ideas for intervention come.

The possible applications, as Minuchin states, are many. "The jump to the systems model frees the therapist for the utilization of every school's insights and techniques. . . . It broadens the approach, using a framework that is more complex than the linear models but which is, for that reason, more consonant with the complex reality of human experience" (Minuchin, Rosman, and Baker, 1978:91). Since the theory does allow for this widespread use of practice models, it supplies a nonlinear framework that is in itself value-free, although the clinician's choice of practice models is usually value-determined. It expands the traditional implications about a traditional disease orientation by assuming that a problem or a solution has arisen not only as a result of a singular cause, but actually may result as the culmination of a number of current interacting forces.

One of the applications of GST has been in the treatment of families; other applications have included group, individual, and organizational interventions. Historically, the family was viewed as being a group of individuals who, if they were experiencing problems, should be treated as individuals. This was a reflection of the view of people as biological entities isolated from the environment. GST suggests other approaches for treating a family. We know from our knowledge of equifinality that there are different points of entry and many ways to bring about change. Bowen (1976) believes in working with the strongest member in order to help others. Minuchin (1978) believes in unsettling the dysfunctional homeostasis of the family and forcing the members to find a new one. Haley (1976) may give homework to the whole family to get them working together. These would all be considered systems approaches; that is, working with one or all members of the family to help one or more members of the family.

The diverse role requirements for the social worker within a systems view are greater for he/she is immediately part of the client's environment. The worker cannot assume that taking the role of an observer is a possible alternative since there is always some impact on the system because of the worker's presence. For that reason, the worker must be aware of the range of the effect that she/he has on the system and that each action from the worker in turn results in a change in the client(s) with whom there is interaction. Clues to possible interventions then appear as soon as the worker meets the system.

As compatible as GST appears to be with the basic tenets of social work, attempts to integrate it have presented problems. Hartman (1970) noted three of the major difficulties. First is the highly abstract level on which systems theory has been conceptualized. This makes the task of integrating it into actual practice ideas difficult. Next is the confusing state of systems theories with many different views and interpretations leading to even more applications. Lastly, the language used by systems theorists has been difficult to assimilate into social work. This semantic confusion adds a burden to the theory and, ironically, obfuscates its integrative capacities. These difficulties may lessen somewhat when ecological concepts are integrated and an eco-systems perspective is adopted.

Having discussed GST and ecology, we can now show how the two combine to enlighten and integrate social work practice. Much of what was discussed previously will be recognized in the following section for there is great overlap between the two systems of thought, both drawing on much of the same body of knowledge.

Eco-Systems Perspective

The marriage of these two fields of thought gives the social work practitioner the capacity for greater understanding of the social environment in which all human beings exist. When locating an individual, family, or group in its ecological milieu and focusing on the nature of transactions, it is possible to assess the strengths of the linkages as well as the distortions. This assessment provides the basis for the action implications from which interventions flow. While different approaches to practice have used GST, only the Life Model of Social Work Practice has used ecology alone as a basis for understanding relationships. The eco-systems perspective is unique in that it furnishes a framework for the worker to use multiple practice models without specific ties to intervention, skills, method, and knowledge.

For a better comprehension of why the perspective evolved in the field, a brief history of social work practice is necessary.

Professional social work practice was never considered a monolith for, since its beginnings as social casework in the 1920s, it has developed around different fields of practice and different methodologies. Until the Milford Conference (1929) the problem definitions, units of attention, and intervention goals developed along the lines of the particular setting in which they were being used. Bartlett (1970: 23) identified the two historical concepts from which practice grew as method and the setting of practice. Method began in the 1920s with Mary Richmond's psychosocial concept of casework. Twenty years later, group work and community organization were formulated as alternative methods for approaching the same human needs and problems through attention to different units of attention. The concept of setting delineated the characteristics of the service based on where the worker was employed. These settings (agencies, hospitals, schools, and so on) had a major impact on practice development and, with social work's growth, spawned various models of practice for differential use within the settings. Although this helped to define practice in terms of setting, and the Milford Conference contributed to the coherence of casework, it also left a fragmented view of practice based on method derived from setting. Thus a unified concept of practice did not develop.

As for clinical methods, social casework has always been committed to the person-situation configuration. This dual commitment has, however, waxed and waned with new discoveries in the social and behavioral sciences and changes in the sociopolitical and economic arenas. Practitioners attempted to integrate the contributions from the social and behavioral sciences but were limited by the perspectives of their specific models which could not account for systemic interaction of case variables. Social workers identified themselves with various approaches to social casework and psychotherapy and focused concern on personality disturbances, often leading to an unbalanced commitment to the person over the person-in-situation.

As noted in the first essay, the 1960s brought criticism to the profession because of its inability to make an impact on the problems of poverty and racism. Germain notes that the practitioners' failure to engage these issues was based on two reasons. First, as mentioned, was the lack of impact that direct service had on problems on "a massive scale such as structural poverty and racism" (Germain 1980: 5). Second was the lack of action principles available to effect envi-

ronmental modification on even a smaller scale. As these action principles have become more available recently, social work has strained
to integrate them. Systems models, task-oriented models, unitary
models, and life models attempted to bridge the person-situation gap
and draw together the fragmented commonalities of practice. Un-
fortunately, all have been limited by the dilemma shared by all
models. They are constricted in their outcome by their initial assumptions, which have to be fairly narrowly defined so as to support
their methodology. The eco-systems perspective sidesteps this issue
by opting instead to provide a common framework which is an organizing approach that all practitioners can use regardless of methodological commitment. It also can be a useful field-wide concept
because it is not restricted to the details of the specific setting.

The first combination of the terms ecology and systems theory can
probably be credited to Auerswald in his article "Interdisciplinary
Versus Ecological Approach" (1968). Ecology and GST both use many
of the same concepts and form a natural partnership; according to
Auerswald:

> Since the people who have been most concerned with constructing
> a model for a unified science and with the ingredients of the hu-
> man ecological field have been the general systems theorists, the
> approach used by behavioral scientists who follow this trend is rap-
> idly acquiring the label of the "systems approach," although a more
> appropriate label might be the "ecological systems approach"
> (Auerswald 1968:203).

In contrasting this approach with the interdisciplinary one, he
points out that the eco-systems perspective is concerned with the interface among various life systems where the other deals with the
systems themselves. Meyer also writes on the combination of GST
and ecology:

> Even though General Systems Theory and ecology derive from dif-
> ferent theoretical bases (while both drawing on the science of biol-
> ogy), together, in the eco-systems concept, they provide a helpful
> perspective for viewing the interconnectedness of variables in cases,
> with special attention to the interrelatedness of persons-in-situation
> (Meyer 1976:129).

Siporin, in a review discussing models of practice, speaks of the two and the breadth they offer social work:

> This ecological systems model is not a unitary theory but is a basic framework, an umbrella-like structure we need for assessment and interventive purposes. It accepts behavior and personality theories. . . . It accepts diverse theoretical orientations, such as psychoanalytic, problem-solving, behavioral, existentialist, and other approaches (Siporin 1979:83).

When applied to social work, the eco-systems perspective provides a framework from which social work practice can derive specialized practice approaches relevant to individualized need. Auerswald, Meyer, and Siporin see it as a broad-based way of looking at phenomena. This application is what makes it a perspective and not a model. Models of practice refer more to a series of steps that include a knowledge base, theory, assessment, intervention, and evaluation. Kettner writes: "Models, to be useful for professional social work practice, need theoretical frames of reference for the purpose of analyzing data and formulating plans of intervention which are consistent with problem analysis" (1975:603). There is need for a problem definition underlying a practice model, for its methodology proceeds from the way it views problems. This is not appropriate where a perspective is applied, since no assumption is being made about problems or a need for change; a perspective only offers a lens through which phenomena are viewed. It is the practice models that are necessary to direct the work.

The eco-systems perspective tells us what is fitting together and the nature of this fit. It gives the user of the perspective information about the fit between the person and the situation with an emphasis on the interface. The focus of social work concern is what is happening at the interface that is causing the societal institution, agency, family, individual or group disjuncture. The unit of attention's adaptive abilities are of special interest because of ecological theory. There is no particular focus on either the person or the environment; the focus must come at the worker's informed discretion based on the perceived needs, and the practice model chosen. The GST orientation tells us how systems interact, while the ecological base grounds the information in a relevant manner that looks at the phenomena holistically and as reciprocally related. Each organism is relevant to some other organism and hence may have to be examined at some point by the social worker. GST would not have as macroscopic a view of the data without the use of ecology.

The integrative capacity of the perspective affects all levels of its conceptual framework. At the theory level, the perspective can provide for various means of organizing and structuring the unit of attention and the environment. This structuring is necessary to understand the transaction taking place at the interface; it is left to the practitioner and client or client group to choose a frame of reference within which to work. In doing this, the perspective augments each practitioner's perception of the world and respects the multitude of conceptualizations that are often necessary to account for the phenomena.

When using the eco-systems perspective with a particular model of practice the knowledge base and interventive repertoire may have to be supplemented or broadened in scope to accommodate various data previously ignored. In setting up the framework for the knowledge base, the perspective guides the practitioner by contributing the concept of "hierarchy" from systems theory. It will be recalled that in a hierarchy systems are nested within other systems and have subsystems within themselves. The eco-systems perspective, in viewing the individual, for example, as the unit of attention, takes this concept into account. The unit of attention, partialized out of the hierarchy, must be understood both as an individual system and as a transactional component of the systemic process within the hierarchy of systems. Whatever the unit of attention is (the person, family, group, or institution), the knowledge base has to provide theories which explain it. This may consist of personality theory, family theory, group theory, organization theory, and so on. Similarly, the environment, or the remaining systems nested in it, is interconnected with the person(s). Their transactions occur through feedback mechanisms, and their relationships are viewed as reciprocal or mutually accommodating. These environmental variables, artificially separated here for convenience, also need to be accounted for as part of the knowledge base and as they affect the unit of attention.

For a broad knowledge base which covers much of these areas see Kahn (1973), particularly article by Sheila B. Kamerman, Ralph Dollgoff, George Getzel, and Judith Nelsen.

Three different conceptualizations of the ecological environment are provided as examples of how various theoreticians have chosen to think about this structuring.

Swap (1975) divides the environment into three settings: the behavioral setting, patterns of behavior across settings, and community and cultural settings. Bateson (1972) has also differentiated three complex systems: the person, the society, and the natural biological surroundings. Bronfenbrenner (1979), who focuses on the matter in great detail, delineates four environmental systems: the microsystem, the mesosystem, the exosystem, and the macrosystem, which basically divide up the areas of the person, family, group, community, society, culture, and institution into operationally defined areas.

The perspective can also be applied in curricula of schools of social work. As a teaching perspective, it can give students a basic framework that can be used regardless of setting or method. As the student gains experience, an increasing amount of information drawn from models could be applied that would expand the worker's repertoire. The worker would not be impeded by having learned one or two practice models that would then prove insufficient to meet the needs of broad-ranging kinds of client groups. The worker using the perspective ultimately would have: (1) greater access to the various knowledge bases dealing with the phenomena; (2) a broader repertoire of methodologies used by different models when creating a strategic intervention; (3) availability of research connected to the field and the intervention; (4) and thus avoid the closure described by Nelsen (1975).

The perspective has proven difficult to master by people attempting to utilize it. Meyer outlines two major constraints when using the perspective. The first is the burden it places on the worker's knowledge base. It forces the worker to look into the dimensions of, at least, his or her field of practice (the various models, research, policy issues). The other constraint is that it compels practitioners to "take a contextual rather than a methodological stance on practice." In organizing the multiplicity of variables and their multiple relations, practitioners will "find there is more to be done than they had noticed before" (Meyer 1979:271). This places greater pressures on the practitioner, the available resources, and types of services offered.

It must be remembered that the perspective cannot, as has been its main criticism, dictate what the practitioner should do. Here the eco-systems perspective does not link the practitioner to models or methods; it means rather that the practitioner should be able to affect a situation by drawing from the multitude of interventions available The purpose of the intervention will be to create a better fit between the client's response and his "task" (Bartlett 1970:94). Again, the client can be a person, family, group, or organization. The perspective acts for the field as a conceptual infrastructure which allows for practice in micro through macro systems. No stance is taken on adaptation, competence, identity, or health. Applications of these concepts must be made by the worker at the time of assessment as the context and the practice model demand. However, adaptation is certainly emphasized metaphorically from the ecological standpoint without given specifics. The perspective is especially effective when it is linked to the assessment stage to widen what the worker looks at before an intervention is chosen. Once the assessment has been made, the limitations of the perspective in practice are only the limitations of the worker's own skill and knowledge base.

The next step in clarifying the use of this perspective is to explore its application to assessment, intervention, and evaluation. The quest is for an appropriate link between the perspective and the real demands of practice. These stages of assessment and intervention have to be linked to the tenets of the perspective in order to utilize actively the information that it offers the practitioner. As Bartlett has stated, the stages of assessment and intervention are not separate and concrete stages. However, because the stages make different demands on the worker, at times it is necessary to make an artificial separation for purposes of clarification.

Assessment

As the eco-systems perspective broadens social work practice parameters, it contributes to the assessment and intervention stages. In assessment, the perspective expands the worker's understanding of the person in the situation, which is the conceptual task of practice. In the intervention stage, the perspective allows for an increased number of choices for interventions by the worker. It can be applied easily to the existing thinking on assessment and intervention and provides further support for what social workers have always been doing. It also adds new dimensions to practice while asking the worker to shift orientations slightly to accommodate different ways of looking at information about the client and the environment. Through this broadened focus, when attention is paid to multiple interacting variables, social workers would see more interventive choices, thus enhancing their practice repertoire.

Bartlett (1970) has written extensively on assessment and intervention. By combining her work and that of Auerswald (1968) one can provide a breakdown of the stages of assessment and intervention that the social worker follows. The first stage following the initial contact involves a collection, organization, and analysis of the data. This helps the worker to identify the major factors being presented by the client so that the second stage, the formulation of the hypothesis, can occur. Bartlett states that in formulating the hypothesis, the worker and client consider the factors which appear most critical, their interrelatedness and their salience, so as to choose which to deal with. This choice is extremely crucial as it leads to the alternatives in social work practice which will be considered. The perspective helps considerably in these two stages of assessment by inviting the social worker and the client to consider all systems that impinge on the client and by providing a background with which to understand the systems in operation.

Meyer (1973b) and Siporin (1979) have highlighted two essential elements of the assessment stage which the worker should bear in mind. Meyer underscores the need for individualizing the case while working toward a mutual understanding between client and worker. Siporin adds the need to look at all dimensions of the situation, emphasizing the networks of the social situation which include the impinge upon the person. This may include primary groups or larger social systems.

The third stage includes the formulation of strategy, choice of techniques and action to be taken. Although intervention takes place at the first worker-client contact, the actual carrying out of the intervention plan that is based upon assessment occurs in the fourth stage. This final stage involves assessing the impact of the intervention and the validity of the original hypothesis. Depending upon the information gained at this stage, the original assessment and intervention may prove to be the correct ones or they may have to be reconsidered. If the need for reassessment is shown, the whole cycle may have to be completed anew. Each intervention provides new information confirming or rejecting parts of the assessment and intervention. At the same time, the relationship between the client and worker is developing and allowing for increased information and a widening choice of interventions.

These stages are essentially what social workers do with clients in practice and can be conceptualized in the flow chart.

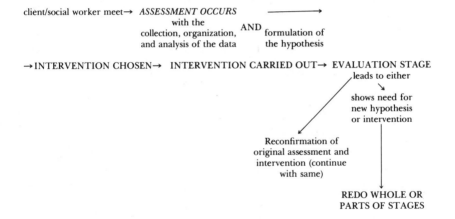

client/social worker meet→ *ASSESSMENT OCCURS* ⟶
with the
collection, organization, AND formulation of
and analysis of the data the hypothesis

→INTERVENTION CHOSEN→ INTERVENTION CARRIED OUT→ EVALUATION STAGE
leads to either

shows need for
new hypothesis
or intervention

Reconfirmation of
original assessment and
intervention (continue
with same)

REDO WHOLE OR
PARTS OF STAGES

Before developing the relationship between the perspective and the assessment more fully we need to discuss briefly the concept of task.

The notion of task has not, as yet, been consensually validated in the field. While all authors seem to agree that the task occurs at the interface they disagree on the definition. This is due to a focus on different phenomenological aspects of the situation-response continuum. We have chosen Bartlett's definition because of its conceptual ability to separate and capture the life situation which presents problems for clients. She defines tasks as those "demanding and critical situations which confront people" (Bartlett 1970:95). These life situations may arise from role transitions, crisis, maturational, interpersonal, or environmental events. In this definition, tasks are not viewed as behavioral. Other attempts to define task have been contributed by Studt (1968), Reid and Epstein (1978), and Germain and Gitterman (1980).

To understand further the possible relationship between the perspective and assessment, we now turn to what the practitioner does when using the eco-systems perspective. The assessment occurs in the first two stages (see the flow chart) and is based on full investigation of the person in environment interface. Following the investigation of the interface the hypothesis can be mutually formulated. The hypothesis is the tentative statement about the nature of the systemic situation in which the client is engaged. From these hypotheses will flow the action implications that are necessary in choosing the goals for the case and the intervention strategy. By action implications we mean the selection of various possible interventions which can be derived from the assessment statement. The action implications tell us what and where action needs to occur. They do not tell us, however, what the actions are or how to do them. Action principles derive from the specific strategies that are tied to a particular practice model.

A brief illustration of these first two stages may be helpful. Puberty can be considered a developmental task for an adolescent. The adolescent's responses to puberty occur at the interface in that the internal (physical and psychological impact of puberty) and external (sociocultural, family and school expectations) forces combine to create the *task,* and the adolescent's response to this task has to be understood in order to form an accurate hypothesis and intervention strategy that is relevant to all the impinging systems (the adolescent, his family, school, and community).

From this formulation, we can see that three fundamental changes occur in the traditional assessment process when using the perspective. First, the perspective brings to the assessment a broad guideline for investigating the person's ecological environment. It holds the social worker accountable for understanding the relatedness of all the systems impinging on the person. The social worker then must decide, based on salience of the phenomena, the client's input, and available resources, including the worker's capacity, what areas they will need to work with. What becomes expanded when the perspective is used would depend on the features of the case and what had been minimized or disregarded by the particular model of assessment the worker previously had used in a particular practice model. This change is required because the perspective asks the practitioner to consider more phenomena than are considered in any single model of practice. As pointed out earlier, the inherent limitation in all practice models is their selective attention when looking at the person-in-situation and deciding what to do. Use of the eco-systems perspective avoids the limitation of methodological closure and permits more specific individualizing of the case through eclectic selection of one or more practice models or other interventive techniques.

The second change signals a more difficult task for the practitioner. It requires a shift from a linear way of thinking about a case. The direct relationship of cause and effect is displaced in favor of a more multirelated way of looking at social work phenomena. When applying the eco-systems perspective one can see the effect of the stages on each other via the flow of information and the feedback process. While the intervention and assessment stages need to be separated for clarification purposes as has been discussed, they are in fact intertwined. Gordon Hamilton noted that assessment starts with the first contact. Interventions may begin in some form at the first contact, too, though they are interventions that do not grow out of a full assessment, but rather out of an immediate interpretation, or telescoped assessment of what the social worker is seeing.

The third change focuses the practitioner on the interface. Gordon defines the interface as "the meeting place of the person and environment . . . the point where there is or is not matching with all its good and bad consequences for person and environment" (1969, p. 7). Here, he writes, the activities of the person and the environment which impinge upon one another create the transactions to be assessed. The person and environment at this transactional point each include their own histories, capacities, and so on. The personal and environmental data pertaining to the task now become emphasized in the interface while other data become limited. This occurs as the worker and client set priorities. The worker judges the impact of the person and environment on one another and formulates interventions to affect the transactional nature of the interface. It is essential to point out that without making an assessment and deciding what issues have to be further dealt with, the worker would be overwhelmed with information, and the interventions chosen would be inadequate or irrelevant. The added focus on the interface rather than on only the separate characteristics of the involved systems elicits the tenets of ecology and GST.

Salience and relevance are still the key factors in determining what to consider as important. The worker's judgments based on epistemology, style, knowledge base, experience, and self-assessment remain as fundamental as ever. Determination of the client's level of functioning, ability to report, strengths and weaknesses is still basic in understanding the client and using the social worker's expertise. The perspective may induce the social worker to examine and intervene in the environment of the client. Finally, the worker's own milieu must be considered in terms of the impact it may have on the client. A depressing office environment, rigidity in setting appointments, political and resource constraints, all have an impact on the worker's impression of the client and the client's impression of the worker.

With an understanding of what the perspective does when applied in the assessment of the client, we can now discuss how it provides new opportunities when looking at the intervention phase of the relationship.

Intervention

The eco-systems perspective provides some unique opportunities for an intervention strategy in that it can draw from many diverse practice models and can, in fact, encourage "the invention of new interventions." Intervention in a particular model of practice is usually a technique defined by that model to solve a problem. The definition of the problem is usually restricted to the model's knowledge base and assessment procedures. The relevance and, indeed, the purpose of the eco-systems perspective are to break through the limitations of a model's narrow focus and provide the practitioner with a more competent armamentarium of interventions.

It is necessary to recall what has already been stated to present a clear understanding of the perspective's application to the use of intervention. First, from ecology we know that transactions occur at the interface; the primary task of organisms is mutual adaptation. Further, ecology identifies the salient elements in the transactions by supplying an adaptation metaphor; it does not, however, tell us how these transactions occur. GST supplies the answers. Their integrated effect is far stronger than their isolated contributions. Combined, we have guidelines for determining the problem plus individualized action implications for solving the problem. Now arises the question of how to do what is deemed necessary. Which is the best method or technique for solving the problem? What are the value, agency, and resource limitations?

It is at this point that the creative capacities of the practitioner working within definite limitations need to be maximized. The choices for intervention are not totally random; they are constrained and defined by the mutually developed problem formulation, availability of resources and organizational purposes. Problem formulation occurs in the second step of the assessment (see the flow chart) after a careful systemic investigation. The problem formulation is based on an analysis of this in terms of the "task" and "social functioning." Emerging from the data, this formulation points to the necessary action implications which are needed to begin planning interventive strategies. Here the worker must decide which transactions of the complex interrelationships between the client and environment he or she hopes to affect. We now begin to see that as the worker can no longer be bound at the outset by models, he or she likewise cannot find action principles in the eco-systems perspective. However, the perspective requires the use of interventions aimed at affecting the impinging environmental demands and the transactional nature of the interface. These elements, of course, change with the changing definition of the client (from individual to institution), but the steps to assessment and intervention strategy remain conceptually the same.

An intervention can, hence, be picked from, to use Meyer's (1973) concept, "a cafeteria model" of all available interventive resources, a blending of direct, indirect and concrete services to provide the greatest impact. To help in understanding the impact of interventions, we conceptualize the systems available for change in four ways: (1) the personal level, which involves the individual only; (2) the family level, consisting of the people in the home; (3) the group or community level, the networks or neighborhood that affect the client; and (4) the institutional level, which includes agencies, laws, schools, city hall, welfare bureaus, and so on. These are similar to Bronfenbrenner's conceptions of the micro, messo, and exo-systems.

In most cases, although it always depends on the problem formulation, the intervention strategy is made up of many interventions which are aimed at creating change with the multiple-identified variables at the different system levels. But an intervention has to take place in at least one of these areas initially. This intervention will eventually, in theory (e.g., reciprocity, in GST) result in some change on all levels. One example of an intervention on an institutional level would be a social worker lobbying successfully to change a welfare law so that that benefits would be increased. This intervention, if successful, would improve conditions for individuals, families, and the community while taking place on the institutional level.

An intervention at the community level might be the establishment of a basketball team that would be pleasurable to teenagers in a particular neighborhood. This might also relieve some of the harassment of an elderly neighborhood woman who is the client. The community intervention would affect the client and the teenagers while, in theory, having a positive impact on the teens' families, the larger neighborhood, and also making greater use of the agency's resources. The worker's active exploration with the client about what was happening in her environment, and help with her ability to cope with the situation or with her relocation to a different neighborhood illustrates intervention on a personal level.

The social worker intervention repertoire can no longer be restricted to known methodological interventions either; that is to the interventions through casework, group work, community organization, and administration. Rosenfeld (1980) has written about interventions that are interventions of necessity when no model and no research are available to follow. He believes the "invention of interventions" is necessitated by the constantly changing demands on practitioners in diverse settings. He sees five sources for interventions as being in: (1) theories, (2) research, (3) successful cases, (4) natural resources, and (5) thinking about how people manage when professionals are not present. Rosenfeld's idea about intervention are not rooted in a method or model but more in a science and technology. What is effective is what should be done, and it does not have to have a knowledge base. When Rosenfeld's ideas are added to our repertoire, the intervention becomes capable of managing the emergence of new needs as well as covering the broad spectrum of phenomena it has already managed successfully.

Fischer (1978) and Bloom (1978) discuss data-based practice, the use of clinically proven techniques that can meet the needs of the situation. This would be another source of possible interventions that could be used in the eco-systems perspective.

In intervening, services are chosen which are aimed at supporting, supplementing, substituting, or eradicating aspects of the situation to create change that will provide for a better adaptive fit for the person-environment interaction. This is the sole reason for an intervention to be formulated and carried out. The more the available resources of the client are used, the greater the likelihood of the intervention being consistent with the client's milieu.

The only constraint on the use of any intervention in the eco-systems perspective for the social worker is that whatever is done should be consistent with the values and purposes of social work. The intervention must do more than produce change, it must produce change in a context that is ethical and reflects the prevailing social work beliefs and values.

Evaluation

Linked to the process of assessment and intervention is the process of evaluation. Evaluation of one's intervention strategy is determined by both empirical and nonempirical data.

Traditional evaluation of the impact of the intervention strategy has been of a nonempirical nature. This generally has included input from supervision, case conferences, and other extra-agency sources. Within the last decade, because there has been a growing demand for empirical validation of practice, several methods of objective evaluation have been developed. The clinical research model (Jayaratne and Levy 1979), for example, provides a manageable design for the practitioner in many cases. The eco-systems perspective itself demands clear operational definitions which, if carried out, would prove to be syntonic with efforts to effect empirical investigation.

Most relevant for the assessment-intervention-evaluation stages in the eco-systems perspective are: (1) theories for understanding transactions of personality and environment, and following assessment (2) that the worker finds a suitable intervention, drawing from all sources.

In summary, the eco-systems perspective directs the practitioner to look at all significant, impinging aspects of the person and the environment while emphasizing the interface between them. It broadens the parameters of assessment and the choices for intervention. Ecology brings attention to the adaptive nature of systems and their mutuality. GST explains how case variables function and interact. Combined, they provide a metaphor for social work practice which is concerned with making the environment and the individual more responsive to each other.

The eco-systems perspective is one attempt to resolve the question of whether there can be a common base to social work. It provides the needed focus to capture the rich and diverse themes of the profession across fields and specializations, and their respective models of practice.

REFERENCES

Allport, Gordon. 1966. "The Open System in Personality Theory." *Journal of Abnormal and Social Psychiatry* (November).

Auerswald, Edgar H. 1965. "Interdisciplinary Versus Ecological Approach." *Family Process* (September).

Bartlett, Harriet M. 1970. *The Common Base of Social Work Practice.* New York: NASW.

Bateson, Gregory. 1972. *Steps to an Ecology of Mind.* New York: Ballantine Books.

Bloom, Martin. 1978. "Challenges to the Helping Professions and the Response of Scientific Practice." *Social Service Review* (December).

Boulding, Kenneth. 1978. *Ecodynamics: A New Theory of Societal Evolution.* Beverly Hills, Calif.: Sage Press.

Bronfenbrenner, Urie. 1979. *The Ecology of Human Development: Experiments by Nature and Design.* Cambridge, Mass.: Harvard University Press.

Dogan, Mattei and Stein Rokkan, eds. 1969. *Social Ecology.* Cambridge, Mass.: M.I.T. Press.

Fischer, Joel. 1978. *Effective Casework Practice: An Eclectic Approach.* New York: McGraw-Hill.

Germain, Carel B. 1973. "An Ecological Perspective in Casework Practice." *Social Casework* (June).

—— 1976. "Time, an Ecological Variable in Social Work Practice." *Social Casework* (July).

—— 1978. "Space, an Ecological Variable in Casework Practice." *Social Casework* (November).

Germain, Carel B. and Alex Gitterman. 1980. *The Life Model of Social Work Practice.* New York: Columbia University Press.

Gordon, William E. 1969. "Basic Constructs for an Integrative and Generative Conception of Social Work." In Gordon Hearn, ed., *The General Systems Approach: Contributions Toward an Holistic Conception of Social Work.* New York: Council on Social Work Education.

Handler, Philip, ed. 1970. *Biology and the Future of Man.* New York: Oxford University Press.

Hartman, Ann. 1970. "To Think about the Unthinkable." *Social Casework* (October).

Janchill, Sister Mary Paul. 1969. "Systems Concepts in Casework Theory and Practice." *Social Casework* (February).

Jayaratne, Srinika and Rona L. Levy. 1979. *Empirical Clinical Practice.* New York: Columbia University Press.

Kahn, Alfred J., ed. 1973. *Shaping the New Social Work.* New York: Columbia University Press.

Kast, Fremont E. and James E. Rosenzweig. 1979. *Organization and Management: A Systems and Contingency Approach.* New York: McGraw-Hill.

Katz, Daniel and Robert L. Kahn. 1969. "Common Characteristics of Open Systems." In F. E. Emery, ed., *Systems Thinking: Selected Readings.* Harmonsworth, Middlesex, England: Penguin Books.

Keeney, Bradford P. 1979. "Ecosystemic Epistemology: An Alternative Paradigm for Diagnosis." *Family Process* (June).

Kettner, Peter, M. 1975. "A Framework for Comparing Practice Models." *Social Service Review* (December).

Klir, George J. 1969. *An Approach to General Systems Theory.* New York: Van Nostrand Reinhold.

Lefton-Greif, Maureen and Greif, Geoffrey, L. "The Application of the Eco-Systems Perspective to Speech Pathology." Paper presented at the 1981 American Speech and Hearing Association Northeast Regional Conference.

Lutz, Werner. 1956. "Concepts and Principles Underlying Social Casework Practice." In *Social Work Practice in Medical Care and Rehabilitation Settings,* Monograph III. Washington, D.C.: NASW, Medical Social Work Section.

Meyer, Carol H. 1973a. "Practice Models: The New Ideology." *Smith College Bulletin* (February).

—— 1973b. "Purposes and Boundaries: Casework Fifty Years Later." *Social Casework* (May).

—— 1976. *Social Work Practice: The Changing Landscape.* 2d ed. New York: Free Press.

—— 1979. "What Direction for Direct Practice?" *Social Work* (July).

Minuchin, Salvador, Bernice Rosman, and Lester Baker. 1978. *Psychosomatic Families: Anorexia Nervosa in Context.* Cambridge, Mass.: Harvard University Press.

Nelsen, Judith C. 1975. "Social Work's Fields of Practice, Methods and Models: The Choice to Act." *Social Service Review* (June).

Reid, William J. 1975. *The Task-Centered System.* New York: Columbia University Press.

Rosenfeld, Jona. 1980. Based on lectures given at Columbia University School of Social Work.

Siporin, Max. 1979. "Practice Theory for Clinical Social Work." *Clinical Social Work Journal* (Spring).

Stauffer, Robert C. 1957. "Haeckel, Darwin and Ecology." *Quarterly Review of Biology* (June).

Studt, Elliot. 1968. "Social Work Theory and Implications for the Practice of Methods." *Social Work Education Reporter* (June).

Swap, Susan M. 1975. "The Ecological Model of Emotional Disturbance in Children: A Status Report and Proposed Synthesis." *Behavioral Disorders* (May).

von Bertalantfy, Ludwig. 1956. "General Systems Theory." In Ludwig Von Bertalantfy, ed., *General Systems Yearbook* of the Society for the Advancement of General Systems Theory. Vol. 1.

—— 1967. "General Systems Theory." In N. I. Demerath III and Richard A. Paterson, eds., *System, Change and Conflict*. New York: Free Press.

—— 1968. "General Systems Theory in Psychology and Psychiatry." In *General Systems Theory: Foundations, Developments and Applications*. New York: George Braziller.

—— 1969. "The Theory of Open Systems in Physics and Biology." In F. E. Emery, ed., *Systems Thinking*. Harmonsworth, Middlesex, England: Penguin Books.

PART TWO

INTRODUCTION

Carol H. Meyer

The next four papers are about four selected practice approaches. These practice approaches or models are discussed within an eco-systems perspective to determine their compatibility with that perspective. They are all written in the same analytic framework so that the reader can, if desired, compare the approaches according to certain dimensions.* All the essays include case illustrations with implications drawn for practice.

The selection of the practice approaches for inclusion in this book was arbitrary to a degree. The four approaches are traditional, well-known, and widely used by social workers. But beyond our striving for familiarity no particular criteria were applied in their selection or in the decision not to include other approaches. We might well have included a selection of group work, family, and generalist social work practice models, but a narrower focus was chosen as a device to control a range of variables. We are attempting to show that the eco-systems perspective, which is not a practice approach in itself, can be viewed as a unifying construct in social work. The practice models presented are to be seen as illustrative of the increasingly large repertoire of practice approaches; it was not our intention to present an encyclopedia or handbook of approaches, especially since

*The analytic framework used here was originally developed by me in Aaron Rosenblatt and Diane Waldfogel, eds., *The Handbook of Clinical Social Work.* San Francisco: Jossey-Bass. 1983.

these may be found in the existing literature (Turner 1979; Roberts and Nee 1970; Roberts and Northen 1976). We believe that the main purpose of the book, to explore the impact of the perspective on the use of clinical practice models, could be adequately served by working out the idea with four practice approaches, leaving to the eclectically minded reader the task of generalizing ideas to other approaches in current use.

The four essays represent each author's individual effort at analyzing the practice models under study. The papers are, therefore, quite different in emphasis. Close reading will indicate that the differences are reflective both of each author's style and of the models themselves. Even though each article includes the same framework for analyzing the practice model, the reader will note different emphases, language, and implications drawn. That is as it should be, for we are considering difference here—difference in practice approaches so as to have a full repertoire from which to choose an eclectic clinical practice. Always able to provide the most appropriate definitions, Helen Harris Perlman says that "eclecticism is a fusion of selected aspects of these diverse (and sometimes embattled) schools of thought" (1970:1291).

The reader also will note the repetition in the essays. This is to be expected since the authors were asked to discuss the practice approaches within the same eco-systems perspective. Recognizing the principles of eco-systemic thinking as they are applied over and over again, with different cases and using different approaches, should help the reader make concrete a perspective that has been so often criticized as too abstract for clinical application.

We hope that it will not pass the reader's notice that in each paper a great deal of attention is paid to the nature of the problem involved in the case illustrations. The impact upon these clients of unemployment, alcoholism and retardation, psychosis and renal failure, and sudden infant death are fully elaborated upon as significant to the case assessments. In the Conclusion more is said about the necessity for clinicians to become expert in their knowledge of such psychosocial problems (the above being illustrative), so as to identify the "social workness" that is unique to this clinical practice. In this Baedecker guiding the reader through this complex book we should note some theoretical signposts along the way. Following the framework used by each author, it will be clear to the reader how the practice models address each item in the framework. Here, we will only note those areas reflected in the papers, but not included in the framework for analysis.

Process and Content

All practice models require that attention be paid to assessment and to intervention; to the nature of the problem, and to the ongoing work done with the client. Yet, one can observe differences in emphasis, as between psychosocial therapy and problem-solving, for example. Hollis places heavy emphasis on the *what* in cases, even though she also presents detailed techniques to deal with the *how*. Perlman, on the other hand, emphasizes the *how* or process, "no matter what the problem is," even though she also includes problem, place, and person (content areas) in her approach. The eco-systems framework is essentially an assessment tool; it broadens the clinician's perspective on the case and contributes to problem definition. It does not take a stand on processes required to intervene; it leaves that to the choice of practice models. Thus, as it addresses *content,* it is further differentiated from The *Life Model,* which uses the transactional processes of ecological adaptation as its focus and the *processes* of beginning, ongoing work, and termination as its model for practice.

Holistic Assessment and Partialization

There is a significant difference to be noted among the practice models that has to do with whether or not the whole case situation or a selected aspect of it is to be assessed. The psychosocial therapy and to a large extent crisis intervention approaches address the whole, while problem-solving and sociobehavioral methods address partialized aspects of cases, those parts that are related to the problem under attention. These differences are rooted in both ideological commitments and in theory, and their differential uses make different intellectual demands upon the clinician.

The eco-systems perspective, as has been mentioned several times in the first two essays, brings the clinician's attention to the *whole* case situation; all the case variables that impinge upon the client are potentially part of the case assessment. The clinical skill required is the ability to select those aspects of the case situation that need or would benefit from some kind of intervention. Using this mode of assessment, partialization occurs *after* understanding the case—to know all is not to do all. Use of the perspective is antithetical to the idea of attempting to understand only that aspect of the case that is assumed a priori to be related to the problem (partialization in assessment). Obviously, the problem for attention cannot be known until the assessment takes place.

Selection of Practice Models

The practitioner will have choices to make when using the eco-systems perspective. Whether one uses one or all of the approaches described in this book, or any of the others in current use, the choices will depend upon the kind of case, the client's need, the practitioner's predilections, the emphasis wanted by the practitioner, and the emphasis offered by the model. An eclectic clinical practice need not overwhelm the practitioner who has the ultimate secret weapons, the ability to think and the power to make informed choices.

The four linear approaches discussed in this book are used only illustratively, to show how the use of the eco-systems perspective affects the models in question. Using this perspective, a practitioner can apply other models directed to families, groups, and individuals. The perspective invites attention to different sizes of systems and different permutations in ways of working. Furthermore, depending upon the needs of the case situation, and the inclinations of the organization and social worker in question new interventions can be "invented" as need arises and imagination flows. The environment of organizations, self-help groups, neighborhoods and so on, becomes through this perspective opportunities for intervention. The perspective, as has been discussed in essay 2, does not assign priority to interventions with the person or environment side of the psychosocial equation, but it directs attention to the multiplicity of events and levels of events which will help the clinician determine the entry points of intervention.

The practice approaches discussed in this book have been subjected to analysis within a framework that, it is hoped, reflects the concerns raised about their utility in this most complex of worlds. Remembering that we believe that no individual practice model can be viewed as useful for all occasions, each one might have relevance for a particular occasion. Thus, in order to help the practitioner evaluate its use and perhaps to compare and contrast them, the framework for analysis is presented as a convenience.

A Framework for Analysis of Practice Models

A framework, through its use of selected words and phrases, induces one to ask certain questions. Apart from yes or no answers, which are sometimes very helpful in just knowing whether or not some information is present, it is also possible to identify profiles of models testing for congruence and consistency. Parts of the framework can be separated out for comparison purposes, one model to the other, and the practitioner can then look up a topic of particular interest. The framework used for analysis of practice models in this book is as follows:

1. *Ideological biases.* What nonempirical commitments are held by the model?
2. *Values.* What beliefs relevant to social work are expressed in the model?
3. *Knowledge base.* What theories and ideas does the model draw upon?
4. *Unit of attention.* Is the model to be used with individuals, families, groups, communities, organizations?
5. *Problem definition.* How does the model determine what is a problem for its attention?
6. *Congruent and explicit interventions.* Is the interventive

methodology consistent with the other parts of the framework, such as those mentioned in nos. 1 to 5? And are the model's techniques of a specific or a general design?

7. *Uses of the professional relationship.* To what degree is the professional relationship used as context and/or process in the model? Is it used as mean or ends in interventions?

8. *Desired outcomes.* What does the model define as its goals of intervention?

9. *Uses of time.* Does the model suggest or require short- or long-term interventions? Is time used as a dynamic in assessment and intervention?

10. *Differential use of staff.* Does the model require that only graduate social workers can practice it, or can it be used by a variety of staff levels and types?

11. *Work with self-help groups.* Can the model be made applicable to nonclient groups?

12. *Availability to effectiveness research.* Is the model explicitly defined, so that its use in practice can be evaluated empirically?

To ask the questions we are asking is not to make judgments, except insofar as the decision to ask those questions reflects a position about what is thought to be important in clinical social work practice.

REFERENCES

Perlman, Helen Harris. 1977. "Social Casework: The Problem-Solving Approach." *Encyclopedia of Social Work.* New York: NASW.

Roberts, Robert W. and Robert H. Nee, eds. 1970. *Theories of Social Casework.* Chicago: University of Chicago Press.

Roberts, Robert W. and Helen Northen. 1976. *Theories of Social Work with Groups.* New York: Columbia University Press.

Turner, Francis J. 1979. *Social Work Treatment.* 2d ed. New York: Pree Press.

III

CASEWORK: A PSYCHOSOCIAL THERAPY

Richard D. Woodrow

Few models of social work practice have been so deeply influential and so widely disseminated as Florence Hollis' *Casework: A Psychosocial Therapy* (1964a). Whether embraced or rejected, it has been a point of departure for countless practitioners, theoreticians, educators, students, and other practice model architects. Its contributions to the understanding of casework methodology have been seminal. Because of its critical impact on the profession, *Psychosocial Therapy* demands serious critical analysis.

"Psychosocial" is a term of multiple referents. As a concept, it suggests a professional focus, perhaps a domain of practice, shared by most practitioners. As a school of thought, it describes an orientation or approach to practice shared by a more delimited group of professionals, historical and current, As a model, as in *Casework: A Psychosocial Therapy,* it refers to a particular representation of this approach to practice and a particular interpretation of the psychosocial concept.

These distinctions are made in order to establish boundaries for analysis. Hollis adopted the psychosocial concept and cemented it in the professional literature and language.[1] She also incorporated theoretical frameworks, practice processes, and principles of the diagnostic or psychosocial school.[2] Yet her model is distinct in its operationalizing of the concept and in its elaboration of theory, processes, and principles. This article focuses on the model at a particular time in its development.

Informed by the developing psychosocial approach to practice, psychosocial therapy was further shaped by a series of impressive research ventures begun in the late 1950s, in which Hollis analyzed process records of actual psychosocial practice. She began to refine the understanding of what caseworkers actually do—to characterize, clarify, and classify the procedures used in the process of treatment—in order to move practice beyond dichotomous claims and disclaimers and enhance the potential for differential interventions. Building upon this ongoing research base, the result was an analysis of *"a particular segment of casework practice—the treatment of individuals experiencing problems in their interpersonal relationships"* (Hollis 1972:3; emphasis added). More specifically, it was an analysis of psychosocial interviews between workers and clients in particular outpatient settings (family service agencies, psychiatric clinics, mental hygiene centers, child guidance clinics) with particular clients (primarily adult individuals and dyads) who sought help for particular problems (marital, individual, or parent-child adjustment). It was truly a model of practice.

But a model *of* specific practice became accepted as a generic model *for* casework practice. First appearing in 1964 and revised in 1972 and subsequently in 1981, *Casework: A Psychosocial Therapy* became the current articulation of the psychosocial concept, the contemporary voice for the psychosocial school, and sometimes for casework itself. "In analyzing a particular treatment approach, we are inevitably also discussing general casework principles. The part cannot be isolated from the whole . . . *when casework is employed to help the client achieve better social functioning, it becomes a form of psychosocial therapy* (Hollis 1972:34; emphasis added).

Psychosocial casework in the 1960s was caught on the cusp of profound social and professional change. Faced by the challenges of that transitional era as the deepening of established methodology became less important than social change, a theoretical model of any kind ran the risk of challenge. In 1972, Hollis revised *Psychosocial Therapy*, responding to reviews of the first edition and to the social and theoretical developments that had occurred. This paper was written prior to the 1981 publication of Hollis' third edition, so this analysis may require the reader's revision. Yet, if the analogy is valid and Hollis is correct, models like people have patterns that persist.[3]

In analyzing the second edition of *Casework: A Psychosocial Therapy,* the following discussion draws upon other writings as relevant. Our main purpose is to explore what happens to this model when an eco-systems perspective is used.

Ideological Biases

Psychosocial Therapy is ideologically committed to several interrelated ideas about human behavior which reflect its values and knowledge base and which have implications for its practice, lending an integrity to the whole. Above all, Hollis reaffirms the historic assumption that social functioning is the result of a complex interplay between "inner psychological and outer social components" (Hollis 1972:7), hence the term "psychosocial." This interplay was reflected in the professional unit of attention, Gordon Hamilton's "the person-in-his-situation." Hollis prefers the term "person-situation configuration" or "gestalt" to suggest the intended dynamic interaction among multiple internal and external variables which influence one's functioning. In psychosocial therapy, "person" refers primarily to the individual's personality system, particularly as it influences one's perception of, expectations for, and reactions to situations. "Situation" includes both "concrete realities and sociopsychological realities" in the client's immediate environment, although it "most often implies a human situation—family, friends, employer, teacher, and so on" (Hollis 1972:10).

For both clients and workers, person and situation are intimately and intricately related. "Clients come for casework help because there has been a breakdown in their social adjustment" (Hollis 1972:23), emanating from the psychological and/or social side of the person-situation. Hollis identifies as possible interacting sources of this breakdown: (1) infantile needs and drives left over from childhood that cause the individual to make inappropriate demands upon the adult world; (2) a current life situation that exerts excessive pressure on the individual; (3) faulty ego and superego functioning. Throughout professional activity there must be a "dual orientation" (Hollis 1972:19), as the social worker keeps vigilant watch over the interplay between internal and external, psychological and social, stress and press, person and situation.

Social work practice always has struggled with the relationship between internal and external factors however variously defined. Even assuming agreement about what is person and what is situation, person-in-situation is potentially at least four different phenomena (see figure 3.1), and the actual if not the articulated tilt of the model in the person or situation direction will be revealed in other components of the analysis.

Another set of ideas incorporated from the psychosocial school is given particular emphasis and shading by Hollis, and is ideological in the sense that it moves the model's values to action (Siporin 1975:355). There is deep commitment to strengthening the individual's capacity to cope and to direct his or her own life in an uncertain world that threatens individual autonomy. It is believed that this capacity can be strengthened through increased understanding of self, of others, of future outcomes, of consequences of one's own behavior on others, of oneself and one's responses to others. While

FIGURE 3.1
Person-in-Situation

Concept	*Practice Implications*
(person)-in-situation	Problems defined primarily within the person; treatment focused on changing the person
person-in-(situation)	Problems defined primarily within the situation; interventions focused on environmental/social change
(person)-in-(situation)	Problems defined within the person/problems defined within the situation; two separate clusters of professional activities (or functions)
(person-in-situation)	Problems defined in the transaction between person and situation; one professional function, multiple professional activities

human behavior is deeply rooted in irrational processes, each human being has the potential for reasoning as ego develops and drives change their form of expression and demand. Through consciously applied reflective understanding, one can gain control over infantile primary process, freedom for self-direction, and mastery over the present demands of the situation, for example, by correcting distorted perceptions or unrealistic expectations. There is an inherent optimism in this idea, drawn in part from Freudian psychoanalytic theory, as "the individual can almost always do something about his problem" (Hollis 1972:18–20). While many people need more than awareness in order to change—for example children, or adults under severe environmental pressure—"the worker always tries to help the client arrive at some measure of increased understanding" (Hollis 1972: 109) since "men are more likely to act wisely in the best interests of others and of themselves when they understand themselves and others" (Hollis 1964b:160).

This idea applies to social work as well as to client functioning. "There is lawfulness in human affairs" (Hollis 1964b:167) since behavior is believed to be governed by psychological and social laws. Growing out of the relationship of casework to the scientific method, this suggests that as behavior and its determinants are understood through rational scientific study, so behavior becomes amenable to change by consciously directed processes. Governing the notion of causality, the idea also reaffirms commitment and adds dimension to the historical casework method. Ever since its roots in Mary Richmond's work, before Freudian theory infused the profession, the psychosocial school has conceptualized casework practice as proceeding through a rational process of study. The central link in Hollis' model is diagnostic assessment, or understanding, the bridge between the collection of data and actual practice procedures at any given time. One must differentially understand each person-in-situation in order to make differential decisions about intervention. Understanding is thus a way to individualize treatment, to support the uniqueness of each individual client.

With the interview as a primary arena for change, the social worker "seeks to engage the client's ego—his capacity to think, to reflect, to understand—in a re-evaluation of himself-in-his-situation (Hollis 1972:34).

Values

Prior to publication of the first edition, Hollis identified eight values that characterized casework practice and which became assumptions for operation in practice. They included the belief that each human life is precious, that individuals have responsibility for enhancing the welfare of others, and that in their essential worth all people are equal. By practice implication, social work carries the collective social responsibility for helping each individual client achieve the greatest possible satisfaction and happiness possible, and to do so without discrimination by race, sex, age, or class (Hollis 1964b:160–61).

In 1972 Hollis reaffirmed the essential value of the individual, including "the right of each man to live in his own unique way, provided he does not infringe unduly upon the rights of others" (Hollis 1972:14). Growing out of this value base, two essential professional attitudes are deeply embedded in practice: (1) acceptance—"maintaining an attitude of warm good will to the client, whether or not his way of behaving is socially acceptable and whether or not it is to the worker's liking" (Hollis 1972:14); and (2) respect for the client's self-determination, or what Hollis prefers to call self-direction—"the right to make his own choices" as well as "the capacity to guide oneself through the maze of interactions that make up the pattern of life" (Hollis 1972:15 and 102). Again, classism, racism, sexism, and ageism are antagonistic to this value base.

Every practice model is exclusive in fact if not by design; every model "values" some kinds of clients as contrasted with others. To the extent that psychosocial therapy emphasizes cognitive procedures which rely upon reflective capacity, face-to-face communication through verbal exchange in interviews most typically held in private offices, and is associated with voluntary services, there may be an unintended "ideal client" who is cognitively and verbally sophisticated and who has both the motivation for, and the access to, help-seeking in the voluntary sector.

Knowledge Base

Hollis draws upon several interrelated sources of knowledge: (1) "practice wisdom" and "practice theory," her own and others; (2) practice research, including numerous case studies, the seminal content analyses of process records through which she developed and refined a typology of treatment, and subsequent utilization of the typology by Hollis and others; (3) theoretical frameworks from behavioral and social sciences. In any practice model that draws upon a clearly defined knowledge base, the theoretical foundation is critical. It guides what and how the practitioner understands, suggests the unit of attention, and thereby frames the professional function, shapes the goals, and influences the procedures of practice.

A practice model that attempts to understand phenomena as complex as person-in-situation, requires a varied and complex supporting knowledge base. In drawing upon a well-integrated personality theory and various "sociological data" (Hollis 1972:13), it cannot be assumed that psychosocial interaction would occur *ipso facto*. In fact, that would be tantamount to premature synthesis. With separate theoretical explanations of "persons" and of "situations," there is the potential for explaining the gestalt by its parts, or for weighting what becomes "figure" and what becomes "ground."

"Knowledge attained early gives perspective to what comes later" (Hollis 1972:283). Since the mid-1920s, Freudian psychoanalytic theory began to enter social work's perception of social functioning, moving clinicians to look beyond and beneath appearances to explain the inexplicable. Freudian psychoanalytic theory became the theoretical center of the psychosocial school (anchored during the functional-diagnostic controversy) and remains at the core of Hollis' ever-expanding knowledge base as "a frame of reference for the understanding of the individual" (Hollis 1972:17). She incorporates numerous aspects of Freudian and neo-Freudian personality theory, including libidinal and aggressive drives (Hollis 1972:29), psychosexual development, the unconscious and its derivatives, ego as defense, and selected concepts from such ego theorists as Hartmann, Erikson, and White.

Consistent with the model's values, emphasis is on the drives as they change their form of demand and expression, including the libidinal shift from infantile narcissism to adult object relations. Consistent with the ideology, emphasis is on the ego as it "moves from primary to secondary modes of thought, develops its superego formation, builds its mechanisms of defense, adapts its perceptions and judgments to reality, and strengthens its capacities for direction and control" (Hollis 1972:18). Personality develops through the oral, anal, oedipal, and genital stages, while derivatives of these stages then affect social functioning throughout life. Powerful intrapsychic forces influence the person's perceptions of, expectations for, and reactions to, situations, and can in fact create their own environment (Hollis 1972:20 and 187).

Hollis emphasizes those aspects of Freudian theory which imply the extension of the developing intrapsychic self to its relationship with reality, noting that Freud conceptualized personality development as both biologically and interactionally determined. While he regarded neurosis as a way of resolving intrapsychic conflicts, "such conflicts themselves emerge from the interactions between the child and his parents or other parent figures. Freud's theory definitely rests upon social interaction as well as upon intrapsychic factors; it is therefore harmonious with the long-standing psychosocial orientation of casework" (Hollis 1972:18–19). Making the link to practice, she suggests that a Freudian orientation will "shift emphasis from manipulation of the environment and a conditioning type of approach to emphasis upon *interaction,* particularly upon the individual's part in the interaction" (Hollis 1972:19). This is the unique emphasis of the practice model.

While Freudian theory is a main tenet of psychosocial therapy, an increasingly expanding list of theoretical ideas and concepts has been woven into Hollis' Freudian perspective. From psychology, Piaget has consistently informed Hollis' understanding of cognitive development. Ideas from learning theory and Gestalt psychology have been utilized. Crisis theory has had a significant recent impact.

Beyond the personality, different levels of knowledge are drawn from many sources, although with a note of caution:

> These sociological data amplify the rich understanding of the internal dynamics of the personality developed by the Freudian school

of thought; they do not replace it. . . . Casework will drastically impoverish itself if it contents itself with accepting explanations of human behavior that rely only upon interpersonal phenomena (Hollis 1972:13).

Hollis demonstrates growing interest in family theories and communication theory. She is interested in issues of culture, class, and race, and she selects ideas from cultural anthropology, particularly as they bear on the development of the personality. Role theory is woven into the psychosocial tapestry, with implications drawn for diagnostic assessment (especially concepts of role expectations as they affect the individual's perceptions through reference groups and norms) and for professional behavior in environmental change.

Crisis theory focuses on the person's response to hazardous events; families are contexts for personal growth; communication theory contributes a systemic view primarily toward dyadic communication; roles extend personality into social behavior. Thus, each of these frameworks extends the person into interaction with the immediate interpersonal environment, the ideas illuminating the individual and not the nature of environmental structures or properties with which the individual interacts.

Lacking a coherent theoretical perspective on "situation" itself, its definition is somewhat fluid, competing in theoretical strength with ideas about the person. Psychosocial therapy does not incorporate theoretical knowledge of physical environments, nor of sociological units larger than dyads or families which tend to be viewed as contexts for individual development and functioning. Hollis was interested in a casework model of practice and did not employ theoretical knowledge of small groups, social networks, and organizations. Theoretically drawn to the individual personality, the model tends to define and explain social structure by the psychological characteristics of its individual participants: "Hence understanding of the person-in-situation requires varying degrees of understanding of the psychology of all the people involved in the gestalt" (Hollis 1972:1–10).

To integrate the expanding knowledge base and conceptualize the complex interplay of multiple variables affecting psychosocial functioning, the second edition makes extensive use of selected concepts from GST: "interaction-or transaction" (Hollis 1972:10); input, feed-back, and reverberation are emphasized, although equifinality and multifinality are not. Hollis refers to the systems of social work atten-tion, including the personality system anchored in Freudian psycho-analytic theory, adding elements of many other theoretical formula-tions, concepts, and data as they seem to fit, expand, or support this perspective.

Unit of Attention

With person-in-situation as the psychosocial focus, "the unit of atten-tion in casework becomes those systems that appear to be of salient importance to the problem for which the individual has sought help or to others that later become the focus of treatment" (Hollis 1972: 11).

Psychosocial Therapy appeared at a time when professional speciali-zation was differentiated by size of client unit, and this "family case-work" approach (Hollis 1950) was clearly designed for individuals and couples, with marital and family structures as contexts for indi-vidual functioning. The individualistic approach is consistent with the model's ideology, values, and theoretical foundation. In the sec-ond edition, with the inclusion of Isabel Stamm's chapter on family therapy, Hollis opened up the unit of attention to the family as a context for treatment and sometimes as "the client." It is possible that one could further stretch the client system to groups. Since psy-chosocial therapy does not theoretically or practically deal with phe-nomena of social collectives qua collectives, however, a group of stu-dents, a unit of residents, or a neighborhood of a community is potentially helped by this model only insofar as the entity serves as an arena for individual change, as in various models of group ther-apy.

Problem Definition

Problems are defined through a complex process of diagnostic as-sessment, which Hollis explicates in unique ways. Within each interview, and periodically during the total client-worker contact, the worker synthesizes and evaluates data about the client's current life, relevant past, and behavior in the casework interview in order to make systematic decisions for planning treatment. The process reflects the model's emphasis on understanding and individualizing through the scientific method. It consists of answering three questions: What is the problem? What is contributing to it? What can be changed or modified?

Problems are also defined in three sequential ways:

1. *Assessment.* "Assessment of the individual and the situation here go hand in hand" (Hollis 1972:261). To locate and conceptualize problems within the person-situation, the psychosocial therapist assesses external and internal factors in light of "average expectables." In the text, Hollis first applies Hartmann's concept to the client's situation or environment, suggesting that the social worker should consider reality pressures outside the range of "normally healthy common experiences" (Hollis 1972:261). She suggests some illustrative situational excesses and potential environmental factors for consideration: realities in income, schooling, medical care, employment, housing, and neighborhood conditions; personal relationships with family and friends; physical condition, as a dimension midway between external and internal factors.

Next, the personality system is placed against "average expectables." Psychoanalytic theory is used to systematize four distinct areas for assessment: drive functioning, ego functioning, superego functioning, and symptomatology. Because norms are influenced by many variables, the worker must guard against inflexible criteria of what is appropriate, evaluating the situation in light of ethnicity and class, and the personality in the context of the situation.

2. *Dynamic-etiological diagnosis.* Next, the worker tries to determine to what extent and in what way causative or contributing factors (current and past) lie within the situation that confronts the client, and to what extent and in what way they lie within the client, always evaluating interaction. The model guards against oversimplification, stressing the need to elaborate with specificity within the general areas of possible causality.

3. *Classification.* Three types of classification are cited as potentially valuable: (*a*) medical classification—a physician's diagnosis of a

medical disorder; (*b*) descriptive problem classification—categories centered on the symptomatic behavior resulting from interaction of person and situation, such as marital conflict, family breakdown, delinquency, unemployment, old age problems (Hollis 1972:273). (*c*) clinical diagnosis—"the only well-developed categorical scheme of diagnosis used in casework," designating major personality configurations (Hollis 1972:274). Predating DSM-III, the model suggests that the social worker distinguish between psychosis, neurosis, character disorder, and normality, making finer distinctions within each of the first three categories with psychiatric consultation where appropriate (Hollis 1972:275).

Psychosocial Therapy repeatedly emphasizes the interplay of multiple factors; however, person and situation emanate from separate and unequal theoretical perspectives, and most phases of diagnostic assessment address personality factors. Without a systematic way to assess interaction, it is therefore difficult to maintain the dual focus sought in the person-situation configuration. Although Hollis repeatedly emphasizes the importance of defining personality strengths as well as weaknesses, the psychoanalytic knowledge base tends to weigh problem definition in the direction of pathology, excess, and disorder.

Congruent and Explicit Interventions

Continuing the commitment to scientific classification that characterized psychosocial theorists in the late 1940s and 1950s, Hollis developed a penetrating typology of practice, based on research, which specifies interventive procedures employed by caseworkers in the treatment process.[4] Assuming this process to include a series of verbal and nonverbal communications, *Psychosocial Therapy* conceptualizes practice as a "constantly changing blend of some or all of these treatment procedures" (Hollis 1972:85).

Hollis' classification begins with Mary Richmond's distinction between direct treatment (helping the client effect change in his situation, interpersonal relationships, or himself through processes that occur directly between client and worker) and indirect treatment (direct change of the client's situation by the worker, including securing of resources and communication processes between worker and collateral). In her research, she studied only direct treatment.

Direct treatment involves a differential blend of six categories of procedures. They differ according to the dynamic which the worker attempts to evoke, that is, the nature of the change component that the communication is generally designed to bring into action. Thus, every step of the treatment process is purposive, seeking to produce an intended effect:

1. *Sustainment.* This category includes procedures designed to lessen client's anxiety, build belief and faith in the worker's good will and knowledge. Much sustainment occurs through nonverbal and paraverbal communication.

2. *Direct influence.* Procedures designed to promote or discourage a specific action or kind of behavior on the client's part constitute direct influence. They form a continuum from mild to extreme forms.

3. *Exploration-description-ventilation.* Such procedures are designed to draw out facts and feelings associated with them.

4. *Person-situation reflection.* This category includes procedures designed to promote discussion of the current or recent situation, client responses to it, and their interaction. This type of reflection is further subdivided into the type of change in the client's perception, awareness, or understanding sought by the communication. One is extrareflective, involving the situation; three are intrareflective, involving the client's own behavior; one lies midway between.

5. *Pattern-dynamic reflection.* Procedures in this category are designed to promote reflective consideration of psychological patterns involved in behavior and the underlying dynamics. Such reflection further extends (deepens) intrareflection.

6. *Developmental reflection.* Included here are procedures designed to promote reflective consideration of developmental factors contributing to dysfunctional psychological patterns. Developmental reflection further extends (deepens) intrareflection back through time.

Hollis specifies interventive procedures or techniques within each category, and elaborates numerous guiding principles for their use that reflect the model's knowledge and values: (1) The worker should keep "his finger on the pulse of the client's anxiety" (Hollis 1972: 315) so that procedures which lower anxiety (sustainment) often accompany or follow procedures that heighten anxiety (pattern-dynamic reflection). (2) The worker should encourage the client to do as much for himself as possible, so that guiding questions are preferable to interpretations in any reflective procedures.

The actual proportion of each of the six components differs from case to case, within each case, and within each interview. This allows for individualizing according to the nature of client problem, client's response to the worker, diagnostic assessment, worker style, agency setting, and time available or set for treatment (Hollis 1970:69). Ongoing research and Hollis' practice principles suggest that most psychosocial therapy usually rests heavily on a continual process of exploration-ventilation and reflective discussion of aspects of the current person-situation. It also assumes that considerable nonverbal sustaining procedures accompany these efforts (Hollis 1970:69; Hollis 1972:174–81).

In an effort to distinguish between psychosocial therapy and psychoanalytic treatment, both of which utilize a similar theoretical foundation, Hollis confronts the question of how deep and how far back to go in the personality dynamics. There seems to be greater emphasis in the Hollis practice model on differentiating professions by relative depth rather than by purpose. Acknowledging disagreement in the field, she takes the position that social work treatment focuses on conscious and preconscious material, but not unconscious content or experiences from infancy or very early childhood; that it does so in face-to-face interviews, usually spread out sufficiently so as not to encourage regression or transference neurosis. Free association, hypnosis, and dream analysis are not utilized. Thus, while understanding is rooted in a psychology of depth, interventions do not reach deeply into recesses of intrapsychic conflict.

While almost all of psychosocial therapy involves some form of direct treatment, Hollis states that more often than not worker-client interviews are accompanied by indirect treatment (alternately called milieu work, environmental work, resource work, collateral work) (Hollis 1972: ch. 9). While indirect treatment is not research-based and is classified somewhat differently, some strikingly similar conclusions are drawn for interventions.

The model begins with a distinction between treatment *through* the environment (involving use of resources and opportunities that exist or are potentially available) and treatment *of* the environment (modifications needed in the client's situation). Hollis postulates three ways to classify indirect treatment:

1. *The type of resources one is trying to employ.* Seven resources are identified. Five refer to the agency or organization, and appear to be subdivided according to the degree of social work control through auspice and presence; two refer to individual collaterals, using a dichotomy of task-oriented and feeling-oriented individuals.

2. *The type of communication used by the worker.* Hollis states that social workers have "tended to think of direct work as psychological and indirect as nonpsychological, or 'social.' This is an absolutely false assumption. Environmental work also takes place with people and through psychological means" (Hollis 1972:81). She therefore concludes that the first four procedures of direct treatment are appropriate for work with collaterals, and that "the skills needed for bringing about changes in the environment on the client's behalf are in many respects identical to those employed in direct treatment with the client" (Hollis 1972:140). In this decision, Hollis does not consider issues of social structure, differential power, or differential nontherapeutic contracts with nonclients.

3. *The type of role the worker assumes with the collateral.* Considered as collateral are the provider, locater, and creator of a resource; interpreter, mediator, or aggressive intervenor. In this regard, psychosocial therapy develops multiple roles for the worker in environmental change, although it does not explicate procedures to operationalize these roles, other than those used for treatment of the client. It operationalizes specific interventions for client interviews, although it does not explicate multiple worker roles in direct treatment.

Thus, the practice procedures and principles are explicit as well as congruent with all other components of this model, including the ideology. Just as psychosocial therapy assumes that understanding leads to action, and just as Hollis constructs bridges from theory to practice, so the knowledge base shapes problem definition and guides intervention. The psychosocial-person-in-situation phenomena are tilted in a decided operational direction.

Use of the Professional Relationship

Psychosocial Therapy conceptualizes the relationship between client and worker as a means of communication, as well as sets of attitudes and of responses, both realistic and unrealistic (including transference and countertransference,[5] defined quite broadly) (Hollis 1972:233–34). While it is not the only means toward change, a positive therapeutic relationship is essential to all practice as it allows honest communication to take place, allows trust to develop, and enables the client to accept and use the worker's help. The relationship requires the worker's acceptance, warmth, good will, and positive regard for the client, as well as confidence in his or her skills and the casework process; the client must be able to trust the worker.

The relationship is developed and modified through these attitudes as well as through specific treatment procedures. There are also special therapeutic uses of elements within the client-worker relationship. Extending Lucille Austin's concept of experiential treatment, the "corrective relationship" utilizes the transference. While the worker helps the client think about the nature of the person-situation configuration—augmented by sustaining attitudes and direct influence—the differences between the client's transferential expectations and the worker's actual responses in their discussion may counteract earlier negative parental effects. Thus, there may be greater acceptance and freedom for clients who experienced restrictive, hostile, or controlling parents; greater ego control for clients whose earlier experiences lacked realistic restraints; improved self-image for all clients, as the worker's attitudes and therapeutic optimism foster the client's own confidence. In a related way, the client's tendency to identify with a worker with whom there is a positive relationship can foster an imitative kind of learning, similar to a child's learning from a parent with whom he or she identifies.

In pattern-dynamic and developmental reflection, relationship phenomena can also be used as one source of increasing the client's self-understanding (although with less intensity and intrapsychic depth than in psychoanalysis, since the nature of the transference is different). By focusing on ego-dystonic preconscious elements in the transference and irrational components affected by experiences later than infancy and early childhood, the client is helped to understand dynamically his or her unrealistic responses to the worker and the ways they repeat earlier reactions to parents and closely related people. The client can use this awareness to correct similar distortions and responses to other people in his or her current life.

Desired Outcomes

Hollis distinguishes between ultimate objectives of treatment (which can be broad or specific) and intermediate or subgoals (which are specific steps toward the ultimate aim). It is difficult to characterize an ultimate objective that describes all psychological therapy; the model's intended inclusiveness, the diversity of persons-in-situations, and the emphasis on individualizing suggest a gamut of possibilities. Choice of objective(s) in any given case depends first on what the client wants, and therefore includes motivation; second, on what the worker thinks is most desirable and possible, and therefore involves diagnostic assessment; and third, on "peripheral factors" (Hollis 1972: 296–98), such as time, agency function and priorities, availability of dynamically oriented consultation, caseworker's skills. Goals must be flexible to change as clients change.

In general, the overall desirable outcome is "always some type of improvement in the client's personal-social life, that is, in his personal sense of comfort or satisfaction in life and often in his functioning as it affects the people with whom he is associated" (Hollis 1972:284). The goals may involve a change in the person or situation or both, in the client's personality and adaptive pattern, in the client's functioning in a specific problem, in realities facing the client, in interpersonal relationships, or in all these areas. It may be very specific and focused on a particular problem, such as helping a mother make a specific decision about her disabled child's education, or quite broad, as in trying to bring about a better parent-child relationship or personality adjustment.

As mentioned earlier, the psychosocial therapist does not elicit unconscious material, and thus does not work with ultimate psychological or social causes, and does not attempt to achieve basic personality structural change. In this sense, the model is concerned with adaptive behavior or behavioral patterns around the problems presented or emerging during the course of treatment, and psychosocial therapy does not seek to "cure" anyone or anything. At the same time, there is an "ideal objective of modifying or removing the causal factors in the client's difficulty" (Hollis 1972:296).

Uses of Time

While the psychosocial approach to practice was equated with open-ended, long-term treatment during the diagnostic-functional controversy in the 1930s and 1940s, crisis treatment and various forms of brief service with limited goals have been embraced as valid alternatives in *Psychosocial Therapy*. More traditional contacts of many months or years must be informed decisions for treatment planning rather than predetermined preferences. Similarly, the traditional fifty-minute weekly interview is not always possible or preferable. However, whenever the objective is substantial change in individual functioning, one usually requires uninterrupted and regular interviewing times (Hollis 1972:297).

Differential Use of Staff

Psychosocial therapy incorporates other clinical and nonprofessional staff in ways that are consistent with the theoretical and operational emphases of the model. Direct treatment is deeply informed by psychoanalytic theory and proceeds within the context of the professional relationship. To assist the professional in this in-depth work, selective use of collaterals is considered potentially helpful for gathering data in the psychosocial study. During diagnostic assessment and treatment, it is recommended that the social worker seek psychiatric, psychoanalytic, or medical consultation for particular problems.

Indirect treatment is less deeply studied, less theoretically grounded, and less fully operationalized in this model. In environmental work, where the worker has multiple roles, there are also possibilities for multiple helpers. Paraprofessional and indigenous staff members "can become experts on resources, on clients' rights, on eligibility procedures. They can be forceful advocates. By demonstration they can teach the client himself to become more effective in his use of resources" (Hollis 1972:140). They can also be useful role models for clients in connection with particular tasks, although Hollis suggests that this requires careful supervision by professionals because of the potential for overidentification and overuse of the transference as well as a tendency by some indigenous workers to impose their own values and goals on clients and thereby threaten self-determination. The graduate worker must carry responsibility for the general direction and coordination of the work, and for making any collateral contact that requires a high degree of differential interviewing skills. Thus, differential ability to interview skillfully becomes a critical factor in the differential use of manpower.

In discussing the potential roles for "feeling-oriented collaterals," the model implies an approach to practice that further extends the boundaries of environmental helpers "to accomplish psychological objectives identical in nature with those sought in direct treatment" (Hollis 1972:154). Following the treatment typology, Hollis suggests that relatives, friends, teachers, doctors, clergy, lawyers, and others may be in better position than the worker to offer sustainment and direct influence, and that consultations with other professionals can be arranged for particular person-situation reflection. There is an implicit potential for an interdisciplinary approach, with the social work therapist in a leadership position.

Work with Self-Help Groups

Although psychosocial therapy was developed prior to extensive professional attention to self-help groups and organizations in social work practice, it is likely that the model would incorporate their differential use with cautions similar to the options for extended manpower. While the dominant theoretical perspective has practice implications of a treating expert and a treated client-patient within the context of a professional relationship, the model's consistent emphasis on self-determination or self-direction is consonant with the philosophy of self-help.[6]

Availability to Effectiveness Research

As an empirically based model with commitment to research, and with a typology tested for its validity and reliability, *Psychosocial Therapy* made a highly significant first step toward the amenability to effectiveness research. Hollis delineates the practice input with clarity and specificity. Therefore, allowing for increasing crossing-over of boundaries between models, one could be at least reasonably confident that what is being tested for effectiveness is in fact psychosocial therapy, and thereby avoid overgeneralization about what works or does not work. Furthermore, to the extent that intermediate goals are always specified and specific, and each step in practice is conceptualized as purposive and goal-directed, the model lends itself to ongoing empirical research during the life of a given case or a cluster of cases. The typology provides marked potential for the role of research-practitioner who investigates what works, in what ways, with which clients, under what conditions. The typology has been used as a research instrument by such eminent professionals as Edward Mullen, William Reid, Francis Turner, Helen Pinkus, Shirley Ehrenkrantz, Ben Orcutt, and Edna Chamberlain. Appropriate outcome measures for psychosocial therapy have not been developed, however, and in this regard the model presents certain inherent problems. As suggested by Hollis in 1976, general social indicators are inadequate outcome measurements for individualized social casework, and the profession needs valid, client-oriented criteria rather than hypothesized social norms. She also identifies the need for measurements related to the type of change which "can reasonably be expected to result from casework treatment" (Hollis 1976:204–22). To the extent that the model's ultimate outcomes are diffuse—potentially very specific, or as broad as "improved communication" or "personality adjustment"—it is difficult to develop measurements for this range of expected outcomes. Despite the empirical base of this model, work would have to be done to make it readily available to effectiveness research.

Psychosocial Therapy within an Eco-Systems Perspective

Perspectives offer vision; models offer methodology. By providing a lens through which to view the relation of parts to one another and to the whole, a practice perspective suggests what and how to see; it does not prescribe what to do. By providing a slice of practice life, a practice model perceives phenomena in a certain way and it further presents a means for action (Siporin 1975:362). This distinction becomes important when one considers how to utilize psychosocial therapy, as presented in 1972, within the eco-systems perspective.

It has been suggested that the eco-systems perspective can encompass diverse practice models used to carry out professional purposes. In this regard, there is a subtle but significant difference between incorporating a model to fit within another perspective and selectively utilizing particular practice roles or interventions of a model within that perspective. *Psychosocial Therapy* provides the social worker with specific processes, procedures, and principles for helping individuals, as well as a framework for differential interventions; this technology can be utilized differentially by professionals who choose to perceive practice phenomena from an eco-systems perspective or from any other perspective. As suggested in the preceding analysis, *Psychosocial Therapy* also reflects a particular theoretical and philosophical view of human functioning which emanates largely from Freudian psychoanalytic understanding and which thereby frames the way problems are defined and procedures are emphasized. While the model is committed to integrating multiple variables, the relative salience of variables becomes settled by such factors as the relative power of its knowledge base. *Psychosocial Therapy* has its own perspective on social functioning and social work practice, and the integrity of the model ought not to be disrupted by trying to adjust it to fit another perspective from another time. To do so would be to create a different model of practice.

In fact, this may be one source of inconsistency in the second edition of *Casework: A Psychosocial Therapy*. As this model was first being developed, social work reliance on Freudian theory was severely criticized as being irrelevant in a time of social upheaval and as being reductionistic in its linear-causal explanations. Its apparent psychic determinism seemed to jar with the rapid changes in society, including roles and mores; focus on early personality development seemed to freeze the inner life in long periods of infancy; its magnificent psychological insights seemed to minimize cultural diversity.

In 1972 Florence Hollis made certain revisions that reflected changing social, theoretical, and professional attitudes. In addition to incorporating the results of subsequent research and refinements of the treatment typology, she added a chapter on environmental work and one on family therapy, added new concepts and theoretical frameworks from modern ego psychology and GST, and sought to be systemic at the same time that she maintained her basic perspective.

In spite of her integrative capacity and intent, contradictions appeared that have practice as well as semantic implications. While she states that the term "therapy" is not descriptive of environmental interventions, and espouses equal concern with person and situation, the title and thrust of the model remain as a psychosocial therapy (Hollis 1972:5). Hollis maintains that "simplistic explanations have yielded to a recognition of the interplay of multiple factors in shaping both the individual and his dilemmas" (Hollis 1972:3), yet within her perspective, she identifies contributing factors or causes of the problem as lodged primarily within the person *or* the situation *or* both. She also selects goals of treatment and points of entry in large part according to a perceived major cause. Given the theoretical emphasis of the model, this decision is also weighted. While she disputes a psychosocial dichotomy between person-change as psychological and environmental change as social, she occasionally reduces both to psychological factors.

The eco-systems perspective on practice in its transactional focus does not separate ever-developing person from ever-developing environment, and does not seek quantitative or linear causal explanations even on multiple variables. In this increasingly complex, fragmented, and sometimes threatening world of the 1980s no human psyche is ever free from, or independent of, "excessive" environmental demands or serendipitous opportunities for growth at any time in the life cycle. A practitioner who perceives the world through the eco-systems lens would not locate problems primarily within the individual or primarily within the environment, but always within the complex relationship between a particular human being and a particular environmental matrix (including physical, and social environments whose boundaries extend beyond immediate interpersonal realities) at a particular time. Help would mean enhancing the process of adaptation between the individual and environment (or family/group and its environment) to achieve a better "fit." The practitioner who perceives phenomena eco-systemically would have to find alternative ways of conceptualizing practice than the distinctions between direct and indirect treatment (or clinical and concrete services), for in a transactional focus, all interventions are clinical when they affect the client.

Furthermore, natural life processes of growth and development imply a potential multiplicity of experts, including clients. Problems with multiple factors imply multiple possible points of entry, not necessarily those that are primarily fixed upon the client. And with the potential for prevention and developmental services, client status does not automatically imply breakdown.

As practice approaches continue to emerge from this perspective—or as individual professionals choose to use the eco-systems lens while they practice—they need not and ought not discard that which has theoretical or operational value. Whereas the perspective offers breadth of conceptual vision, diverse models offer depth of theoretical understanding and operational practice. In this regard, *Psychosocial Therapy* provides a distinct methodology to engineer practice within the eco-systems perspective, as part of an interventive repertoire.

Hollis provides by example a rigorous, disciplined approach to the helping process, including the precarious bridge from understanding (synthesizing and evaluating data) to operationalizing (planning and executing practice interventions) at any given time. The eco-systems perspective would ensure the wide-angle focus on what is being understood (person-and-environment) and widen the possibil ities for points of entry, targets of intervention, aims of intervention and repertoire of interventions as this discipline is adapted throughout a case. The concept of an interventive "dynamic" is useful at all levels of practice, no matter what the target of intervention. With each intervention conceptualized as purposive, the practitioner must hold himself or herself accountable as the immediate response provides feedback regarding the actual effect or effectiveness. Thus, practice can become technical although not reduced to technicianship.

Furthermore, if the assessment of a total ecological system suggests the point of entry or target of intervention as an individual client (or individuals within a dyadic or family context), a differential blend of the six treatment procedures can be used during interviews with these clients, with selective use of practice principles as guidelines for action. The psychosocial therapy approach seems particularly relevant when it is determined that changing a client's awareness and understanding—influencing expectations, perceptions, knowledge—can enhance adaptation in particular interpersonal relationships. Such cognitive-emotional mastery may be essential when overwhelming stress has temporarily blocked an individual's ability to think rationally and this interferes with coping, or when personality characteristics are maladaptive for particular tasks facing a client. Thus, a blend of procedures may comprise most of the practice in some select cases, or some of the work in many cases.

In addition, the practice roles conceptualized under indirect treatment can be incorporated as an expandable range of possibilities for all practice activity within the eco-systems perspective. However, one needs to be cautious about utilizing specific techniques of sustainment, direct influence, exploration-description-ventilation, and person-situation reflection when attempting to influence or modify aspects of the environment. Collaterals are not clients, and an environmental change is not always reducible to worker-collateral dyadic communication.

Case Illustration [7]

The following case illustrates the utilization of psychosocial therapy within an eco-systems perspective. It demonstrates how a social worker adapted the model during a critical period of case activity to help a client cope with a highly stressful problem. The case seems appropriate as an end to this discussion of Florence Hollis' work, since she seemed to appreciate the interplay of work and self-esteem long before it was fashionable to do so.[8]

The agency is a social work unit in a labor union for workers whose blue, pink, and occasionally white collars had faded from changing industrial conditions. It was a time when economic and political uncertainties threatened the personal and interpersonal well-being of workers and their families, just as growing pressures in family and community affected work performance. The agency was committed to increasing the accessibility and relevance of services to these workers who underutilized help that they needed from the voluntary and public sectors. A comprehensive social work program emphasized crisis intervention, liaison, and advocacy with appropriate community resources, and counseling around health, mental health, family, and particularly work-related problems. Furthermore, social workers were placed at strategic sites throughout the total union organization, becoming part of the fabric of the work environment. Within this setting, social workers with an eco-systems perspective had a natural environment for practice, including potential for unique and multiple points of entry within a natural life space.

They also had the challenge of helping people who were initially suspicious of social work, as they defined and distrusted the profession at its caricatured extremes of welfare and psychotherapy. No matter how problem-ridden, these working people were not and would not be treated as dependent or pathological parts separable from a complex, fragmented urban condition. Social workers had to be very sensitive to the attitudes that accompanied or precluded seeking or taking help, flexibly negotiating roles, and actively involving clients in mutual problems definition, with solutions that often built on action.

The client in this case was a union member of eighteen years whose initial utilization of service followed a pattern common in this setting. He sought help during periods of felt emergency, and over time developed trust in the social worker. Elements from psychosocial therapy were used primarily during a later period of worker-client contact that could only have emerged from a context of brief, intermittent episodes of service which combined crisis intervention, mediation, and advocacy.

> Mr. F. was a 50-year-old, white, European-born, Jewish, married, skilled worker who had suffered a serious back injury that temporarily disabled him. After several months of rehabilitation, he was unable to perform his usual job, which required manipulation of heavy materials and machinery. At first he turned to his union, and several alternative positions were located, despite a bleak market in an industry that was soon to enter a seasonal period of lay-offs.
>
> Mr. F. left each job after several days or weeks, finding the work too difficult (requiring painful physical exertion or new skills that affected his performance and salary) or too humiliating (carrying lower status and less pay).
>
> Mr. F. became despondent, and behaved in dependent ways that were tinged with guardedness and suspiciousness. He began to frustrate and alienate others, and he whined and begged for help, but shared only partial information about himself and his job losses, vacillated between daily frantic appearances at his union local and subsequent failure to follow-up or maintain necessary contact, behaved as if he were doomed and being victimized, and vaguely implied that the union did not want to find him the "right job" in order to force early retirement and thereby save pension costs.
>
> He registered for unemployment benefits, and entered a short but vicious cycle: he began a new job, was fired or quit, withdrew to an increasingly tense family environment—his wife resented his growing passivity, and he remorsefully accepted his adult children's needed financial contributions, although doing so was culturally alien to him—and then started all over again. Within several months

his social supports disintegrated, his appetite for life decreased, and his despair deepened.

During this three-months period Mr. F. was receiving medical care sponsored by the union, and periodically sought help from the social worker in the same building. Mr. F.'s requests were always vague but urgent, often focused on forms or bills that he could not understand and that seemed to represent his feeling victimized and helpless in the face of those in power or authority. He seemed to be an isolated, dependent, overtly passive but deeply enraged and profoundly pained man, desperate for someone on whom to depend at the same time that he mistrusted nearly everyone.

In early contacts Mr. F. was evasive and guarded, slipping into a thickened accent, discussing tangential issues, or changing the subject whenever the worker explored for detail. The worker stayed very close to the client's overt concerns. Mr. F.'s injury had thrust him up against and between the cracks of multiple new systems with which he had to negotiate: new departments and personnel in his union, hospitals and private physicians, the insurance company. It also thrust him up against incomprehensible and inhuman policies of Workmen's Compensation/disability/unemployment that seemed to punish the newly disabled worker. The social worker helped Mr. F. decipher and fill out his bottomless pile of forms, helped him mediate systems, connected him to resources, and consistently kept an open-door policy. As he withdrew from others, Mr. F. began to turn episodically to his social worker and began to trust explorations as concerns rather than control.

In the period under discussion, Mr. F. returned to see his social worker after he had been through a medical procedure to relieve the pain in his back. Although physicians found no physical basis, he had begun to somaticize and generalize pains to other parts of his body. Within several weeks, he appeared agitated and depressed; he repeatedly referred to the loss of his manhood, expressed vague suicidal wishes, and reported early morning awakening. As the worker empathically stayed very close to his feelings during this time, missing pieces of past and present poured out, further clarifying and complicating an already highly complex person-environment problem. What had begun with a single event had multiple contributing factors and multiple reverberating consequences among Mr. F., his family, his work organization, and his past and present.

Mr. F. was a survivor of the concentration camps, a fact known to the very few whom he most trusted. He had begun to associate his injury and job loss with past traumas and atrocities over which he also had no control, and yet over which he also felt overwhelming and unspeakable guilt as senseless as the holocaust itself. As he slipped into the workless role, the hell of the recent past began to be relived in recurring nightmares of victimization. The war had destroyed his adolescent hopes for a future; the injury threatened the fragile equilibrium in a middle-aged man whose self-esteem and sanity hinged on his customary work. His job as a skilled worker, obtained through a union with protective powers, provided a critical and dependable role, with opportunities for security and some measure of status recognized by Mr. F., his family, and his work organization; it also provided a structure to seal off and defend him against the traumatic past. As he was forced to confront his inabilities to regain his former powers and position, his frustrations with himself seesawed with rage at others upon whom he now depended or had to combat (union, lawyers, doctors, wife, children) and whom he expected to turn on him (as his country of birth had), disappear (as his family of origin had), or abandon him (as he felt his paternalistic union now had). As he began to lose control, he paradoxically gained it by creating his most dreaded expectations of abandonment; he lost the very social supports so desperately needed to attenuate the consequences of loss of work.

Yet Mr. F. was not the only victim. His family could not tolerate the disruption to its fragile equilibrium over which its members had no apparent choice and limited options. The threats to family roles and norms occurred at a time when the stage of family development already demanded changes in roles and norms. His work organization could not secure an endless stream of jobs, and could not tolerate the behavior of a member who would not keep a job at a time when jobs were scarce and the power of unions was being severely challenged. The worker decided to enter this case at all three levels.

With support, Mr. F. agreed to a psychiatric consultation arranged by the social worker. He received a diagnosis of psychotic depression, a prescription for Mellaril, and a recommendation for vocational rehabilitation for the disabled and for job retraining in another industry. The social worker disagreed with this recommendation. In private conference, he shared his own knowledge and perceptions that while this plan might be advisable in the near future, at present it could be tantamount to an ultimate rejection and abandonment by his union, reinforce Mr. F.'s own redefinition of a physical injury as a personal failure, and turn his suicidal thoughts into actuality (judgments verified by Mr. F.'s own perceptions and feelings). Since victimization is experienced as externally imposed and environmental, it requires environmental as well as personal "adjustment." The psychiatrist agreed, and continued to work together with Mr. F. and the social worker, monitoring medication and providing ongoing consultation.

Hollis states that treatment goals are based not only on what is desirable, but what is modifiable; but what is modifiable is affected by one's perspective, including one's curiosity about, and creativity in, areas of change outside the range of immediate vision. The social worker met with Mr. F. to clarify alternatives, careful not to impose his own standards, rescue fantasies, or uninformed prognostic pessimism. Mr. F. could try to : (1) find another job through the union; (2) find another job through his own resources; (3) find another job in another industry; (4) apply for early retirement; (5) wait until he was eligible for permanent disability payments. The worker made a critical decision: rather than help Mr. F. "adjust" to the permanent limitations of his disability, he would begin by trying to help him reach his articulated goal, no matter how unrealistic it seemed to be.

The ultimate goal of this case was to locate or create a job in the same industry, one that Mr. F. could physically perform and with status and salary comparable to his former position. This was far beyond the worker's own function, power, or capacity; it was fraught with risk and unpredictability in an industry and market that were themselves out of control. No matter what the actual outcome, however, it was critical that Mr. F. begin to mobilize and experience support.

To work toward this aim required closing gaps between Mr. F. and his union, as well as between Mr. F. and his family, in order to develop the multisystemic resources essential for the job hunt or the job loss, no matter what the actual outcome. As part of this process, it would be necessary that Mr. F.'s perceptions and expectations of a hostile world be attenuated, that he begin to handle his fears and suspicions in ways that did not alienate those he needed and thereby deepen his isolation and sense of victimization.

The practice, therefore, included a psychosocial therapeutic process aimed at helping Mr. F. communicate his needs more effectively and function in more adaptive ways with his family, his union representatives, and other systems involved in his disability. "Intermediate goals" and actual practice then focused on helping Mr. F. in several related areas: (1) to reassess the realities of his work situation and work capacities, including the fact that in most jobs he could not initially work as fast or efficiently as he had before his injury; (2) to reevaluate his expectations and perceptions of these capacities, and the extent and personal meaning of his limitations, including unrealistic and distorted aspects; (3) to consider alternatives to his ideal goal, including work that would carry lower pay and status, at least temporarily, as a step toward work reentry; (4) to understand when and how his own behavior (negativism, exaggeration of his infirmities, begging for help but providing only partial information and then withdrawing, helplessness and passivity, isolation) perpetuated crises and worked against his articulated goals; (5) to understand that some of this behavior suggested understandable ambivalence about his work goals, because of his own limitations and barely suppressed rage at himself and others.

The social worker utilized all six procedures of direct practice in different proportions at different times. He was guided by principles of monitoring anxiety and knowledge of psychodynamic, biological, and cultural factors related to agitated depression. Given Mr. F.'s own level of anxiety and guilt, a traumatic past reactivated in the present, class and cultural expectations, and predilection to crisis, the worker emphasized rather active techniques of sustainment and direct influence to accompany person-situation reflection.

Sustainment, for example, ranged from ongoing encouragement and recognition of Mr. F.'s attempts to find and maintain a job while paying careful attention to his own perceptions of the efforts, to active demonstration of concern such as helping Mr. F. arrange medical appointments at times compatible with his interim work schedule.

Direct influence included active advice and more extreme urging through confrontation during periods of crisis, to help Mr. F. regain control.

Exploration-ventilation was used differentially, depending on the specific content and Mr. F.'s response to it; whatever mobilized his massive anxiety or guilt was avoided.

Person-situation reflection was used whenever possible as the core of the interviews. In various ways, the social worker focused on Mr. F.'s perceptions of others, himself, and the relationships between them, around the five areas of content indicated previously. It was important that Mr. F. understand that he was in fact the victim of circumstances beyond his control *and* that he was not helpless or out of control in all areas. The worker also monitored carefully the client's fragile reaching out for the object of his rage.

The practice selectively used pattern-dynamic reflection and rarely used developmental reflection. These procedures could mobilize massive anxiety and guilt, deepening the client's association between past and present, and perpetuating his retreat to feelings of helpless and defenseless victimization. There were times, however, when awareness of his patterns helped Mr. F. mobilize some control over particular tasks, such as approaching a union official.

The worker also utilized the relationship, including elements in the unique transference (in which Mr. F. had literally transferred earlier experiences from childhood and adolescence to the paternalistic union and the social worker).

The worker realized that while Mr. F. conveyed gratitude, he had grave fears of being controlled or abandoned by those in perceived power. The worker carefully timed interventions to open discussion of the worker-client relationship when he sensed Mr. F.'s unvoiced dissatisfaction or fears were interfering with their work together. He also identified areas in which Mr. F.'s own help was needed in order to help him; this conveyed the work as a mutual process. Finally, he used Mr. F.'s growing trust in the professional relationship to extend his interest back to the union; for example, he often contacted union officials in Mr. F.'s presence, and then discussed what had transpired, including Mr. F.'s perceptions of the worker as part of this union. Disagreements (too often called distortions by others) were discussed openly and freely.

In addition, the social worker attempted to reach out to Mrs. F. She would not agree to marital or family social work, but maintained periodic telephone contact with the worker. The model was helpful in identifying certain psychodynamic factors involved in Mrs. F.'s transactions with her husband and children, and in providing several procedures for intervention.

Psychosocial therapy was very useful, but not sufficient. In the first place, direct influence and active thinking did not always lead to action, and this client needed more than understanding. He needed specific problem-solving skills, often required through structured tasks, within interviews (including role play, role rehearsal), and within his own life, to "practice" alternate ways of coping with specific problems. Furthermore, the multiple systems involved required an active liaison; Mr. F. and the worker *together* negotiated various systems related to his disability and work status, and in this regard indirect and direct treatment were indistinguishable. Most important, Mr. F.'s inability to find and maintain a satisfying job was not only a result of his inability to accept reality, his lack of reality-testing, his lack of judgment, or his lack of interpersonal skills, but also of his lack of power.

The social worker also lacked ascribed power and direct access to resources within Mr. F.'s local; but there are other types of power and other routes available in formal and informal systems. He consulted with officials from various union settings, to understand the political way of life in this organization which helped him reconsider strategies with Mr. F., his family, and the union. He contacted the social worker who was directly connected to Mr. F.'s local; together they developed an organizational assessment of latent pockets of formal and informal resources, and they began to work as a team. Through skills of interdisciplinary collaboration, persuasion, mediation, advocacy, and occasional bargaining, a formal and informal network of helpers was created. As more complete knowledge was differentially shared, at Mr. F.'s initiative or with his informed consent, this "case" opened up, and Mr. F. shifted from being a private annoyance to something of a public symbol, his cause a mission to his local and others in the union. Mr. F.'s changing experience reverberated with changing expectations, and he was enabled to maintain himself during several months of severe stress. Against apparently impossible odds, over time a job was created through the political process, a job in which Mr. F. was to examine the production of merchandise he once produced himself. Within a week, his depression lifted.

Conclusion

In 1964 and 1972 Florence Hollis reflected an integrative mind and intent as she constantly reached for synthesis between polar ideas, including the link from theory to practice and person to situation. Influenced as she was by the era of Freudian theory, her practice model was weighted in a direction that deepened the understanding of personality, while environmental and transactional understanding was less refined. The linear perspective could not but narrow the view of causation and subsequent practice decisions. Her research and practice interventions focused sharply on changing people, but the model· had limited operational specificity for changing "situations" and for changing the deep and complex transactions among people and their physical and social environments.

The psychosocial bridge is a precarious one to traverse in any theoretical or practice model. The difficulties are not Hollis' alone. On the contrary, she is a significant part of professional continuity and development. Models are not discovered; they develop in and through time, and reflect the larger issues of their time. Psychosocial therapy emerged at a particular time in the development of social work. The eco-systems perspective has been another attempt to "reformulate, refine" (Hollis 1972:8), and rework that which has been the hallmark of this profession. If the perspective provides a framework for the relationship of multiple parts, it does so through time as well as space. The present cannot be disassociated from the past any more than the person can be dichotomized from environment. At the level of professions, what is "traditional" cannot be rejected for apparently new ideas or paradigms. The answers are quite different, but the question and the quest are not dissimilar: the relationship of people and environments.

NOTES

1. According to Turner, the psychosocial concept was first used in 1930 by Frank Hankins of Smith College, embraced by Gordon Hamilton, and established as the professional preference by Hollis (Turner 1974:85).

2. For an overview of the psychosocial school of thought, see Hollis 1970, 1971, 1977 and Turner 1974.

3. When one reviews the span of Hollis' writings, the continuity and integrity of her ideas become apparent. Earlier works trace out some of the central themes, contributions, and constraints that subsequently develop in her model. For example, Hollis has consistently been concerned with the meaning of behavior for diagnostic assessment, the relationship between diagnostic assessment and treatment, and the quest for specification, classification, and "universally accepted principles of treatment" (Hollis 1931:1). See Hollis 1931, 1939, 1949, 1950, 1951, 1958, 1962, and 1963.

4. Hollis was dissatisfied with classifications that categorized by type of ultimate objective (e.g., clarification vs. supportive treatment), or that confused means and ends. Suggesting a need for a more fluid model of classification, she focused on the alternative means by which a desired effect at a specific moment could be achieved. In her content analyses of process records, she classified each communication according to four dimensions: who is communicating; the content; the change context (for client communication) or change objective (for worker communication); the dynamic. It is the

dynamic ingredient which led to the explication of interventions (Hollis 1968:70).

5. Hollis defines "clear and specific transference reactions" as those in which the client displaces onto the worker feelings and attitudes experienced in early childhood or later life, with parents or other closely associated people, and responds as if the worker were that person. Less specific distorted ways of relating to people that have become part of the personality can also enter treatment, whether or not the client identifies the worker with early figures. Countertransference is broadly defined as any "countertherapeutic" response, whether realistic or unrealistic (Hollis 1972:233–4).

6. In "Casework and Social Class," Hollis refers to Riessman's concept of "helper therapy" in reference to helping low-income clients (Hollis 1965:463–71).

7. This case was developed from materials being prepared for the Industrial Social Welfare Center, Columbia University School of Social Work. Certain details have been changed or omitted to protect the confidentiality of client and organizational participants.

8. Although Hollis did not have the conceptual tools to elaborate this interplay, the importance of work for self-esteem is interspersed throughout her work. This is demonstrated at the beginning of her writing (Hollis 1939) and throughout her career. The presenting problem in this case illustration is strikingly similar to a case briefly cited in Hollis 1972:63–64.

REFERENCES

Hollis, Florence. 1931. "Emotional Factors in the Attitudes of Clients Toward Relief: Seven Case Studies." *Smith College Studies in Social Work* (December).

—— 1939. *Social Case Work in Practice: Six Case Studies.* New York: Family Service Association of America.

—— 1949. *Women in Marital Conflict—A Casework Study.* New York: Family Service Association of America.

—— 1950. "The Techniques of Casework." In Cora Kasius, ed., *Principles and Techniques in Social Casework: Selected Articles, 1940–1950.* New York: Family Service Association of America. Reprinted from *Social Casework* (June 1949).

—— 1951. "The Relationship Between Psychosocial Diagnosis and Treatment." *Social Casework* (February).

—— 1958. "Personality Diagnosis in Casework." In Howard J. Parad, ed., *Ego Psychology and Dynamic Casework*. New York: Family Service Association of America.

—— 1962. "Analysis of Casework Treatment Methods and Their Relationship to Personality Change." *Smith College Studies in Social Work* (February).

—— 1963. "Contemporary Issues for Caseworkers." In Howard J. Parad and Roger R. Miller, eds., *Ego-Oriented Casework: Problems and Perspectives*. New York: Family Service Association of America. Reprinted from *Smith College Studies in Social Work* (February 1960).

—— 1964a. *Casework: A Psychosocial Therapy*. New York: Random House.

—— 1964b. "Principles and Assumptions Underlying Casework Practice." In Jean S. Heywood, ed., *An Introduction to Teaching Casework Skills*. London: Routledge and Kegan Paul.

—— 1965. "Casework and Social Class." *Social Casework* (October). Reprinted in Francis J. Turner, ed. *Differential Diagnosis and Treatment in Social Work*. 2d ed., New York: Free Press, 1976.

—— 1968. *A Typology of Casework Treatment*. New York: Family Service Association of America. Four articles reprinted from *Social Casework* (June 1967, October 1967, January 1968, March 1968).

—— 1970. "The Psychosocial Approach to the Practice of Casework." In Robert W. Roberts and Robert H. Nee, eds., *Theories of Social Casework*. Chicago: University of Chicago Press.

—— 1971. "Social Casework: The Psychosocial Approach." In *Encyclopedia of Social Work*. New York: NASW.

—— 1972. *Casework: A Psychosocial Therapy*. 2d ed. New York: Random House.

—— 1976. "Evaluation: Clinical Results and Research Methodology." *Clinical Social Work Journal* (Fall).

—— 1977. "Social Casework: The Psychosocial Approach." In *Encyclopedia of Social Work*. New York: NASW.

Siporin, Max. 1975. *Introduction to Social Work Practice*. New York: Macmillan.

Turner, Francis J., ed. 1974. *Social Work Treatment: Interlocking Theoretical Approaches*. New York: Free Press.

IV

CASEWORK: A PROBLEM-SOLVING PROCESS

Sandra Abrams

The problem-solving approach in social work practice was developed by Helen Harris Perlman in 1957. The model was considered, at that time, a radical new restructuring of casework, a branching off from the dominant diagnostic casework process which emphasized psychodynamic theory within an open-ended, analytic framework. Perlman sought a new way of organizing and synthesizing an action theory of the casework process which would enable the individual client to address immediate presenting problems while extracting resources from the surrounding environment. This approach to practice has remained intact, although the traditional individual unit of attention has expanded to include family and group problem-solving processes.

The framework for the problem-solving model has four parts: person, problem, place, and process.

Person. The person is viewed as "a by-product of his inherited and constitutional transaction with persons and forces in his life experience. . . . Thus, he is a product of his past, not a final product, but a product in the process of becoming" (Perlman 1977:1293). The assumption in this model is that in people's everyday roles certain aspects of the personality are exposed to powerful stimuli at crucial times and then undergo modification in behavior and affect. "A person is knowable and understandable to himself and others only in the context of a given set of psychosocial circumstances, within the boundaries of a given situation or life-space and in transaction with given forces" (Perlman 1977:1293). Thus, while the person is viewed as a living whole, a biopsychosocial system , it is only the part of him or her that is engaged in a problem-solving event that is diagnosed or worked with.

Problem. "The problem-solving model is, by definition, based on the presence and identification by both help-seeker and helper of a problem for which help is being either sought or referred. For the situation to be a problem to the help-seeker, he or she must feel some discomfort about it, and it is not necessarily the major problem or basic cause of the person's difficulty" (Perlman 1977:1293). Problems identified through this practice model are usually difficulties found in person-to-person or person-to-task relationships.

Place. The place "is the specific organization or agency that utilizes casework as its mode of helping people. The agency's purposes define its functions, services and areas of social concern it considers to be within its purview and expertise" (Perlman 1977:1298). As part of Perlman's framework, place is the setting for practice.

Process. This element includes the therapeutic relationship, viewed as "the most potent in human change . . . a continuous and dynamic context in which problem-solving takes place" (Perlman 1977:1294). The process also includes professional responsibility to determine need for material provision and to make resources available to the client. The process stimulates and supports ego functioning through four steps: (1) clear identification of the problem, (2) expression and clarification of emotions, (3) clarification of possibilities available to the client, (4) participation by the client in defining and acting on the problem. The process does not start with study of the problem, but with dealing with the client as the client takes action in defining the problem.

Ideological Biases

The problem-solving model is ideologically committed to a particular set of ideas which clearly establish the structure for the selection of knowledge, use of the professional relationship, assessment and interventive processes, and other components which make up a unified casework approach to practice. Basic to problem-solving ideology are philosophical views of existentialism and concepts of social psychology that deal with the social self through social role transactions. Perlman assumes that all of human life is engaged in a problem-solving process, a natural struggle toward the goal of better adaptation, and that the person, through use of ego functions in daily conscious and unconscious decisions, imitates life in "doing" problem-solving. An implicit assumption is that when a person fails to cope with a problem it is due to some lack of motivation, capacity, or opportunity to solve the problem in appropriate ways. Perlman does not view failures in social functioning as being due to a person's weak ego, psychopathology, or derivative intrapsychic conflict; rather, such failures are considered deficits in problem-solving means. The process makes no attempt to cure or to ameliorate problems totally. The approach suggests that people, individually and collectively, can alter their own behavior if they possess a clear idea of what to do and if their wishes regarding problem definition are respected. The model is positive in its view of people as capable of acting in a responsible, independent manner in their own behalf.

In the problem-solving model casework clients are those whose problem-solving capacities or resources are maladaptive and thus must use social agencies for material or psychological help with their present problem. The person is viewed as transacting with the environment, "continually a person-becoming within the transactional field" (Perlman 1970:143). This social becoming is a product of the interaction between the person and his or her specific social reality. Thus, the model views the person as developing his or her identity through continuous transactions with social realities, particularly with others and through the performance of everyday tasks.

The model assumes further that a person extends him or herself in a drive for effectance or mastery. All people are thought to possess an autonomous problem-solving apparatus which is found in the conflict-free functions of the ego—the functions of perception, judgment, cognition, memory, and choice. People actively engage in a search for the expansion of a sense of self, a struggle which is continually impeded by such punitive life experiences as poverty of stimuli, lack of opportunity, and self-destructiveness. The person, in changing some aspect of negative life experiences, can improve his or her current social functioning and sense of personal well-being. The individual must, therefore, be motivated to pursue solutions to problems and to cope with the emotional and material obstacles which block drive to attain competence and personal growth.

In this regard, the problem-solving model takes the view that the special arenas for casework operations are the social role tasks and role transactions by which the individual expresses his identity and quest for competence. The approach is, therefore, biased in its study of the present-day interpersonal functioning of the individual and his or her immediate role transactions with others as the major field through which the autonomous ego struggles in the drive for competency. The study of intrapsychic conflict, or use of psychodynamic theory to uncover unconscious motivation, is not considered central to the problem-solving process. The approach attempts to make maximum use of the person's conscious and conflict-free ego functions in order to develop new ways of coping which may better enable the individual to address the new problems one inevitably encounters during the living process. Therefore, problem-solving is committed to a rational view of life.

Values

The problem-solving model clearly holds to the idea of an open value system which does not discriminate against participants on the basis of sex, race, age, or class. Perlman sought a way to modify the traditional, psychodynamically oriented casework approach that reached primarily those clients capable of engaging in a long-term relationship with the worker so as to work through intrapsychic conflict or gain self-awareness. The problem-solving model broadens the potential clientele to include persons who can benefit from a shorter term, goal-oriented treatment focused on current social functioning.

In fact, Perlman thought the problem-solving model could be particularly effective with multiproblem families because of the attention paid to client-defined problems, clear delineation of courses of action, narrow limits in decision-making offered to the client, short-term goals, small but accessible rewards, and the nutritive supports of a helping relationship (Perlman 1977:1298). In keeping with this orientation, the model values action and the heightened motivation to engage in action-focused activities in order to achieve the goal of self-competence. But the person is not left to deal with external environmental deprivation on his own. Rather, the model calls for the worker to identify potential emotional and environmental resources which will aid in adaptation to problems in addition to providing the necessary emotional and material support to the individual throughout the casework process.

Perlman believed strongly in a democratic, humanitarian society. She advocated provision of social resources for the poor and thought that institutions and helping professions must establish strong networks of services to provide physical, financial, and educational support to multiproblem individuals and families, recognizing that a person can cope with problematic social realities only when services are made available and resource networks are in operation.

Thus, the model attempts to expand the casework process, which Perlman thought had been primarily focused on the inner or intrapersonal dynamic, to include a recognition of the impact of environmental deprivation on personal functioning. Although the problem-solving model is still restricted to those persons who are motivated to engage in problem-solving activity and are sufficiently verbal to engage in interaction with the caseworker, the model does allow for more immediate goal gratification through adaptation to problem areas which have been broken down or partialized into their discrete, more manageable parts. The emphasis on action and the focus on partialized and more easily accessible goals can allow the less verbal and less motivated client with multiple problems to become more quickly involved in his or her own problem-solving process. Thus, while the model may address any population within its specialized rubric, problem-solving may be viewed as particularly suited to work with disadvantaged populations whose life circumstances have made them poor prospects for traditional, more introspective modes of therapy.

Knowledge Base

The problem-solving model is eclectic in its synthesis of several major knowledge bases with the intent of bridging the gap between the focus on internal psychological processes and what was in 1957 a new concern with the impact of environmental stimuli on interpersonal functioning. The approach maintains its roots in psychodynamic theory, but incorporates what were then new developments in ego theory. To this end, Perlman combined theories of ego psychology that were evolving from Erik Erikson and Robert White among others, John Dewey's theories of social philosophy, and existential perspectives from the functional school of social casework.

Specifically, Perlman was interested in the Eriksonian concept of human development which wove together the psychodynamic theories of Freud with social cultural forces. Erikson described the stages of ego development through specific interaction with the physical world and social, cultural, and institutional environments. A person is viewed as born with an "innate adaptiveness" which requires a favorable environmental and emotional climate in order that the person may achieve an adaptive fit within the surrounding world.

Perlman incorporated the then emerging concept of one's innate drive to master life's experiences. The post-Freudian ego-psychological theorists further developed the concept of the existence at birth of an autonomous, conflict-free ego that is available and ready for use without resolution of an unconscious conflict. The powers of perception, apprehension, cognitive grasp, anticipatory memory, impulse control, judgment, and selection are subsumed under the concept of ego, and were considered by ego psychologists to be the essence of the ego's conscious and conflict-free efforts to cope with problematic decisions. A person is able to become an active agent on his or her own behalf while attempting to cope with stress through exercise of the energies of the ego. Repeated and successful efforts to master particular problems reinforce the ego's ability to develop a sense of mastery and competence.

Perlman also drew heavily on the social philosophy and learning theories of John Dewey which formed a behavioral science knowledge base that emphasized concepts of social role. Dewey said that "man developed through active engagement in social transactions in pursuit of problem solution" (Perlman 1970:170). Social role is the vehicle through which the individual expresses his or her personality in action. Role is closely related to a self-concept or personal identity, and the exercise of ego functions is thought always to take place within some social role transaction. Dewey's orientation focused on people's consciousness and their ability to change their social environment. Individual and social goals are accomplished through experimental search for knowledge and use of human action to "test ideas, their consequences and effectiveness" (Somers 1976:335). Social betterment is achieved by assisting persons to become conscious of attainable goals and the obstacles which stand in their path.

Thus, problem-solving became a model for translation of ego psychology and social role theory into action principles. The unknown energies of the free ego can be tapped as the individual is helped to resolve the problem at hand. The problem-solving process, consciously undertaken, educates the person in the use of decision-making capacities. The model provides the means for which the client is able to take responsibility for his or her actions while gaining new confidence in the ability to cope through problem mastery.

Unit of Attention

The problem-solving model, as originally conceived by Perlman, did not encompass varying size systems as units of attention, nor did it analyze the environmental milieu in systemic terms. The model does not offer a framework or language for the analysis of the total environment in which all persons exist. The individual, in Perlman's view, is not in any sense located within the surrounding milieu, thus there was no attempt to conceptualize and clarify all facets which might bear on the particular problem at hand. Rather, the approach adhered to the more traditional concept of the person as the focal point of intervention. The problem-solving process could only begin when the person, beset by a conflict with which he or she could not cope, came to the agency in search of assistance.

The person, as the unit of attention, is looked upon as an open system in the process of becoming. Behavior, self-esteem, capacity for growth and adaptation can change in response to changes in life situations. The problem is worked on with the narrower focus on the individual in order to facilitate regained competence and increased internal integration which will positively affect interpersonal relations and role transactions. The problem-solving process is cognizant of the reciprocal need and relationship between the individual and society. The person cannot be fully understood except within the transactional field which calls forth a response. The individual is assessed in relationship to social transactions which are shaped by role requirements and expectations within a particular role system. Thus, problem-solving activity centers on the person and the individual's perception of the problem as the field from which all problem-solving activity emanates.

Problem Definition

The problem-solving model is focused on the manner in which psychic and interpersonal difficulties are played out in everyday life through social role enactment. All individuals are confronted with daily problems in living which they find insurmountable at a given moment, transactions with others often being experienced as stress. Problems are defined in relation to what exists and what is emerging at the time rather than to preoccupation with historical psychological conflict. The overall aim of the process is to enable the individual to cope with the daily tasks and problems that are currently alive and disturbing.

The approach is one of admitted partialization. Problems are broken down into manageable components with the realization that, as the nature of the problem changes as it is reinterpreted and acted upon by the client and worker, the area under assessment will change. The particular problem of concern leads to other problem situations, and the whole can be viewed as related parts of interlocking problems. Thus, Perlman viewed problem causation as circular, with present transactions both the consequence and the cause of further problem formations. The breakdown of individual problem areas into manageable, discrete components is based in the problem-solving assumption that reduction of stress in one aspect of living will have an effect upon some other aspect or parts of the personality system, enabling the person to regain some measure of self-confidence and mastery.

Congruent and Explicit Interventions

The problem-solving model encompasses a broad repertoire of interventions in both the person and environment, shaped to the presenting problem, with the particular intervention varying according to the needs of the individual. In a general sense, the process attempts to engage the client in his or her own problem-solving process while supplementing the individual's own problem-solving resources.

In keeping with the underlying assumptions that motivation, capacity, and opportunity define the client's "workability," the problem-solving approach uses interventions to: (1) free ego energies for investment in the task at hand so as to release, energize, and give direction to the client's *motivation;* (2) release and repeatedly exercise the client's mental, emotional, and action capacities for coping, as required by the problem; (3) make accessible to the client the opportunities and resources necessary for mitigation of the problem, this being essential for satisfactory role performance (Perlman 1977: 1292).

Specific interventive skills are not prescribed by the model, but the approach recognizes that overwhelming problems in living can threaten physical and emotional stability, making it essential that the problem be partialized and clarified quickly by both client and worker, and that small sectors of a problem be singled out for immediate intervention. The search for alternative solutions to problems are considered. Generally, the worker is directed to: (1) address the presenting problem as defined by the client, (2) utilize treatment and diagnostic efforts to draw out and enhance motivation, (3) focus on small sections of multiple problems, (4) define clearly all possible choices of action, (5) encourage/support clients in their decision-making efforts, (6) set short-term attainable goals for the client, and (7) offer a casework relationship of support and acceptance. It is assumed that within this broad prescription for problem-solving intervention the worker will draw upon a repertoire of diagnostic skills, interventive modes, and treatment techniques relevant to the particular client and problem presented. The worker is free to develop a personal style of relating to individual clients within the problem-solving framework.

Use of the Professional Relationship

Problem-solving operates within the context of the worker-client relationship in which the professional relationship acts as a supportive backdrop for intervention, in addition to providing the continuous context within which problem-solving takes place. The model presupposes a person's need for social connectedness, human nourishment, and support in times of stress that may bring about helplessness and vulnerability. Thus, problem-solving is not an intellectual exercise separated from a supportive, empathetic, and involved worker-client relationship. Such a relationship offers the client a sustaining emotional experience with a concerned helper who provides the means of meeting material/emotional deficits or underdeveloped opportunities.

The relationship "is a catalytic agent in the under levels of personality, of conscious shifts and changes in the sense of trust, the sense of self worth, the sense of security and the sense of linkages with other human beings" (Perlman 1970:151). The relationship is the vehicle through which the worker engages the client in the client's own problem-solving processes. The casework process, within the context of the supportive relationship, becomes the means by which frail or distorted ego capacities may be restored to effectiveness. This makes it possible for the person to take responsibility for his or her actions while gaining new confidence in the ability to cope through problem mastery.

The client is described as the major change agent within the framework of the professional-client relationship which supports change. The client is responsible for presenting the initial problem and for adhering to problem-solving activities, since these actions are the means through which gradual competence is effected. The client is the primary worker in action accomplishment, not merely a passive recipient of service, and must engage in the agreed-upon actions necessary for problem-solving.

The function of the worker is to assure responsibility for helping the client focus on and define problems and to assist in creating actions for alleviating them. The process emphasizes that the client's request for assistance must be considered in relation to the model's framework; that is, that the practitioner's role of offering service should be that of an agent or helper who assists the client in satisfying requests within the limits of the model's structure.

Within the framework of the therapeutic relationship, the problem-solving process consists of actions on the helper's part which aim to: (1) provide support and encourage the client to lower disabling ego defenses in order to free ego energies for investment in the task at hand; (2) give direction to the client's motivation while assisting him or her to exercise the ego function of perception cognition, judgment, and choice of action; (3) make accessible to the client opportunities and/or resources necessary to mitigate the presenting problem.

The worker aims to make available environmental opportunities essential for satisfactory role performance, and has the right to challenge the client's perception of the problem to be addressed. However, the worker cannot pursue problems which are unrelated to the client's request; the area the client chooses as the target has validity because it is a personal choice regardless of the worker's judgment regarding the client's selection of the initial problem. Thus, the social worker in using this model of practice relates to the client in the role of supporting, clarifying enabler.

The problem-solving approach encourages the worker to make immediate contact with a client whose emotional and material resources may be in a state of collapse. Engagement around the presenting problem helps the client to feel that he or she is not alone but can rely on a concerned professional who will work with him or her to resolve the problem at hand. The practitioner can make a unique contribution in the area of identifying and analyzing the transactions which take place between parts of the problem and their effect on the total individual. Within the supportive framework of the relationship, worker and client are free to develop forms of intervention that will contribute to more positive social transactions and enhance overall adaptation.

Desired Outcomes

The overall goal of the problem-solving process is to assist the person in coping effectively with stressful problems in living. The approach "aims not at total amelioration or elimination of the stresses and tensions in interpersonal functioning but in setting in motion ways of more satisfactorily coping with them" (Perlman 1970:175).

An attempt is made to positively help the person confront the anxiety-provoking experience and develop the capacity to tolerate and deal more effectively with anxiety and change. What the person "sees, wants, feels, thinks, and does in the response to an identified problem and to the now present provisions of compassionate support, guided consideration and services that the worker offers, are the content of problem-solving work no matter what the problem" (Perlman 1970:138). Within the professional-client relationship, the worker must appraise the person's capacity and motivation to become involved in the problem-solving process. Does the inability to cope lie in the external environment, the lack of material resources, or in the emotional-intellectual makeup or life experiences of the client? The worker attempts to make accessible to the individual a variety of resources, services, and interventive modes necessary to aid the problem-solving process which will strengthen the ego's capacity to cope through mastery of the problem at hand.

Uses of Time

The problem-solving approach to practice has a particular attitude regarding the ability of clients to benefit from long-term therapy.

Namely, a majority of clients do not seek casework help to achieve fundamental behavioral change. Rather, clients, and especially hard-to-reach populations, tend to seek alleviation of discomfort from specific problems and relief from the daily pressures of living in highly complex environments. The model encompasses the Rankian or functional belief in "the potential potency of the present moment" (Perlman 1970:172) wherein the casework encounter can be a transactional experience of a crucial moment in the changing adaptation of a human being. The personality, exposed to powerful stimuli at a crucial moment in time, may undergo modification and shifts resulting in change of behavior and affect.

According to recent effectiveness research, the greatest change in client functioning may occur relatively early in the treatment process. Given this awareness, the model, while not directly limiting the number of client contacts or period of intervention, explicitly focuses on a shorter term approach to treatment whereby the significant client-worker encounter within the problem-solving framework attempts to mobilize the energies of the ego within a projected time limit. When a more easily reachable, partialized goal is achieved the client is free to go on to the next problem, if that is the client's choice. When several short-term goals are achieved, the problem may be satisfactorily mitigated. However, the time required to achieve a particular outcome may be extended when both the client and the worker feel the need to do so. Time is used in this model to heighten focus, expectations, motivation, and outcome.

Differential Use of Staff

Although the problem-solving model is concerned primarily with the person as the focus of intervention, and the professional relationship as its context, the process does incorporate a view of the larger environmental field in which to examine the client's problematic transactions. Depending on the particular scope and needs required by the problem at hand, a variety of professional and nonprofessional staffing patterns conceivably could be utilized to assist the professional in helping the client to engage in the problem-solving process.

The model can be viewed as particularly efficient in its possibilities for the utilization of an array of helpers who could address themselves to the realities of shortages of professional staff and large caseloads which are often found in larger institutional settings and in community work. The effective scanning of possible resources and aides to assist the client in problem-solving efforts could be achieved, using this model, through the increased use of paraprofessionals and allied helpers who could identify environmental deprivations. Such allied helping professionals as visiting nurses, outreach community workers, or trained indigenous "friendly visitors" could be employed to provide greater initial contact and service accessibility to clients so overburdened as to be unable to make the initial contact on their own with the professional worker or agency. Such personnel might be trained to make initial preliminary assessments with the client regarding the immediate problem to be addressed.

In problem-solving staff "extenders" could become active in guiding the client through less complex problem-solving tasks, thereby increasing the number and opportunity for such interventions. The utilization of varieties of staff could increase the focus on economic-environmental conditions and psychosocial stresses which give rise to maladaptive behavior, while leaving the social work clinician free to invest time in particularly difficult problem-solving which may require more in-depth exploration and delineation.

Work with Self-Help Groups

Although the problem-solving model does not focus on the utilization of potential self-help groups or networks external to the professional encounter, it is entirely possible that such supportive networks could function as a real aid to the more traditional problem-solving process rooted in the context of the professional-worker social work relationship. For example, a patient self-help group focused on the problematic issues involved in coping with a chronic disease, might form a kind of advisory council whereby patients make themselves responsible for talking with their fellow patients about particular problems experienced within the treatment situation or the outside community. In this manner, such a group would be better able to alert medical personnel and the surrounding community to the specific problems experienced in relation to their illness. Organized self-help and consumer groups could have an effect on overall patient management in relation to improved patient-staff interaction, lessening of conflict, and improved treatment conditions. The problem-solving process, applicable to groups, could contribute to problem definition, partialization, and clarification of options available to self-help groups as well as to individuals.

Availability to Effectiveness Research

The problem-solving approach, as originally conceived by Perlman, does not directly or adequately address itself to issues regarding the empirical evaluation of the effectiveness of the problem-solving process. In earlier writings, Perlman stated that the social work profession had shirked its responsibility to engage in scientific research. Such research, she felt, should be directed to studying specific populations in need in order that more effective resources and interventions could be developed or redesigned which would more usefully address various populations. The early literature states that in 1957 aspects of the problem-solving process used specifically with hard-to-reach poverty populations were tested and found useful. However, in the 1950s Perlman was not primarily concerned with testing the workability of the model itself through more empirical measurement of desired outcomes.

Although no recent research appears to have concentrated on the effectiveness of the problem-solving method per se, the problem-solving process bears close affinity to more recently emerging social work practice approaches and models that are becoming subject to research: those of short-term treatment, crisis intervention, and the life model. In later writings Perlman points to the shift from long-term to short-term treatment, noting particularly William J. Reid and Ann W. Shyne's research (1969) which compared long-term to short-term treatment of clients with similar problems in family agencies. Study results indicated more client progress in resolution of interpersonal problems when goal-oriented, short-term treatment was utilized. Short-term treatment approaches utilized by Reid and Shyne are related to many factors characteristic of the problem-solving process: clear identification of the problem, the breakdown of the problem into manageable parts, realistically limited goals, and the focus on problems of current interpersonal transaction. It appears that since the problem-solving process is rather explicitly defined regarding its ideology, knowledge base, problem definition, interventive processes and desired outcomes, an objective instrument should be devised which could more scientifically investigate the effectiveness of the model.

The Problem-Solving Model within an Eco-Systems Perspective

The problem-solving approach provides the client and social worker a method of breaking down a complex situation into its more manageable components. Its focus on partialized aspects of problematic individual functioning does not seek to analyze, as a part of case assessment, the impact of concurrent multienvironmental variables on the presenting problem. Thus, the process can be considered reductionist and prone to distortions in assessment when one does not view cases in a broad, interlocking person-environment context. The intricacies and uncertainties of the modern world, and the multiple threats such a world poses to individual survival, make a linear or partialized assessment of presenting problems seem inadequate.

The problem-solving emphasis on man's innate adaptation and coping abilities and the assumption that environmental stress can overwhelm people make this model syntonic with the eco-systems framework, which provides a structure for the understanding of the complex transactions between individuals and their environments. The eco-systems perspective, used in mapping out and analyzing the relationship of phenomena relevant to a particular case, meshes with Perlman's belief that the individual cannot be fully understood except in relationship to his environment. In this respect, Perlman's model is quite modern in its grasp of the link between the individual

and his environment in relation to problem causation and adaptation.

Perlman viewed the caseworker as influencing the environment
indirectly by strengthening the client's coping abilities and capacities
to draw on existing outside environmental resources to aid the process of problem adaptation. Perlman assumed, at a time when systemic principles and language were not yet integrated into social work
thinking, that adaptation in one partialized problem area could affect the functioning of the whole. As an example of the GST principle of reciprocity, this particular behavioral response could alter in
varying degrees the larger environmental system of which the individual was a part—even though the individual was not diagnosed or
treated directly.

The use of the problem-solving process within an eco-systems perspective provides a practice model with its helpful prescriptive interventions, but expands the concept of the whole beyond the individual to include work with many other systems that contribute to
problems. In this perspective the unit of attention is reformulated as
a field of action in which the "client, his biological and personality
subsystems are in transaction with a variety of biological, psychological, cultural and historical environments" (Colman and Bexton 1975:
408).

The individual organism can be placed in a field of other connecting organisms which make up the larger whole. The unit of attention can be the whole system under study or any subsystem which
presents a difficulty that affects the balance of interventions in other
systems, beyond the individual: those which may impinge upon or
cause the presenting problem. The individual, as a subsystem, is
placed squarely within the surrounding environment and becomes
part of a network of related others, thereby avoiding isolation of the
individual and a dichotomy between the person and his or her environment. Linear thinking in relationship to problem causation and
selective intervention with the individual is challenged when the
problem-solving process is governed by the broader eco-systems
framework that analyzes human behavior in relation to the influences of multiple variables.

The problem-solving model's awareness of the interconnection and

circular influence which exists between an individual and the surrounding world as he or she adapts to problems makes the process
a useful approach within an eco-systems framework of analysis.
Problem-solving can effectively utilize the eco-systems structure in
mapping out entire fields of related problematic phenomena as a
whole, while also allowing the worker-client to intervene partially in
a variety of systems to mitigate the immediate problem at hand.

Case Illustration

The following example illustrates the utilization of the problem-
solving approach within an eco-systems perspective. This model of
practice was chosen for this particular case because there was a clearly
identified problem, and an immediate task to be accomplished. The
client was not accessible to, or interested in, personal change, and
provision of resources (opportunity) was essential in order for the
client to heighten his motivation and capacity for dealing with the
crucial problem at hand.

The population from which the case was drawn is composed of
chronically ill renal patients who required hemodialysis three times
weekly in order to sustain life. The social worker was aware of the
effect of the interaction of staff and patient on overall patient adaptation to chronic disease within the network of the larger dialysis
organization. The eco-systems perspective offered the social worker
a coherent, analytic framework in which to identify related problems
in patient adaptation, and a framework to understand the complex
transactions between the patients and their immediate organizational
environments which were at the same time both threatening and potentially life-saving.

The adaptation to a chronic catastrophic illness is an ongoing process. Throughout this process, the patient is integrally linked to a
network of connecting individuals, usually intimate support groups
and professional helpers, all of whom mutually affect one another
in their striving to help the patient cope with the impact of kidney
disease. Faced with the overwhelming reality of impending death
and an uncertain future connected to a hemodialysis machine, the

renal patient is often temporarily unable to cope effectively with the everyday tasks of living. The malfunctioning biological system affects the patient's emotional balance, which can be overpowered in the face of physical breakdown, suffering, material loss, and feelings of helplessness and dependency. Indeed, the entire human organism may be irrevocably altered by the intrusion of terminal disease. Preexisting problems can become intensified, while the patient and his family may develop a new set of needs triggered by the onset of illness. In the case of the hard-to-reach or "unworkable" patient who resists help, the catastrophic illness can, without intervention, upset the already delicate balance existing between the patient and the external environment. The practice of the social worker in renal dialysis, therefore, is directed to facilitating adaptation to the new set of variables created by the onset of disease in order to mitigate the handicap of the chronic illness and the terrible experience of dialysis.

The dialysis center served primarily an indigent black and Hispanic population who lived in a devastated inner-city area. This population presented multiple economic, housing, nutritional, and health problems. The patient population was not verbal, and they generally thought of help in concrete terms. The majority of the patients had little understanding of the psychotherapeutic process and tended to attribute their difficulties to external conditions. Patients were oriented toward action and gaining immediate, concrete relief, tending to view the social worker as caring only as they recognized action and not words as meeting their presenting needs directly and easing their overwhelming reality. The social worker viewed the majority of the population as essentially normal, healthy persons at the onset of illness who lived on the margins of a society which offered little environmental support. The social worker's concern was that each individual should begin to gain some mastery over the illness that threatened to destroy his or her world.

The social worker adopting the eco-systems perspective is pressed to locate the problematic forces impacting upon the individual's ability to cope and make necessary adaptations. Depending upon the practice model used, the patient's internal psychological conflict may or may not be viewed as one of these forces, but all practice models would recognize the reality of hemodialysis as a problem demanding clinical attention. Multiple bases for defining problems allow for multiple approaches, and the eco-systems perspective brings to the foreground the awareness of multiple events, problems, and relationships. In the following case, the problem-solving model was used to define the problem and to direct the helping process of dialysis and other significant staff work so as to enable a reluctant patient to accept medical treatment.

Mr. G. was a single, 68-year-old hemodialysis patient. He had a history of mental instability coupled with a long record of transient work history and living arrangements. The patient had been living in a private nursing home since the onset of his kidney disease and was maintained on large dosages of thorazine. Mr. G. had no outside contacts and could not care for himself. His only living relative, a sister, had not seen him in years and wanted no involvement with the patient.

Mr. G., reacting in his usual manner, was extremely suspicious of all staff members while undergoing hemodialysis, making it difficult for technicians to connect him to the dialysis machine for treatment. He was verbally abusive, demanding of attention, and accusing the staff of deliberately trying to cause him pain. Technicians became anxious while connecting Mr. G. to the machine and infiltrated his arm on numerous occasions, causing painful swelling. At other times Mr. G. presented a flat affect and appeared detached from the surrounding environment. His eyes were glassy, and he had difficulty swallowing. All attempts to establish a relationship with him were futile.

The medical staff was aware of the patient's psychiatric problems prior to his coming to the center for treatment, so they expected to have difficulty treating him—and the patient fulfilled their expectations. He did not fit the concept of the "good" or cooperative, dialysis patient; rather, he was hostile and unpredictable in his moods. The staff groaned when Mr. G. was scheduled for treatment.

Gradually, medical personnel began to withdraw from the patient and only interacted with him when absolutely necessary. They labeled him a "hopeless case," effectively isolating him from other patients by seating him as far as possible from the nurses' station. Naturally, the patient became more hostile and finally withdrew from the staff. Technicians refused to monitor his treatment, and the interactions between the patient and staff became so unbalanced that the equilibrium of the center was threatened. The social worker eventually was approached by the center director to eject Mr. G. from the medical system—presumably to any other dialysis facility that would accept him.

The social worker was faced with several difficult problems, for transfer to another facility was not a possible solution. The worker asked for time to investigate the matter further in order to attempt to find alternative solutions to the presenting problem of extremely poor patient-staff interaction.

Mr. G. exhibited suspicious and argumentative behavior when the social worker approached him. He wanted to be left alone in his misery, seeing no role for himself in the problems he was having with the dialysis staff. His only comment that even suggested his involvement in solving his problem was, "I just want them to get on with it" (his dialysis). Beyond this, he was not interested in changing his behavior so as to enable the staff to do their work, in becoming aware of his feelings, or even in relating better. Yet, in wanting the staff to "get on with it" he was implicitly identifying obstacles to that goal even though he would accept no responsibility for his difficulties. The social worker accepted his definition of the problem as an obstruction to his treatment, albeit the problem was projected onto the staff.

Since Mr. G. was not "workable" as a client in the problem-solving sense and would talk no further with the social worker than he would with the technical staff, the worker shifted the unit of attention from the patient to the staff. This shift was made possible through use of the eco-systems perspective which helped the worker to identify and analyze all the impinging variables that influenced the patient and his central problem—getting on with the dialysis. Among the related problems were: the patient's inability to adapt on any level to his chronic illness, partially due to clinically defined psychopathology; the effects of his chronic disease; the hemodialysis treatment; and poor staff response. These were major factors which contributed to the disruptive staff-patient interaction.

The nursing home, which isolated the patient, and the dialysis staff's preconceived attitude regarding management of this difficult patient contributed greatly to the patient's inability to adapt to his surrounding environment, notably, the dialysis treatment procedures.

The social worker determined to apply the problem-solving process to the staff involved and began by exploring the nursing home where the patient lived. The home was short-staffed and overburdened with the needs of many patients, and personnel had little conception of renal disease or hemodialysis treatment. Mr. G.'s psychiatric history was well known and that, coupled with his kidney disease made him an object of apprehension. Nursing home staff rarely interacted with Mr. G.; he was left to his own devices, spent most of the time isolated in his room, and was highly medicated by the part-time visiting psychiatrist. The transactions between the patient and staff within the nursing home were, naturally, mutually disruptive and provoked anxiety in all related nursing home personnel and in the patient himself.

The social worker in the dialysis center began the initial intervention in the nursing home by inviting Mr. G.'s primary caretakers to the dialysis agency to discuss their concerns actively with the medical staff. Both staffs commiserated with each other and shared their frustrations in working with Mr. G. The worker gave the nursing home staff a tour of the dialysis center and explained the treatment process and the ramifications of the disease.

Nursing home personnel identified a major problem as "patient medication" with its apparent negative effects on the patient, and after much discussion both staffs agreed that a reduced dosage might be more beneficial to Mr. G. The social worker and the center's liaison psychiatrist spoke to the nursing home psychiatrist, and he agreed to reduce the thorazine dosage for a trial period. Thus, communication was gradually established between the two major caretaking systems. Nursing home staff began to call the center with questions about a special diet and the advisability of including the patient in activity programs. Both places mutually began to support one another in this case of a particularly difficult patient, and nursing home personnel began to feel more competent in their management of Mr. G.

The dialysis staff began to notice some change in the patient's physical appearance. After the reduction of medication he appeared to be more in contact with his surroundings. His eyes were no longer glassy and fixed, and he no longer made excessive demands for water and attention, so technical staff were less reluctant to monitor him. The social worker then approached the dialysis nursing administrator with a proposal for several short-term staff sessions to be centered on staff interaction with the patient. All staff who had direct contact with Mr. G. were encouraged to attend, and the social worker shared with them some information regarding Mr. G.'s background and difficult life experiences. The staff psychiatrist discussed psychodynamic functioning, explaining some of the reasons for his difficult interactions with others. Staff were able to ventilate their concerns and feelings regarding the patient's care, and as personnel became more familiar with Mr. G.'s history, they became less fearful of his outbursts, which they formerly had taken personally.

The patient was eventually moved into a less isolated dialysis chair, and technicians were able to relax more easily around him and to experience less difficulty in connecting him to the machine for treatment. Other personnel were able to greet Mr. G. upon his arrival to the center for treatment but did not press him for the intimacy that he could not tolerate.

Although still suspicious, the patient's accusations of staff grew less frequent, and he became relatively calm during treatment; all of the staff involved considered the subsiding of his agitated and hostile behavior an indication of his enhanced capacity to deal more effectively with his dialysis. The request for patient transfer was withdrawn, and Mr. G. remained within the agency system, able to receive his life-saving dialysis treatment.

The worker utilized aspects of the problem-solving process within an eco-systems perspective in order to direct attention, analyze, and intervene in the transactions between the patient, the dialysis center, and nursing home. The patient, while the object of help, did not become the focal point of intervention. This was particularly pertinent because the patient was suspicious and unresponsive to direct attention. Rather, each system was studied and worked with in its relationship to one another and with respect to the multiple variables which affected the presenting problem and the harmonious balance within and without each system.

Major problems were identified by the social worker and the other staffs involved in the care of Mr. G. As problems were partialized, addressed, and resolved to some degree by the social worker and others involved, other problematic concerns were clarified and explored. Multiple interventive modes were utilized in relationship to the systems which impinged on Mr. G. in order to reshape maladaptive transactions and to generate positive inputs and outputs between the individual patient and a variety of staffs responsible for his care. Emotional and external supports were given to each staff until a bond of mutual trust and support could be created naturally among everyone involved. A sustaining worker-staff relationship was gradually formed and afforded staff needed reassurance. Less hostile responses from staffs related directly to Mr. G.'s medical care.

These interventions directly affected the patient's overall adaptation to the medical system. Reduction of medication enabled the patient to remain more in contact with his immediate environment and to function in a manner less offensive to the medical staff, who were than able to withdraw less from the patient.

Education of all staff related to management of kidney disease and the hemodialysis process allowed staff to become less anxious and more aware of the realities associated with chronic disease. Staff group sessions afforded the staff a vehicle to express their frustrations regarding the care of Mr. G. All parts of the dialysis system began to interact in a more adaptive manner, and the equilibrium of the patient and the center and its parts was preserved.

Conclusion

Problem-solving within an eco-systems perspective offers a model for analysis of cases and for interventions. Without requiring excessive motivation for behavioral change on the client's part, the goal of the problem-solving process is improved coping, and adaptation to the defined problem at hand, not to change lifelong patterns of client behavior or even organizational rules. Creative, multiple modes of intervention that address this adaptational goal can result in problem-solving, sometimes (as in the case of Mr. G.) through making the environmental variables (the staffs, in this case) the unit of attention. The problem-solving model alone would not have accomplished the task defined in Mr. G.'s case because Mr. G. was "unworkable" as a client from the standpoint of motivation and capacity. The broadened perspective made it possible to "see more" in the case; that is, to note the need for the nursing home and medical staffs themselves to "problem-solve" so as to maximize Mr. G.'s opportunities for dialysis.

REFERENCES

Colman, Arthur D. and W. Harold Bexton, eds. 1975. *An. A. K. Rice Institute Series: A Group Relations Reader.* San Rafael, Calif.: Associates Printing and Publishing Company.
Perlman, Helen Harris. 1957. *Social Casework: A Problem-Solving Process.* Chicago: University of Chicago Press.
—— 1970. "The Problem-Solving Model in Social Casework." In Robert W. Roberts and Robert H. Nee, eds., *Theories of Social Casework.* Chicago: University of Chicago Press.
—— 1977. "Social Casework: The Problem-Solving Approach." In *Encyclopedia of Social Work.* Vol. II. New York: NASW.
Reid, William J. and Ann W. Shyne. 1969. *Brief and Extended Casework.* New York: Columbia University Press.
Somers, Mary Louise. 1976. "Problem-Solving in Small Groups." In Robert W. Roberts and Helen Northen, eds., *Theories of Social Casework with Groups.* New York: Columbia University Press.

V

BEHAVIORAL APPROACHES TO SOCIAL WORK PRACTICE

Meredith Hanson

Behavioral practice approaches, which are relatively new to social work, became prominent in the profession during the 1960s, a time when traditional practice methods based on a medical disease model of human behavior were attacked as unresponsive to the needs of social work clients and ineffective in attaining beneficial outcomes. In the context of rapid social change and increased client activism, the behavioral approaches emerged as a series of empirically based technologies which not only could produce rapid, verifiable changes, but also could actively involve social work clients in the problem-solving process.

The behavioral approaches, arising in an intellectual tradition with roots in the animal laboratories of the early experimental and learning psychologists, are grounded firmly in an orientation stressing empiricism and positivism. Most of the "critical principles of learning" were spelled out fairly elaborately between 1898 and 1938 by researchers like Pavlov, Watson, and Thorndike (London 1972); however, intervention based on learning principles did not enter the general "therapeutic market place" until the 1950s (Thomas 1970) and did not appear on the social work scene until much later.

It was during the 1950s that the effectiveness of psychotherapy was called into question in psychology and psychiatry. Many critics found support for their criticisms in the work of learning theorists, and behavioral therapy developed as a practice system within which to direct the new emphasis on therapeutic effectiveness. When social work itself came under renewed attack in the 1960s, it was understandable that many educators and practitioners would turn to the "new schools" of behaviorism for alternatives to their traditional approaches.

Ideological Biases

Contrary to the belief of many practitioners, behavioral interaction is not a single approach to practice with one uniform body of knowledge and technology. Krasner (1971) lists fifteen different "streams" or "schools" of behavioral therapy; Thomas, on the other hand, refers to five behavioral schools, citing the sociobehavioral eclectic approach, which "uses techniques derived from behavioral therapy, behavioral modification, social psychology, other areas of behavioral science, and from practice" as the approach having the most "promise" for social work (1970:190–91).

In general, however, social work educators agree that a three-way classification of behavioral orientations is most informative for social workers (Schwartz and Goldiamond 1975; Fischer 1978). Behavioral intervention—the parsimonious, "planned, systematic application of experimentally established principles of learning to the modification of maladaptive behavior" for purposes of decreasing undesired behaviors and increasing desired behaviors (Fischer 1978:157)—can be categorized into three perspectives: the respondent approach, the operant approach, and the social learning (modeling) approach.

The respondent (classical conditioning model) approach, which reflects the experiments of Pavlov, postulates that behavior is elicited by antecedent stimuli. It is from this approach that the familiar S→R (stimulus produces response) paradigm was developed. In this approach, which addresses reflexive behavior of the automatic nervous system like eye blinks, salivation, and anxiety responses, "the strength, the speed, the very presence of the response, depend upon the presence, strength and other aspects of the stimulus. In other words, the stimulus *must* be present for the response to occur" (Schwartz and Goldiamond 1975:10). By pairing different stimuli, behavioral responses can be generalized to a number of different stimulus conditions. (An in-depth discussion of conditioning and learning is beyond the scope of this article. The interested reader should consult more comprehensive texts, such as Bandura 1969, and Kanfer and Phillips 1970.)

In the *operant approach* (instrumental learning, Skinnerian behaviorism), the occurrence of an action is said to be governed primarily by its consequences. According to Schwartz and Goldiamond:

> We may salivate [a response] at the sight of a box (conditioned stimulus); this is a conditioned reflex, according to the Pavlovian scheme. However, our behavior of reaching (a response) into the box (a stimulus) is governed by the consequences of getting a peanut (a reinforcing stimulus according to the operant orientation). We continue to reach only so long as the reaching has the consequences of providing us with peanuts (has a reinforcing consequence) or until we do not want any more peanuts (we are satiated) (1975:11).

As this example illustrates, while the respondent approach applies to reflexive (automatic) actions, the operant approach is most relevant for directed actions, under the control of the voluntary nervous system.

The *social learning approach* assumes that behavior can be acquired vicariously without the occurrence of overt responses. Because people have the capacity to develop and use symbols, Bandura (1977), who is most responsible for the articulation of this approach, asserts that symbolic, that is, cognitive, processes must be considered in any explanation of behavior. The presence of cognition and self-reflection enables people to regulate the stimuli that impinge upon them, transforming, selecting, and organizing the stimuli. Within the social learning approach human behavior and psychological functioning are seen as "a continuous reciprocal interaction between personal, behavioral, and environmental determinants" (p. 194).

> The relative influences exerted by these interdependent factors differ in various settings and for different behaviors. There are times

when environmental factors exercise powerful constraints on behavior, and other times when personal factors are the overriding
regulators of the course of environmental events (Bandura 1977:
10).

Schwartz and Goldiamond (1975) refer to the approach as a "me-
diational" one, since what is learned is thought not to be a set of
specific stimulus-response relationships, but rather the imagined and
verbal representations of modeling the stimuli.

From these overviews of the major behavioral paradigms it is apparent that the approaches draw one's attention away from an excessive, if not exclusive, focus on the individual and intrapsychic
processes of a focus on the environmental contingencies which are
shaping and maintaining the individual's actions. The perspectives
have been attacked severely for this shift. Many critics claim that the
"black box" approach to individual and intrapsychic factors is overly
simplistic and ignores crucial variables that affect a person's behavior. It is claimed that it is in error to ignore man's ability to think, to
fantasize, and to self-reflect. This ability makes human behavior
qualitatively different from that of the laboratory animals upon which
many behavioral principles were originally based.

A related criticism is that due to their stress on environmental determinism, the perspectives are linear and mechanistic in nature. This
argument asserts that humans are not passive reactors but active
beings who transform the stimuli that impinge upon them. Von Bertalantfy's criticism of the psychology of the first half of the twentieth
century illustrates this argument's main themes:

> Psychology, in the first half of the twentieth century, was domi-
> nated by a positivistic-mechanistic-reductionistic approach which can
> be epitomized as the robot model of man.
> Basic for the interpretation of animal and human behavior was
> the stimulus-response scheme or, as we may call it, the doctrine of
> the primary reactivity of the psychophysiological organism. Behav-
> ior is a response to stimuli coming from the outside (1967:7).

Von Bertalantfy continues his criticism by observing that although
"hypothetical mechanisms, intervening variables" have been introduced into the formulations, the basic concepts and outlooks of the

perspectives have remained unchanged. "In the end, the effects of modern psychotechnics and behavioral engineering amount to a functional decerebalization, that is, exclusion of higher cerebral centers and mental faculties—almost as efficiently as if these were removed by surgical operation" (1967:16).

Behavioral theoreticians have countered these criticisms in a number of ways. For example, they note that, although for purposes of analysis and theory development behavioral processes can be separated into discrete stimuli and responses, and environmental contingencies can be outlined, behavior is appropriately considered to be a function of the interactions between persons and their environments; the person impinges on the environment as much as that environment impinges on him/her. As Kanfer and Saslow argue, there is an interdependence between personal and situational factors:

> The unit of analysis is a relationship between environment and behavior, with attention not only on antecedent variables but also on the impact of behavioral acts on the patient's environment. The patient is . . . a member of several social systems, differing in significance to him (e.g. his family, friends, co-workers, club), and it is assumed that his behavior contributes to the maintenance or disruption of these systems, just as the group norms of these systems affect his behavior (1969:426).

Krasner extends this argument by observing that behavioral approaches imply that a person's behavior "is a function of, is elicited by, and is controlled by environmental stimuli. [However], man does not have a basic predetermined nature; his behavior is characterized by learning and change" (1969:549). To say that behavior is lawful, predictable, and controllable is not to say that it is completely predetermined or mechanistic, and that the person is a robot lacking self-direction.

> The kind of control which makes man fully a robot does not exist; it is only theoretical. . . . [Man] is . . . free to the extent that there is no systematic manipulation of his behavior and to the extent that he acts as if he were free . . . To the extent that a human being has alternative behaviors available to him, to that extent he is "free" and not a passive reacting robot (Krasner 1969:550).

As the behavioral approaches have developed and as scientists have moved out of the animal laboratories and into the human arena to apply and test their ideas, more consideration has been given to the person as an active participant in the reinforcement process. With the development of social learning approaches and cognitive behavioral interventions the trend toward the more complete explanation of the individual's role as a thinking actor, rather than a passive re-actor, is likely to continue (see, for example, Bandura 1981).

Values

Behavioral approaches have emerged as case-oriented practice technologies and as such usually do not focus explicitly on how practitioners allocate their services. Only in recent years have behavioral practitioners raised important ethical questions about their procedures. In part these questions and the consequent attempts to establish guidelines for ethical practice have been a response to the public's misconception of behavioral practice as being associated with punitive and aversive procedures like shock therapy and being dominated by a "Clockwork Orange," behavioral control mentality.

Published research and case reports indicate that behavioral approaches have been utilized effectively with a wide range of people from all social classes. Behavioral interventions have been applied to problems such as fear of public speaking, obesity, impotence and frigidity, addictions, delinquency, marital discord, and deficits in social skills to list just a few. As Fischer observes:

> The focus of behavior modification, contrary to many stereotypes, is one of the full range of human responses, from feelings and cognitions to overt behaviors. . . . Perhaps even more importantly, some classes of problems previously thought to be "hopeless" have responded positively to behavioral procedures, including childhood "autism", retardation, severely disturbed behavior of adults and children ("psychotic" behavior), long-term, apparently entrenched phobias, and specific sexual problems (1978:158–59).

It is apparent, therefore, that behavioral approaches do not overtly discriminate against any category of persons. However, certain value questions about the approaches can be raised. For example, with the emphasis on behavioral specificity an unintended message can be communicated to the client; that is, that what is important is his/her behavior not him/herself. Clients who are reluctant to approach their life problems in this way may not benefit from behavioral intervention. Related to this issue, clients who are unable to specify their problems and or needs and or who experience a general malaise may not benefit greatly from these approaches.

Another value issue concerns the emphasis on action and "homework" assignments in the approaches. To be effective many behavioral approaches require that clients perform homework assignments such as relaxation exercises, dating, and asking for a raise, between sessions. Carrying out these assignments requires a certain skill and motivation on the part of the clients. Although the behavioral procedures are designed to prepare the clients for carrying out these assignments, a person who cannot or will not complete the assignments may not be reached by the interventions.

A more serious value issue is raised by Epstein, who asserts that, although behavioral theory places priority on environmental factors in explaining behavior,

> Observation of behavioral practice and a reading of practice papers . . . reveals an ominously familiar pattern. For while behavioral theory rejects invidious labels for client behavior, practitioners almost universally view their task as the identification and reduction of "problematic," "deviant" or "maladaptive" client behavior. In other words the client remains culpable (1975:140).

Behavioral practitioners, in short, can fall into the trap that they have accused traditional psychosocially oriented practitioners of being caught up in. The individual client is focused on, with the implicit message that he or she is at fault for the condition. Environmental manipulations that are undertaken are done so to modify the client's behavior and only secondarily to change the social situation. This type of emphasis can lead to a normative approach to practice in which the social worker is more an agent of social control than an advocate for the client and in which the full implications of the person-situation gestalt are overlooked.

Knowledge Base

The behavioral approaches utilize techniques derived from principles of learning which were established initially in the animal laboratories of experimental and learning psychologists and more recently in experiments with both clinically and nonclinically defined
human populations. Although the primary criterion for knowledge
utilization is that it have empirical support and can be made operational for purposes of establishing intervention strategies, psychological principles of learning still constitute the major bases for behavioral techniques.

Thomas notes that unlike some behavioral therapy approaches
which are applied mainly in face-to-face practitioner-client contacts,
the sociobehavioral approach, which advocates for social workers, is
a more general one. It draws "upon knowledge from social systems
. . . role theories . . . performance and motivation theory in psychology as well as . . . theories of organizations, socialization, and
deviance" (1967:17). In spite of this argument and although learning principles have been incorporated into sociological theories like
Homans' (1974) exchange theory and behavioral sociology (Burgess
and Bushell 1969; Akers et al. 1979) behavioral approaches remain
overwhelmingly psychological in nature. Environmental factors are
explained in psychological terms and examined from the perspective
of the individual.

In part, this tendency is by design. There is an archindividualism
in many of the approaches, exemplified most clearly by the work of
Skinner (1950):

> Skinner differs markedly from the average experimental psychol-
> ogist in his *concern for the individual subject.* . . . It is not enough
> that his studies produce average results that occur with expectation
> and future observation. The behavioral law or equation must apply
> to each subject observed under appropriate conditions (Hall and
> Lindzey 1970:480).

Although the benefit from such an orientation is obvious in that
individual differences are not overlooked and are not averaged into
group performance rates, the orientation may impede the fuller ex-

ploration of the impact of societal and institutional factors on individual activity. Consequently, the full implications of behavioral approaches as social movements that can generate societal (macrosystemic) level interventions have yet to be realized (Krasner 1969), while conceptually practitioners are not limited to intervention methods which must be mediated through the individual client, as Scheff (1966) and Epstein (1975) have noted, in actual practice change techniques tend to be focused on the person rather than on the person and the social institution.

Unit of Attention

As observed above, priority in the behavioral approaches is placed on formulating behaviorally specific descriptions of action as they occur in specific situational contexts. Within this framework the unit of attention for the practitioner becomes the behavior—the actions— of individuals. Emphasis is placed on understanding how the person interacts with important members (family peers, agencies) of one's environment with an attempt to specify one's own current behavior in terms of skills possessed or must be acquired, and habits to be altered.

Contrary to the accusations of some critics, this emphasis on individual behavior "is not a narrow conception of human activity. . . . All behavior is pertinent—thoughts; 'affect,' as well as motor action—providing that it is discernible through the senses of the observer and can be reliably denoted" (Thomas 1970:186–87). Although the more radical behaviorists, like Skinner, would limit the unit of attention to observable, empirical behaviors, most behaviorally oriented practitioners acknowledge the existence of covert responses (cognitions, imagery). Their use of covert responses differs from that of more traditionally oriented workers, however, in their avoidance of highly elaborate, hypothetical constructs about man's "mental life."

Problem Definition

For the most part, initial problem definition, which follows logically from the focus on specific behaviors, is based on determining the presence and absence of both adaptive and maladaptive behaviors as defined by the client, a significant other (parent, guardian, spouse), a referring agent (teacher, probation officer, employer), and/or the practitioner. Assessment involves an ongoing functional analysis of the client's behavior. That is, analysis "endeavors to ascertain the explicit environmental variables which control [or influence] the observed behavior" (Kanfer and Saslow 1969:426). Since a person's behavior is assumed to be a function of antecedent and consequent stimuli which occur in a given situation, his/her history of reinforcement, his/her skills, and his/her motivation, attempts are made to describe each of these variables within its specific sociocultural context.

> A preliminary formulation attempts to sort out the behaviors which are brought to the clinician's attention with regard to their eventual place in the treatment procedures. . . . Since no objective frequency tables are available for reference, behavior items can be viewed either as excesses or as deficits, depending on the vantage point, from which the imbalance is observed. . . . Preference viewing behavior as excessive or deficient is often determined by cultural valuation of the behavior based on its consequences to other people (Kanfer and Saslow 1969:430).

In short, from a behavioral perspective problems can be defined in terms of excesses and deficits in the client's action repertoire. Analysis, therefore, focuses on clarifying those factors that are seen as contributing to the excesses of deficits with the objective of altering them to achieve behavioral change. Although in theory a person's actions often are described in terms of antecedent and consequent stimuli—a practice which reinforces a somewhat linear and mechanistic view of behavior—in reality, by focusing on the current situation and the multiple impinging factors which influence the person, behavioral practitioners recognize that no simple cause-and-effect relationship actually exists. Rather, by describing the client as totally involved in a specific situational context—one in which he/she is influenced by the environment and in turn shapes it—practitioners are acknowledging the presence of a reciprocal arrangement in which the individual and his/her environment are mutually influential; that is, are in transaction.

Congruent and Explicit Interventions

The intervention techniques which are utilized are congruent with the problem formulation and evolve directly from the initial assessment. In general, behavioral approaches are characterized by a large body of precise and explicit technologies which can be applied to a broad range of specific problem situations. As Fischer notes:

> The hallmark of behavior modification is the development of specific techniques which the caseworker can differentially apply depending on the nature of the client, problem, and situation. . . . No longer need the novice, when faced with applying a complex theory in practice, cry: "Yes, but what techniques do I use?" The development of techniques is a high priority for behavioral theorists, researchers, and practitioners (1978:158).

The intervention technologies that have been developed reflect the problem definitions in that they are designed to prepare the client for behavioral change (relaxation training, assertion training), teach the client new skills (behavioral rehearsal, *in vivo* practice), eliminate maladaptive actions (self-control procedures, thought stopping), and alter environmental contingencies (token economies, work with teachers, employers, and significant others, alternative schedules of reinforcement). No other social work approach has developed such a wealth of internally consistent and explicit intervention strategies.

Use of the Professional Relationship

Traditionally, social workers, following the lead of their psychoanalytic colleagues and social work theorists such as Virginia Robinson

(1930), Florence Hollis (1972), and Helen Harris Perlman (1957) have placed tremendous emphasis on the therapeutic relationship which has been valued as curative in its own right and as the context in which client change occurs. The behavioral approaches, however, place less emphasis on relationship factors.

Behavioral practitioners are, however, sensitive to the worker-client relationship, since they realize that the manner in which the client interacts with the practitioner is a valuable source of information about him/her, and because they recognize the need to establish a solid working alliance to enhance the likelihood that the client will continue to seek assistance and will cooperate with the intervention strategies. The client's relationship with the practitioner is a factor which facilitates his/her expectations and motivation for change. From a behavioral perspective, however, change is not thought to occur via the professional relationship per se but through the application of specific intervention techniques in the precise context in which the client's problems arise.

Because of this belief, behavioral practitioners devote much of their effort at enhancing relationships and social exchanges that occur outside the context of the worker-client interaction setting. The behavior of significant others and the characteristics of the client's ecological context are viewed as more powerful influencers of the client's activities than is the worker-client relationship itself.

The Desired Outcomes

An objective of behavioral practice is to alter the "terminal behavioral repertoire" (Gambrill, Thomas, and Carter 1971) of the client so that he/she is better able to manage in the specific problem areas that have been identified by him/her and the practitioner. In achieving this terminal repertoire the practitioner intervenes in a planned way with the client and with the environment to enhance its reinforcement and enabling potential. An axiom of behavioral interventions is: "All behavior is learned and can be modified through the application of principles of learning" (Stuart 1967:19).

The client's terminal behavioral repertoire is not determined *a priori* but rather is a result of a negotiation process that occurs among the practitioner, the client, and the other significant participants in the case. The focus is not on "curing" the client but on altering and developing behavioral patterns and modifying the environmental contingencies so that the client is better able to cope with the impinging environment, and the environment and the client are more mutually adaptive and reinforcing.

Reflecting the explicit nature of behavioral approaches, goals are often divided into long-term, intermediate, and short-range objectives. Further, they are outlined in specific treatment contracts which contain precise statements of each participant's responsibilities, tasks, and privileges. As intervention proceeds and as objectives are attained, the contract and outcome goals are renegotiated, thus reinforcing the notion that there are no absolute, desirable outcomes, but only those which reflect the needs and desires of the participants and the constraints of the situation. (For examples of behavioral contracts applied to specific problem complexes see Miller 1975, Rose 1977, and Stuart 1969.)

Uses of Time

With their stress on precise and explicit specification of the means and objectives of interventions it is obvious that the concept of time plays a central role for behavioral practitioners. As Germain observes, time "refers to pacing, duration, and rhythm" (1976:419). In behavioral approaches the importance of time and timing is apparent in the manner in which environmental contingencies and reinforcement patterns are determined. For example, in the case of operant, goal-directed behavior, reinforcement that affects the emission of the behavior is defined as taking the form of two major types of reinforcement schedules. First, reinforcement can occur at specified intervals (time periods), as when a mother gives her child a cookie only after she feels that sufficient time has elapsed since the child's last cookie. Second, reinforcement can be contingent upon the occurrence of a specified number of responses (in effect, the behavior serves as its own timing device), as when a mother rewards her child with a cookie after he has correctly spelled three words in his spelling lesson. Reinforcement with each of these schedules can be variable or it can be fixed. In general, however, the time interval between the response and its reinforcement is crucial; shorter time intervals are more potent than longer ones in shaping and maintaining a response.

The role of time is further demonstrated by the manner in which behavioral interventions are designed. A common method for setting up and evaluating behavioral interventions is the use of time-series research designs (see for example, Campbell and Stanley 1963, and Jayaratne and Levy 1979). During the preintervention, baseline period the occurrence of the problem behavior is recorded and measured—often through the use of timing devices (see Butterfield 1974). Following the baseline period the intervention occurs, and the behavior is again measured under the intervention conditions. Finally, during a postintervention follow-up period the behavior is measured to determine if the effects of the intervention are maintained. As Jayaratne and Levy assert:

> The ideal of the clinical research model requires a series of measures over time (time series) within each phase . . . [A] *series* of measures must be taken before intervention and the same series of measures must be taken after intervention. By the same series we mean that the same units that were observed before intervention must be re-evaluated after intervention within the same physical and time frameworks (1979:53).

In short, the use of time is central to the approaches. The manner in which it is used, however, is highly structured. There is a tendency to see time in a Newtonian style. That is, time is thought of as moving linearly as cause and effect. Auerswald observes that:

> Processes are thought of and described separately from things and are recorded in clock time. Data collection consists of describing, classifying, counting (using numbers), and qualitative weighting of things, again using numbers or hierarchical positions. Methods of data analysis are aimed at cause-effect relationships arrived at by linear induction and/or deduction (1980:119).

Although this manner of using time is valid and yields important information about the functional relatedness of phenomena, the practitioner utilizing the approach (a form of cognitive epistemology) must be wary lest the essence of the phenomena that is being observed is overlooked in the haste to measure, alter, and analyze their occurrence.

Differential Use of Staff

The essential concepts involved in the behavioral approaches are clear and explicit. Thus, they can be transmitted and taught fairly easily to various staff members, the client, and other significant participants in the case. In effect, this permits the intervention process to be broadened beyond the one-to-one, worker-client exchange to include a large support system of change agents. The roles of the potential participants in the intervention process are clearly defined, each requiring certain skills and each equally important to the intervention. Examples of a differential and integrated use of service manpower can be found in classroom management strategies, token economies, and social skills training.

Kanfer and Goldstein (1980) identify four levels of helpers: (1) the behavior analyst, who develops programs, research, and new intervention methods; (2) the behavior technology coordinator, who conducts helping programs in schools, prisons, and other institutional aid facilities; (3) the behavior technologist engineer, who carries out helping strategies and programs; and (4) the behavior cotechnician, who assists in implementing the intervention strategies. The helpers at the different levels possess differential expertises, competencies, and training. Together, they make up the intervention team.

> In this sense, a pyramid operation can be developed with a supervisor or consultant whose role is greatest at the beginning of treatment, who can monitor progress of treatment, and who can offer the paraprofessional any supervision or advise needed. Developing a team of helpers varying in skill and competence . . . permits the delivery of psychological services to large numbers of people who previously could not have afforded expensive psychotherapy (Kanfer and Goldstein 1980:5).

Kanfer and Goldstein conclude their discussion by observing that although total management of the case requires the skills of a trained professional, "paraprofessionals with limited training can . . . make substantial contributions to successful treatment" (1980:5).

The possibilities for the differential use of manpower extend beyond the boundaries of the professional and paraprofessional personnel employed by human service agencies. The use of behavioral approaches permits the mobilization of natural helpers in the client's own environment on his/her behalf. Tharp and Wetzel describe how these possibilities have emerged in the behavioral practice models:

> A different model of practice has emerged naturally from the assumptions of the behavior therapies. In behavior modification techniques, the professional specialist need not have direct interaction with the "patient." Rather, he may instruct, or advise, or consult to other individuals who bear some normal role relationship to the "patient". . . . The logic of behavior modification dictates that those individuals who do indeed possess the reinforcers should occupy a position intermediate to the consultant and the patient who is the ultimate target of behavioral intervention (1969:47).

As Tharp and Wetzel elaborate, the assumptions of behavioral approaches permit the development of a triadic model of practice within which the actual interventions are implemented by a natural helper. The professional practitioner acts as the consultant who assesses need, supervises the helper, and manages the intervention process.

Implicit in the behavioral approaches is the understanding that there are multiple ways and multiple levels on which to intervene in any case. This view permits the behavioral practitioner to employ a full range of professionals, paraprofessionals, and other persons in the intervention process. The agency itself is transformed from a site which provides the practitioner with a base from which to operate—and little else—to a dynamic resource which the practitioner can draw upon in assisting the client. Other staff members, both social service and associated personnel, become equal partners in service delivery and assume essential roles in that effort, thus opening to behavioral practitioners the option for systemic and organizational interventions that potentially can address a broader range of client needs. By making use of colleagues in the intervention process, the behavioral practitioner is able to devote more time and energy to situational assessments and case management, and assistance can be delivered to a larger group of people.

Work with Self-Help Groups

Many behavioral practitioners work collaboratively with various self-help groups. The rationale for this collaboration is similar to that for the use of natural helpers—these persons possess reinforcers (social support, resources, information) that the practitioner does not possess, and they are able to form a network which will help the client alter his situation and maintain any change which has occurred.

According to Stuart, many of the problems which clients present to professional practitioners cannot be resolved effectively in professional settings because:

> Situational factors contribute significantly to the etiology of the problem and problem mastery requires important life-style change by the troubled person. . . . The primary treatment [for problems like drug abuse, child abuse, obesity, and alcoholism] can and should be the responsibility of self-help groups because these groups have recently demonstrated the skill and resources to produce good results. *Indeed, the time has come to consider the self-help approach to be the treatment of choice for programs aimed at helping people to make lasting changes in their patterns of living* (1977:285; emphasis added).

Self-help groups possess several assets, often not associated with the professional practitioner, that contribute to their potential utility for troubled people: (1) They tend to focus on problem behavior, compelling their members to find ways of coping with the problem rather than fixating on why it is present. (2) The groups are informal in nature, thus permitting the attainment of social support in addition to aid in problem resolution. (3) The group leader, who usually has experienced the same difficulties as other group members, can be a role model for all members. (4) Membership is fluid, and entry to, and exit from, the group (access) is easily accomplished. (5) The groups are successful in helping members accept their problems and deal with them as "normal" reactions to the pressures of living; they help the members to attribute the problem to external conditions, thus facilitating their ability to develop methods of coping more effectively with them. (6) They stress skill mastery which enhances the likelihood that changes which occur will be maintained by the process (Stuart 1977).

Because of these characteristics and because the behavioral approaches focus on the contextual factors which influence individual behaviors, self-help groups and other natural helpers are considered valuable resources in behavioral intervention. In recent years, however, several authors have been concerned about the way in which members of the natural support system are taught the techniques of helping others and about how the effectiveness of self-help programs are evaluated. Although self-help groups and natural support efforts are worthwhile in their own right and do not need to justify their existence beyond the fact that participants feel that they benefit from them, it is reasoned that if the professional is going to utilize them he/she has a responsibility to determine how appropriate they are for his/her client, the means they use to provide assistance (how they self-help), and how effective they are in attaining their objectives. Consequently many professionals collaborate closely with self-help organizations, such as Weight Watchers International (Stuart 1978), assisting them with the development of intervention strategies and helping them to evaluate their effectiveness. Other researchers are studying various self-help approaches and raising critical issues about the vast quantity of self-help programs and materials that have been marketed in attempts to assess their utility. (Many self-help manuals and publications claim to produce remarkable results; yet, few have been subjected to rigorous evaluation. See, for example, Rosen 1979.)

Availability to Effectiveness Research

In general, behavioral researchers and theoreticians place a high priority on effectiveness research. The behavioral approach is unique in social work, since, with the possible exception of task-centered practice (Reid 1978), no other approach is tied as closely to an empirical base. Certainly, no other approach has been researched as extensively. In its short history literally thousands of effectiveness studies and case reports have been published (Fischer 1978). Increasingly, these studies are emphasizing refinements in practice technologies and models.

The development of operational practice models—paradigms—is important to behavioral practitioners, who strive to create and operationalize explicit, prescriptive intervention strategies which can be disseminated within the professional community. It must be recognized, however, that the models which are developed are not "grand" formulations about human behavior and change. Most behaviorists eschew grand theories as being irrelevant and unnecessary for understanding and changing behavior. Skinner makes this point very clearly in his discussion of theory building:

> [In "Are Learning Theories Necessary?" (Skinner 1950)] I defined theory as an effort to explain behavior in terms of something going on in another universe, such as the mind or the nervous system. Theories of that sort . . . are [not] essential or helpful. . . . But I look forward to an overall theory of human behavior which will bring together a lot of facts and express them in a more general way (Evans 1968:88).

The practice models developed by behavioral practitioners are consistent with this line of thinking since they articulate specific methodologies which integrate a number of practitioner tasks in an explicit and directed manner. Their conception of model development is similar to that of Reid, who has developed a "practice system" which can be used in two ways by social workers: as a system that "can be employed in its entirety by certain practitioners, in certain settings, or for certain types of cases;" and as "a cohesive package of theory and methods that can be taken apart by discerning practitioners who can select from it those pieces of value to them" (1978:3).

Behavioral intervention models specify procedures for measuring and assessing the occurrence of a problem, for developing change strategies, and for evaluating the impact of those strategies. Because they usually specify not only the techniques to be employed and the desired end state, but also the general time frame in which the change is to occur, behavioral approaches can be self-correcting and are ideal for developing a clinical research orientation to social work practice. By using the client as his/her own control by measuring the baseline frequency occurrence of the problem, practitioners can estimate the effectiveness of their interventions. By continuing to monitor the situation after intervention has ceased, they can evaluate whether or not the change is maintained (see Jayaratne and Levy 1979).

The use of self-correcting, explicit practice models must not be construed to mean that behavioral practitioners have resolved the effectiveness issue, however. Due to the nature of ongoing clinical practice the criteria and controls necessary to set up well-designed effectiveness studies often cannot be instituted. In addition, ethical issues are involved in the use of some research strategies. For example, although it may be desirable from an experimental standpoint to remove the variables which are thought to have produced a change to verify whether they are in fact responsible for the change observed (as when an older client's mood becomes more positive after he becomes an active participant in a senior citizens' center), from a clinical perspective such an action may not be desirable. Therefore, tension often is present when one questions the effectiveness of many practice procedures. For the clinical practitioner the most that can usually be demonstrated is that client change is correlated with worker assistance and that it seems likely that the change has resulted from the assistance that the client received. By introducing more controls in the practice, by precisely describing and monitoring the intervention process, and by repeating the procedures on similar clients and under similar circumstances (see, for example, Gambrill and Barth 1980), the practitioner can be more confident that the specific interventions are, in fact, producing the results, the behavioral changes, that are observed.

A Synthesis

This overview of the behavioral practice approaches has illustrated how they offer social workers the potential for transcending the bounds of a reductionistic, linear approach to practice and for intervening rationally in the person-environment complex. The approaches are empirically based, self-correcting, oriented toward environmental contingencies, and suggestive of explicit practice strategies for inducing and maintaining change and for incorporating the significant elements of the person's environment (other staff, family, support network) into the intervention process. However, as is also apparent from the discussion, the approaches can revert to linear, individualistic orientations which postulate naïve cause-effect relationships and which hold the client culpable for the dilemma.

Conceptually, the behavioral approaches effectively include environmental factors in the assessment and intervention process. However, there is a possibility of an inconsistency in behavioral formulations that may lead the undiscerning social worker away from a true person-environment focus. This inconsistency arises from the fact that although the behavioral ideology stresses environmental contingencies the manner in which environmental variables are operationalized tends to be through psychological laws. The use of stimulus-response patterns, reinforcement schedules, and other psychological explanations can lead to a practice in which environmental contingencies are mediated only through the person, and the direction of the intervention is aimed at helping the person to change and adjust rather than on working directly in the environment itself.

As mentioned, part of this tendency is due to a behavioral theory and research orientation which concentrate on the individual subject rather than on aggregate statistics. This type of a tradition does not prepare its disciples well for an adequate appreciation or understanding of social systemic (structural) factors that do not operate on the individual level. As Repucci and Saunders observe:

> The principles of behavior modification are insufficient and often inappropriate for understanding natural settings—their structures, goals, traditions, and intersetting linkages. . . . Behavior modification was never intended to be a basis for describing, understanding, or changing natural settings. . . . There is nothing in behavior modification that guides us in answering these questions: Where should one seek to enter a setting? Where will the points of conflict arise? What will constitute a viable support system? What is a realistic time perspective for change? (1975:337–38).

Although these writers take the extreme position, and although approaches such as Thomas' sociobehavioral approach (which admittedly is broader conceptually) more adequately address these questions, their argument highlights an important issue: "Application of principles of behavior modification may be frequently necessary; they are rarely sufficient" (Franks and Wilson 1975).

It is at this point, by broadening the practitioner's viewpoint so that he or she is more fully cognizant of institutional, cultural, and organizational factors, that the eco-systems perspective is most advantageous for the behavioral practitioner. While the behavioral approaches provide the tools for a detailed situational analysis and the development of explicit practice interventions, an eco-systemic orientation ensures that the practitioner's perspective remains sufficiently broad to include all the relevant environmental factors in his or her practice.

Behavioral Practice in an Eco-Systems Perspective

Since the use of an eco-systems perspective does not prescribe interventions, but merely aids in focussing the practitioner's attention upon significant variables for assessment, a practice approach can be used independently or eclectically with other approaches. Behavioral approaches, however, share some features with ecological and general systems theory, so it may be quite compatible for behavioral approaches to be used in the eco-systems framework.

First, behavioral approaches place a high priority on action. An assumption of ego theorists for example, White (1963) which suits behavioral practice is that competence and individual growth and development can be achieved through activity by the person creating an effect on the environment. The eco-systems perspective encompasses person and environment in transaction, laying the groundwork for the behavioral practitioner to engender action by the client upon his environment and for interventions to make the environment responsive in turn to the client. Behavioral theorists also stress the role of action—behavior—in the acquisition and maintenance of new learning patterns.

Second, emphasis is placed on contemporaneous rather than historical events in the assessment and intervention processes. The behavioral orientation, while acknowledging the impact and importance of historical factors in learning, places primary importance on those variables which are operative in the person's immediate environmental context when explaining, and trying to change behavior. The eco-systems perspective, having no theoretical position on the uses of history, draws attention to apparent variables—those which are readily discernible in the person's current situation—behavioral practitioners believe that these are most influential to understanding the dynamics and interrelatedness of the immediate situation.

Third, the behavioral approach asserts that the client must be involved in goal selection, contract negotiation, assessment, intervention, and evaluation. Likewise, the eco-systems perspective highlights the client's presence "in the picture." This allows for the client's perspective, which to the behavioral practitioner, is critical for accurately and meaningfully defining the situation. Therefore, the social worker must not act upon the client; instead, the worker must act *with* the client.

Fourth, attention is directed at the exchanges and interaction patterns in which the client is currently involved. Both the eco-systems perspective, through the description of processes such as reciprocity, multifinality, and equifinality (Meyer 1976) and behavioral intervention, with its emphasis on environmental contingencies and reinforcement patterns, draw the social worker's attention to the multiple levels (individual, family, neighborhood) of factors that are influencing the client.

Fifth, the behavioral approach is interactional. Conceptually, both the behavioral orientation and the eco-systems perspective transcend a linear, reductionistic orientation toward problem definition and resolution. This complementarity between the two must be reflected in intervention efforts that focus on the mutually dependent—reciprocal—nature of maladaptation, problem maintenance, and problem resolution.

There are two major tensions between the behavioral approach and the eco-systems perspective: the contrast between a specific and a holistic conceptualization; a reactive vs. an interactive view of people. The eco-systems perspective postulates that the function of the parts of the system is meaningful only when viewed in the context of the whole. The behavioral approaches, on the other hand, emphasize partialization through behavioral specificity. The eco-systems theorists insist upon a holistic perspective for the understanding of action; the behaviorists emphasize the specifics of the acts.

The second major difference deals with the theorists' view of people as actors or reactors. Although many behavioral theorists and practitioners incorporate cognitive and affective factors into their analyses and no longer accept the simple S-R (cause-effect) notion, there remains a tendency toward environmental determinism that can lapse into a view of people as reactors only to stimuli. Emphasis is placed on discovering how the stimuli affect and shape behavior. Less attention is placed on the unique, perceived meaning of the stimuli, and insufficient emphasis may be placed on developing the concept of people the actors as opposed to people the reactors. The eco-systems theorists, on the other hand, place greater emphasis on the relatedness of all variables—people and environments—in interaction. Although, as an organizing framework, the perspective makes no substantive claims, theorists sympathetic to a view emphasizing the situational/systemic nature of assessment and intervention (see for example Germain 1979 and Siporin 1970, 1972) tend to describe people as actors who initiate contact with the environment and interact with stimuli, whose meaning emerges from the individual's unique definition and perception of the situation.

While at first glance these differences may appear irreconcilable, they may in fact be only a function of the current state of knowledge. Developing as they did in an experimental tradition, the behavioral approaches have a vast store of empirical research about behavior which is precisely described under controlled conditions. They have yet to develop a more comprehensive theory of social systems which can account adequately for the degree of stimulation in social situations. General Systems Theory, upon which many of the eco-systems formulations are based, developed from another direction in that it was conceived as a meta-theory or way of conceptualizing events. As such it need not develop the content and degree of specification that are present in behavioral approaches. In any event, the use of behavioral approaches within an eco-systems perspective will help to remind behavioral practitioners of the presence and effect of impinging, nonspecific, and possibly unknown variables on the intervention process. To use an analogy, by combining the "wide-angled lens" of the eco-systems perspective with the "microscope" of the behavioral approaches, the practitioner can have the flexibility of a "zoom lens" in which he/she can both examine closely the specifics of the situation and also step back to place the specifics in their broader situational context.

Case Illustration

The following case presents one way a behavioral approach to practice can be informed and enhanced by the eco-systems perspective. The assessment and intervention strategies that have been employed draw from the work of Bartlett (1970) and Gambrill, Thomas, and Carter (1971). The specific intervention paradigm which is followed is based on the paper by Gambrill and her colleagues.

Mr. Granti, a 43-year-old, single Italian Catholic, was referred to an out-patient alcohol clinic after being hospitalized and treated for acute alcohol withdrawal in the hospital's alcohol detoxification ward. At the time of his initial contact with the clinic he was living with his sister, her husband, and the couple's two children, aged 3 and 5. Other relevant information about Mr. Granti included: he had a high school diploma; he was a disabled, semiskilled factory worker, having crippled his left hand in a toy factory accident five years earlier; his current income source was Supplemental Security Income.

Mr. Granti's medical record revealed a fifteen-year history of problem drinking. After the factory accident his drinking increased and, according to his sister, his condition deteriorated. Prior to his hospitalization he engaged in daily, solitary drinking, drinking "everything that was available" and often consuming more than "four pints of wine and two six packs of beer" each day in his room. Clearly, he had developed an alcohol dependence. His sister observed that prior to his hospitalization he began "roaming around," "getting lost," "not remembering things," and "mumbling to himself."

This was Mr. Granti's first treatment for alcoholism and was precipitated by his sister's request and her feeling that "we can't take care of him anymore if he stays like this." Until his hospitalization Mr. Granti had been responsible for caring for the family's two children—a task he enjoyed—while his sister and her husband worked. Now, his sister expressed concern about his ability to look after the children; and his brother-in-law was extremely angered by his condition, threatening to "kick him out if something isn't done." The brother-in-law refused to participate in the intervention process, however, citing lack of time.

Mr. Granti presented himself at the clinic in a quiet, nonverbal manner, speaking in short phrases and appearing confused. His affect was flat, and he never initiated a discussion. He appeared to rely on his sister, who always accompanied him to the clinic, for guidance. His sister reported that his behavior at home was similar. He remained in the house all day and watched "his soaps." He could not travel alone, since he frequently got lost; therefore, he had to attend evening sessions at the clinic with his sister, who worked during the day. Psychologists indicated that Mr. Granti was moderately retarded and experiencing some organic brain damage secondary to the alcoholism. Although he did not resume drinking after his discharge from the hospital, his condition remained essentially unchanged.

Mr. Granti's counselor, a recovering alcoholic paraprofessional, met with him and his sister on a weekly basis. The focus of their contacts was on the importance of continued sobriety, education about the effects of alcohol, and helping Mr. Granti make plans for the future. Mr. Granti, who enjoyed caring for his niece and nephew while his sister and her husband worked, wanted to work with the children in the future. Due to his impairments, the feasibility of this goal was questionable. However, his counselor wanted to have psychological and other vocational skill and aptitude tests completed before ruling out the option. At best, employment seemed to be a long-range goal.

A critical problem in the treatment of alcoholism (and

other substance abuse) is relapse. Although Mr. Granti was currently abstinent, his counselor was aware that up to two thirds of all relapses occur within three months following treatment (see for example, Hunt, Barnett, and Branch 1971). Further, studies have indicated that a large proportion of all relapses are due to interpersonal conflicts and negative emotional states, such as depression and frustration (Marlatt 1979). Mr. Granti's situation, in which he was housebound and totally dependent on his family, seemed ripe for such conflicts.

After assessing the situation with him, the counselor's supervisor (a professional social worker) suggested that Mr. Granti enroll in the alcohol day treatment center, a five-day-a-week center with structured group activities. The recommendation took into consideration several factors: (1) Enrollment would effectively expand Mr. Granti's social network. Not only did the center have group activities which would increase the likelihood that he would receive positive social reinforcement for continued sobriety, but also several of the day center participants were Italian and residents of Mr. Granti's community, which would make it easier for the effects of the center to be generalized beyond the day center setting to his nontreatment environment. (For more information on the beneficial impact of interpersonal activities and peer group support see Johnson 1980, Mitchell and Trickett 1980.) (2) It would alleviate some of the stress in his home that resulted from his being housebound. (3) It would give him an opportunity to learn new skills that would help him maintain sobriety and would help him attain his ultimate goal of employment. (4) Enrollment would give the staff an opportunity to observe Mr. Granti more closely and better assess his needs and rehabilitation potential. The counselor discussed this recommendation with Mr. Granti and his sister, and they were both receptive to the idea. There was a major obstacle to implementing the program, however; Mr. Granti could not travel alone by bus to the day center daily and his sister could not escort him because of her job.

It was decided, therefore, to insert an intermediate step in the plan. The supervisor suggested that a behavioral procedure of skill instruction and behavioral rehearsal be used to teach Mr. Granti how to travel to and from the center alone (it was located in the same building as the alcohol clinic) and how to sign in daily at the center (Mr. Granti had to learn how to approach the receptionist and inform her of his appointment; his sister had been doing this for him). The use of skill instruction requires that a task analysis of the skills involved in the desired activity be completed. This is followed by designing and implementing an instructional program in which the client is successively taught each task involved in the total activity and reinforced (in Mr. Granti's case, by social reinforcement and praise) for the successful attainment of each step. Behavioral rehearsal, in turn, involves the simulation of the skill in the practice setting by role-playing the real-life situation and then carrying out the skill in the actual context in which it is to occur. Generally, behavioral rehearsal is broken down into steps in which the client first learns adequately one part of the skill and then incorporates other segments into the "skill package" when he is comfortable with them. (For research evidence on the effectiveness of these interventions for increasing self-care skills among severely disturbed populations see Gambrill 1977.)

These procedures were suggested in this case for three reasons: (1) Possession of the skills was necessary if the client was to participate fully in the day center program. (2) Teaching him these skills would improve his self-esteem and sense of competence. (3) Training instructions could be transmitted to the counselor, enabling him to continue to work with Mr. Granti. To transfer Mr. Granti to another practitioner with whom he had no relationship seemed counterproductive at this time, especially since he was going to make a second transfer—to the day center—shortly. (4) The skills could be taught over a short period, and it was important to help the client make some visible gains, not only to increase his motivation for continued intervention, but also to ease some of the tension in the household.

It was decided to involve the client, his sister, and an agency receptionist in the intervention process to expand the learning and reinforcement opportunities for Mr. Granti.

In addition, since it was realized that any change in Mr. Granti's activities would also require an adaptation by his sister (a tenuous steady state existed between Mr. Granti and his sister; intervention was disrupting it), explicit efforts were made to keep her informed of the process, to involve her in the process, and to interest her in Al-Anon, a self-help group for the family and friends of alcoholics. Moreover, Al-Anon held meetings on the clinic premises on the nights of Mr. Granti's appointments. This direct intervention with his sister would simultaneously help both parties to adapt to the changes which were taking place in their life as they occurred.

Following the procedural model of Gambrill, Thomas, and Carter (1971), when the staff, based on their assessment of the needs and desires of the client, decided that intervention aimed at developing travel skills and "sign-in" skills was the most appropriate point in which to enter the situation, the rationale for their selection of these as priority areas, including a description of the procedures involved in the intervention, was discussed with Mr. Granti and his sister. A verbal commitment to cooperate was obtained from each of them.

The procedure then involved the specification of the target behaviors and the situations in which they occurred. Among the behaviors which were specified in the problem complex were: The sister controlled the travel to and from the clinic. She paid the bus fare and signaled the driver at the appropriate stop. At the receptionist's desk she assumed full responsibility for the exchange, greeting the receptionist and giving her the appointment card while Mr. Granti remained quietly in the background. In place of these behaviors it was desired that Mr. Granti would pay his own bus fare, he would signal the appropriate stop, he would greet the receptionist, he would present his appointment card, and he would request to see his counselor. A baseline of the target behaviors, compiled from the sister's reports, the receptionist's feedback, direct observation of Mr. Granti in the reception room, and the client's own verification, indicated that Mr. Granti had never initiated or performed any of these actions prior to intervention.

The following issues were taken into consideration in identifying some of the controlling conditions (contributing factors) to the problem situation: traveling to and from the clinic and greeting a stranger—the receptionist—although they are automatic and routine for most people, are quite complex behaviors and are difficult for a retarded person to carry out. His sister was very protective of Mr. Granti; by acting for him, both she and he received some stress relief and other secondary gains. Several environmental resources were available, however, which could be used in the intervention process. Most important, the sister could be used to mediate much of the change process (see Tharp and Wetzel 1969). In addition, the bus route involved was a direct one, requiring no transfers, thus simplifying the instruction process. In the clinic itself there were several resources, including the counselor, who could be the skill instructor; the receptionist, who could aid the practitioners and reinforce any gains that Mr. Granti made, and Al-Anon, a support network for the sister.

Among the behavioral objectives which were specified were: (1) for traveling alone—walking to the bus stop, boarding the bus and paying his fare, identifying the stop near the clinic, signaling for the stop, walking to the clinic, and repeating the steps to return home; (2) for entering the clinic—greeting the receptionist, identifying himself, presenting his appointment card, waiting to see his counselor, and retrieving his appointment card from the receptionist at the appointment's end. Since the counselor thought that the objective of entering the clinic was less complex and risky and more likely to be successfully attained, the intervention plan was implemented to teach these skills first. As Mr. Granti made gains in this area, intervention expanded to include the objective of traveling alone.

In implementing the plan a process of successive approximations for response acquisition was employed. The counselor and Mr. Granti spent several sessions rehearsing the behaviors involved in greeting the receptionist and identifying himself. Difficulties were identified as they arose. The counselor maintained a sympathetic, supportive stance, encouraging Mr. Granti's efforts and reassuring him when he was proceeding well. When Mr. Granti was ready to try the behavior *in vivo,* his sister was instructed to let him carry his appointment card and to encourage his efforts. Prior to the day that Mr. Granti carried out the procedure, the receptionist was alerted and taught how to cue the appropriate responses in case he faltered.

Once there were gains made in accomplishing the task of entering the clinic, intervention proceeded to the second target area. Mr. Granti was encouraged to describe the bus route to both the counselor and his sister. His sister was asked to identify any "landmarks" on the way that would help him to remember the route. On the actual bus ride his sister was instructed to allow him to deposit the bus fare. She was also instructed to talk to him about the route, asking him to indicate when their stop was approaching and praising him when he was correct. She was instructed to ask him to signal for the stop; eventually, he was responsible for signaling for the stop without being prompted by his sister (a similar procedure was used for the return trip).

After fifteen weeks of intervention Mr. Granti was able to travel to the clinic alone and to greet the receptionist. At this point the next step in the intervention process—enrollment in the day treatment center—was implemented. Follow-up on the travel and entry procedures indicated that one year after they were successfully instigated, Mr. Granti had yet to miss an attendance day at the center.

This case illustration demonstrates how a behavioral intervention plan, consistent with both the eco-systems perspective and the behavioral orientations, can be implemented. From the behavioral orientation came the attention to detail, the specification of the conditions influencing the case, and the intervention procedures. From the eco-systems perspective came a broadened viewpoint in which the practitioners were alerted to the impact of their interventions on the family balance and to the range of environmental resources which could be incorporated into the intervention plan. Both the perspective and the behavioral approach sensitized the practitioners to the importance of active client involvement in the change process and oriented them to procedures designed to improve the client's sense of competence and self-efficacy. The entire change process was seen as a reciprocal one in which the practitioners could influence client change by intervening with the sister and one in which it was realized that a change by any member of the system necessarily entailed a change in other members of the system. Finally, intervention was extended beyond the immediate client system to include the agency itself. In effect, involving staff members of the agency, like the receptionist, in the change process amounted to a temporary restructuring of the organization to make it more responsive to the needs of a client. Intervention on each of these levels was merged to produce a holistic approach to the client in his situational context.

Conclusion

The behavioral approaches to social work practice have been described briefly, highlighting the historical-societal context in which they emerged and indicating their assets and liabilities. The behavioral approaches offer social workers the potential for developing a more rigorous, self-correcting practice that addresses the needs of their clientele in an accountable fashion. However, they can revert to reductionistic, linear formulations when they are applied by insensitive and undiscerning professionals. It is at this point that the eco-systems perspective can be most useful to behavioral practitioners, by broadening their perspective and suggesting multiple points and means for social work intervention. If one thinks of the behavior approaches as being microscopic, with their attention to detail, and of the eco-systems perspective as wide-angled in breadth, combining the two gives the social worker the flexibility of a zoom lens with which to view his/her practice.

There is a great deal of similarity and overlap between the behavioral approaches and the perspective in which it rests, and further study of both might yield valuable points of convergence. (Kirk and Gambrill 1975 present an interesting discussion of how the two views converge in deviance research and theory.) Since the eco-systems perspective has developed as a "meta-theory" emphasizing the ways of conceptualizing social work practice, it has broadened the base of practice. If one uses the behavioral approaches, adoption of an eco-systems perspective requires that one reject simplistic S-R notions of behavior in favor of the more comprehensive view of action as an interactional and interpretational process (see for example Finlay 1978 and Goldstein 1973). The eco-systems perspective thus may give direction and breadth to behavioral approaches. On the other hand, the behavioral approaches may complement the eco-systems perspective by providing a practice approach whose features of definition and precision anchor the abstract concepts in the perspective.

REFERENCES

Akers, Ronald L. et al. 1979. "Social Learning and Deviant Behavior: A Specific Test of a General Theory." *American Sociological Review* (August).

Auerswald, Edgar H. 1980. "Drug Use and Families—In the Context of Twentieth Century Science." In Barbara Gray Ellis, ed., *Drug Abuse from the Family Perspective: Coping Is a Family Affair.* DHHS Publication No. (ADM) 80–910. Washington, D.C.: GPO.

Bandura, Albert. 1969. *Principles of Behavior Modification.* New York: Holt, Rinehart and Winston.

—— 1977. *Social Learning Theory.* Englewood Cliffs, N.J.: Prentice-Hall.

—— 1981. "In Search of Pure Unidirectional Determinants." *Behavior Therapy* (January).

Bartlett, Harriett M. 1979. *The Common Base of Social Work Practice.* Washington, D.C.: NASW.

Burgess, Robert L. and Don Bushell, Jr., eds. 1969. *Behavioral Sociology: The Experimental Analysis of Social Process.* New York: Columbia University Press.

Butterfield, William H. 1974. "Instrumentation in Behavior Therapy." In Edwin J. Thomas, ed., *Behavior Modification Procedure: A Sourcebook.* Chicago: Aldine.

Campbell, Donald T. and Julian C. Stanley. 1963. *Experimental and Quasi-Experimental Designs for Research.* Chicago: Rand McNally.

Epstein, Irwin. 1974. "The Politics of Behavior Therapy: The New

Cool-Out Casework?" In Howard Jones, ed., *Toward a New Social Work*. London: Routledge and Kegan Paul.

Evans, Richard I. 1968. *B. F. Skinner: The Man and His Ideas*. New York: E. P. Dutton.

Finlay, Donald G. 1978. "Alcoholism and Systems Theory: Building a Better Mousetrap." *Psychiatry* (August).

Fischer, Joel. 1978. *Effective Casework Practice: An Eclectic Approach*. New York: McGraw-Hill.

Franks, Cyril M. and G. Terrence Wilson. 1975. "Commentary: Behavior Therapy and the Natural Environment; Community-Societal Issues." In Cyril M. Franks and G. Terrence Wilson, eds., *Annual Review of Behavior Therapy: Theory and Practice*. New York: Brunner Mazel.

Gambrill, Eileen D. 1977. *Behavior Modification: Handbook of Assessment, Intervention, and Evaluation*. San Francisco: Jossey-Bass.

Gambrill, Eileen D. and Richard P. Barth. 1980. "Single-Case Study Designs Revisited." *Social Work Research and Abstracts* (Fall).

Gambrill, Eileen D., Edwin J. Thomas, and Robert D. Carter. 1971. "Procedure for Sociobehavioral Practice in Open Settings." *Social Work* (January).

Germain, Carel B. 1976. "Time: An Ecological Variable in Social Work Practice." *Social Casework* (July).

—— 1979. "Introduction: Ecology and Social Work." In Carel B. Germain, ed., *Social Work Practice: People and Environments*. New York: Columbia University Press.

Goldstein, Howard. 1973. *Social Work Practice: A Unitary Approach*. Columbia: University of South Carolina Press.

Hall, Calvin S. and Gardner Lindzey. 1979. *Theories of Personality*. 2d ed. New York: John Wiley.

Hollis, Florence. 1972. *Casework: A Psychosocial Therapy*. 2d ed. New York: Random House.

Homans, George Caspar. 1974. *Social Behavior: Its Elementary Forms*. Rev. ed. New York: Harcourt Brace Jovanovich.

Hunt, W. A., L. W. Barnett, and L. G. Branch. 1971. "Relapse Rates in Addiction Programs." *Journal of Clinical Psychology* (October).

Jayaratne, Srinika and Rona L. Levy. 1979. *Empirical Clinical Practice*. New York: Columbia University Press.

Johnson, David W. 1980. "Attitude Modification Methods." In Frederick H. Kanfer and Arnold P. Goldstein, eds., *Helping People Change.* 2d ed. New York: Pergamon Press.

Kanfer, Frederick H. and Arnold P. Goldstein, eds. 1980. *Helping People Change.* 2d ed. New York: Pergamon Press.

Kanfer, Frederick H. and Jeanne Phillips. 1970. *Learning Foundations of Behavior Therapy.* New York: John Wiley.

Kanfer, Frederick H. and George Saslow. 1969. "Behavioral Diagnosis." In Cyril M. Franks, ed., *Behavior Therapy: Appraisal and Status.* New York: McGraw-Hill.

Kirk, Stuart and Eileen D. Gambrill. 1975. "The Convergence of Interactionist and Behavioral Approaches to Deviance." *Journal of Sociology and Social Welfare* (September).

Krasner, Leonard. 1969. "Behavior Modification—Values and Training: The Perspective of a Psychologist." In Cyril M. Franks, ed., *Behavior Therapy: Appraisal and Status.* New York: McGraw-Hill.

—— 1971. "Behavior Therapy." In P. H. Mussen and M. R. Rosenzweig, eds., *Annual Review of Psychology.* Palo Alto, Calif.: Annual Reviews.

London, Perry. 1972. "The End of Ideology in Behavior Modification." *The American Psychologist* (October).

Marlatt, G. Alan. 1979. "A Cognitive-Behavioral Model of the Relapse Process." In Norman A. Krasnegor, ed., *Behavioral Analysis and Treatment of Substance Abuse.* NIDA Research Monograph 25. Washington, D.C.: GPO.

Meyer, Carol H. 1976. *Social Work Practice: The Changing Landscape.* 2d ed. New York: Free Press.

Miller, Peter M. 1975. "A Behavioral Intervention Program for Chronic Drunkenness Offenders." *Archives of General Psychiatry* (July).

Mitchell, Roger E. and Edison J. Trickett. 1980. "Task Force Report: Social Networks as Mediators of Social Support." *Community Mental Health Journal* (Spring).

Perlman, Helen Harris. 1957. *Social Casework: A Problem-Solving Process.* Chicago: University of Chicago Press.

Reid, William J. 1978. *The Task-Centered System.* New York: Columbia University Press.

Reppucci, N. Dickson and J. Terry Saunders. 1975. "Social Psychology of Behavior Modification: Problems of Implementation in Natural Settings." In Cyril M. Franks and G. Terrence Wilson, eds., *Annual Review of Behavior Therapy: Theory and Practice.* New York: Brunner Mazel.

Robinson, Virginia. 1930. *A Changing Psychology in Social Casework.* Chapel Hill: University of North Carolina Press.

Rose, Sheldon D. 1977. *Group Therapy: A Behavioral Approach.* Englewood Cliffs, N.J.: Prentice-Hall.

Rosen, Gerald M. 1979. "Self-Help Approaches to Self-Management." Paper presented at a symposium on self-control and modification of emotional behavior. University of Toronto, Erindale Campus.

Scheff, Thomas J. 1966. *Being Mentally Ill: A Sociological Theory.* Chicago: Aldine.

Schwartz, Arthur and Israel Goldiamond. 1975. *Social Casework: A Behavioral Approach.* New York: Columbia University Press.

Siporin, Max. 1979. "Social Treatment: A New-Old Helping Method." *Social Work* (July).

—— 1972. "Situational Assessment and Intervention." *Social Casework* (February).

Skinner, B. F. 1950. "Are Learning Theories Necessary?" *Psychological Review* (July).

Stuart, Richard B. 1967. "Applications of Behavior Theory to Social Casework." In Edwin J. Thomas, ed., *The Socio-Behavioral Approach and Applications to Social Work.* New York: Council on Social Work Education.

—— 1969. "Operant Interpersonal Treatment of Marital Discord." *Journal of Consulting and Clinical Psychology* (December).

—— 1977. "Self-Help Group Approach to Self-Management." In Richard B. Stuart, ed., *Behavioral Self-Management.* New York: Brunner Mazel.

—— 1978. *Act Thin, Stay Thin.* New York: W. W. Norton.

Tharp, Roland G. and Ralph J. Wetzel. 1969. *Behavior Modification in the Natural Environment.* New York: Academic Press.

Thomas, Edwin J. 1967. "The Socio-Behavioral Approach: Illustration and Analysis." In Edwin J. Thomas, ed., *The Socio-Behavioral*

Approach and Applications to Social Work. New York: Council on Social Work Education.

—— 1970. "Behavioral Modification and Casework." In Robert W. Roberts and Robert H. Nee, eds., *Theories of Social Casework.* Chicago: University of Chicago Press.

White, Robert W. 1963. *Ego and Reality in Psychoanalytic Theory.* Monograph 11. New York: International Universities Press.

Von Bertalantfy, Ludwig. 1967. *Robots, Men and Minds.* New York: George Braziller.

CRISIS INTERVENTION

Barry Panzer

There is a fundamental issue underlying the use of an eco-systems perspective as an organizing conceptual device for various practice models, and indeed for understanding human behavior. That issue is the unstated extension of Kuhn's thesis regarding paradigms and scientific revolutions (Kuhn 1970). For a perspective, whether linear or systemic, does not alter the nature of occurrences in the world or in any way attest to a greater truth. Rather, it embodies a certain style and consistency of perception based on the belief that people and societies function in a particular manner. Clearly, if a perspective is adopted by many it has achieved consensus, but does its use accomplish more than that?

A review of the literature points out that crisis intervention, both historically and in current usage, incorporates both linear and systems principles. Crises have been defined largely in a linear, deterministic manner, beginning with Lindemann's disease model of grief, its symptoms, time limits, and so forth (Lindemann 1944). The systemic aspects are to be found in interventions dealing with equilibrium, steady state, and overload.

This paper will illustrate the duality and the practice consequences of adopting either perspective. Thus, the linear thinker risks obsolescence by not incorporating social science findings which alter early crisis theory ideas, while the systemic thinker loses credibility by advocating equifinal strategies without addressing the hierarchy, parsimony, or effectiveness of the range of interventions.

It is important to mention from the outset that the most widely used paradigm for the study of situational crises is Hill's classic formulation (Hill 1949). See figure 6.1.

FIGURE 6.1

A	Interacts with	B	Interacts with	C	Produces	X
Event		Family Resources		Definition of Event		Crisis

Expanded by Burr in 1973 and more recently by McCubbin et al. (1980), this model has guided crisis research and practice for nearly three decades. The use of an eco-systems perspective and its concepts can produce a significant modification of this paradigm, and this will be presented along with practice implications.

Any presentation of crisis intervention needs to consider Fischer's strong position (1978:152):

> Unfortunately, the research literature is not clear as to just what crisis intervention contributes to positive outcome over and beyond the effects of time limits. Beyond this, Rapoport has pointed out that crisis intervention has no real treatment methodology of its own. Thus, the body of knowledge called crisis intervention may be superfluous to outcome since time-limited intervention has demonstrated its effectiveness independent of any link with crisis intervention. That crisis theorists understand this possibility might be inferred by the attempt to tie crisis intervention to short-term treatment (Rapoport 1967, 1970; Parad and Parad 1968).

Fischer's view appears to reflect a shortcoming in theory development rather than an inherent weakness in the formulation. Specifically, crisis theory holds the potential for using the construct of tasks to identify coping strategies and clinical guidelines for a catalogue of stressful life events. This approach, which would indeed constitute a distinct methodology, was evident in some of the early crisis literature (Lindemann 1944, Rapoport 1963, Kaplan and Mason 1960), but apparently it gave way to more general formulations (Aguilera and Messick 1970; Smith 1978; Golan 1978, Burgess and Baldwin 1981).

In addition, crisis intervention as a field of study and practice can enable social work to incorporate more effectively the large body of research and clinical concepts related to stress. As will be noted later, the stress construct may serve as one of the vital theoretical notions in an eco-systems perspective.

This article reviews the traditional crisis intervention model and then examines the modifications of this approach, using an ecological and systems orientation. The discussion is geared toward analysis of situational crises since these are qualitatively different from the stresses of maturation and the life cycle which are also termed crises. The former characteristically involve stressful life events, identifiable precipitants, rapid, often sudden change, and usually loss. Bereavement is the archetypal crisis situation, and a separate section considers eco-systems principles in relation to grief and coping with the sudden infant death syndrome.

Ideological Biases

The history of crisis intervention suggests that over the past forty years the ideological biases have shifted from a focus on the individual to a focus on the event, to a focus on both via the concept of coping tasks (Bartlett 1970). This dual emphasis draws attention to the exigencies of the stressful event (*task*) as well as to the adaptive response of the individual or family (*coping*). The current literature, however, tends to reflect the predominance of the "person" half of the person-environment equation, and this bias has resulted in a primarily psychodynamic, treatment-oriented formulation, with less understanding of the multiple environments which produce, shape, and affect stressful life events and adaptation.

Values

A number of beliefs have evolved with crisis practice, primarily in two general areas: the nature of crises and the nature of intervention, including the role of the professional and the persons to be served by the model. Basic tenets of crisis intervention would include the following:

1. Crisis situations are usually initiated by a hazardous event which may be either an external blow or internal pressure.
2. The hazardous event disturbs the individual's homeostatic balance, resulting in a vulnerable state.
3. If usual problem-solving efforts are unsuccessful, a precipitating factor can further distress the individual leading to disequilibrium and disorganization—the state of active crisis.
4. Stressful events may be perceived as primarily a threat, a loss, or a challenge, and each perception will evoke a different emotional and cognitive response.
5. A crisis situation may reactivate earlier unresolved conflicts, causing the individual to react currently in an exaggerated or inappropriate manner. There is thus the clinical opportunity to resolve both the current and the past conflict.
6. There is a sequence of predictable stages for each type of crisis.
7. The state of active crisis is usually limited to four to six weeks.
8. During the crisis period, individuals and families are particularly responsive to help.
9. Brief clinical intervention at the time of crisis can be more effective than longer treatment after the crisis has passed.
10. Crisis methodology is best suited for those individuals and families who are functioning normally until befallen by crisis (Porter 1966, Rapoport 1970, Golan 1978, Smith 1978).

These assumptions and observations are repeatedly cited in the crisis literature and have served as guidelines for clinicians responding to persons in distress. It is interesting to note that these assumptions have persisted despite the lack of supporting evidence, or even when contradicted by new data (Lukton 1974). For example, the "state of crisis," the central concept in Hill's and other formulations, is extremely difficult to operationalize both for clinical and research purposes (Bloom 1963, Golan 1974). Clients may show no emotional distress amid overwhelming trauma, and are therefore presumed to be in crisis, or an external trauma may not be apparent and the crisis is traced to some internal issues.

The notion that crises are time limited and follow predictable stages is derived from Lindemann's prototype. However, those original time guidelines have not been validated in other life crises, and have been questioned in bereavement itself (Wikler 1981, Caplan 1974, Lewis et al. 1979).

In addition, while stage theories of adaptation provide practitioners with useful conceptual tools, such approaches are not without their limitations:

> Stage theories assume a single primary path of movement which can impede the discovery of alternate approaches, and can stereotype uncommon or idiosyncratic patterns as deviant. Also the stage approach sometimes fails to distinguish between what *usually* happens and what *should* happen. . . . There is a disturbing tendency for description to be converted imperceptibly into prescription (Kastenbaum 1975:44–45).

The theoretical weaknesses and inconsistencies of stage approaches would include: that stages may be considered both overlapping and separate entities; that stages do not necessarily occur in succession; that it is not considered necessary to experience each stage; and that the intensity and duration of any one stage can vary idiosyncratically (Bugen 1977).

Other crisis notions of increased psychological accessibility and the opportunity for resolution of previous conflicts have not been tested empirically. It is significant to note that the available evidence does not verify the view that brief intervention at the time of crisis is more helpful than longer treatment at a later time or that crisis therapy produces improved coping mechanisms (Bloom 1977). The overall effectiveness of crisis therapy remains an unanswered question (Mechanic 1969, Umana et al. 1980).

Knowledge Base

Crisis theory has always been an eclectic enterprise, drawing on a spectrum of academic disciplines and helping professions for its concepts and principles. Significant contributions have come from various personality theories, role theory, learning theory, stress theory, social work theories about community, clinical psychology, psychiatry, nursing, pastoral counseling, public health, experimental and developmental psychology, physiology, as well as the short-term and family therapy treatment methodologies.

Two additional comments regarding theory-building are in order. First, as noted earlier, the emphasis in crisis theory appears to have shifted from efforts to delineate tasks for specific life crises toward the development of general strategies of crisis management. Second, some theorists have drawn a distinction between individual and family crisis intervention (Bonnefil 1979, Umana et al. 1980). It will be interesting to follow the impact of this issue on the evolution of the crisis knowledge base.

Unit of Attention

Crisis theorists have expanded the unit of attention from its original focus on the coping of individuals and families (Lindemann 1944), to the effects of social networks (Erickson 1975, Rueveni 1979, Speck and Attneave 1973), to the community response to natural disasters and catastrophies (Bloom 1977, Golan 1978). For the clinician, the unit of attention is clearly the coping responses of the individual or family. As Morley notes: "If the person had had a repertoire of coping mechanisms adequate to deal with the life stress, he or she would not have gone into crisis in the first place" (1980:18–19). Consistent with this emphasis on the individual's or family's adaptation, some have taken the position that the use of traditional psychiatric diagnoses in crisis work is unnecessary and even misleading for the practitioner (Butcher and Maudal 1976).

Definition of the Problem

In keeping with the unit of attention, the case problem would be defined in terms of problematic affective, cognitive, and behavioral reactions to crisis situations. The performance of the delineated coping tasks is often used as a diagnostic yardstick, and for some stressful life events, syndromes have been identified which specify normal vs. pathological responses. These reactions are most often viewed as properties of the individual or family, and intervention is directed toward their alleviation or modification. The environmental influences and determinants of these responses, both past and present, may include broad societal forces and ideologies as well as more immediate social network factors. Clinicians are aware of this, yet well-developed methods of assessment and intervention are lacking at present.

Congruent and Explicit Interventions

One of its leading proponents has noted that crisis intervention has no real treatment methodology of its own (Rapoport 1970). There does appear, however, to be a configuration of practice principles and guidelines which address the how, where, and when of intervention.

Much of the crisis literature depicts the interview as the most common method or technique. (When interviews are patterned and consist of specified persons, they become the treatment modalities or therapies of the mental health providers.) Clinical strategies which rely on interviewing as the major therapeutic and change mechanism will have clear implications regarding the central role of the professional and the nature of the client-worker relationship. Thus, the term "crisis therapy" or "crisis treatment" underlies such traditional psychotherapeutic services.

The "how" of intervention has direct bearing on the "where" or location of practice efforts. The interview situation imposes temporal and spatial limits, and requires at least a basic level of verbal exchange. Crisis sessions with individuals will usually focus on the expression of distressing emotions, and the examination of cognitive impasses to problem-solving. With families, the emphasis is on communication, affective, and decision-making processes.

Lastly, the timing of intervention has been one of the major features of the crisis model. Corresponding to Caplan's secondary prevention level, crisis intervention calls for rapid diagnosis and treatment during the period of disequilibrium. This is based on the previously discussed concept of the crisis state as a time-limited phenomenon, and on the beliefs both that clients are more receptive and that help can be provided more parsimoniously during this period. There is implied a "reachable moment," if you will, mandating early provision of clinical services.

Thus, at its not-so-extreme, the traditional approach would restrict the how, where, and when of the crisis model to clinicians serving articulate clients during a fairly specific period of time.

An additional restriction is implied by theorists who suggest that the crisis model is most appropriate for individuals and families who were functioning well during the precrisis period (Smith 1978). This might eliminate large numbers of recipients of mental health care, especially those with chronic psychosocial problems. An alternate approach sees crisis concepts as applicable to a broader range of persons and situations, this perhaps being a major strength of the model. Thus, clients labeled alcoholic or schizophrenic may be helped to cope with the tasks of bereavement, divorce, or having a handicapped child, in much the same way that nonlabeled persons will, allowing for a wider variation in coping responses (Panzer 1978).

Use of the Professional Relationship

Crisis intervention concepts have been credited with dislodging social work practice from its strong reliance on psychoanalytic and long-term treatment approaches (Siporin 1975). Most theorists indicate that unlike traditional casework formulations, the helping relationship in crisis practice is not an interpersonal exchange which is intended to produce insight, growth, change, or "working through" of conflicts. Rather, involvement with the clinician is used to relieve distress and bolster coping, mainly through verbal discussion. The relationship is clearly a means to an end, and not an end unto itself.

Another aspect of relationship includes the concepts of support and a supportive relationship. Both have permeated social work theory and practice for over thirty years (Selby 1979), and recently various kinds of support have been described as a necessary condition for change (Nelsen 1980). There is a basic practice issue concerning what to support, and the traditional crisis model answers that question in vague or universalistic terms. It would appear that the idea of support could provide a framework and practice guideline which require that all crisis strategies and interventions be based upon a relationship providing support of the particular coping tasks and processes. Given this framework, it becomes apparent that the distinction between the use of the relationship in supportive and insight-oriented treatment is indeed overstated (Hollis 1972, Reid and Shyne 1969) since both techniques and processes may be practiced in support of specific coping tasks.

Desired Outcomes

The crisis literature is almost unanimous in delineating the goals of intervention as helping the client to resolve the crisis successfully by alleviating the immediate impact of the stressful life event and restoring the individual or family to at least the precrisis level of functioning. There appears to be general agreement that personality reorganization and characterological revamping are not intended objectives of the crisis approach. Some traditionalists have suggested that a current crisis may offer opportunities to master previously unresolved conflicts, as well as improve coping skills to prevent or better handle future crises. Despite the familiarity of such ideas, they remain hypotheses which have yet to be validated empirically.

Uses of Time

As previously noted, time and timing are clearly central concepts in crisis theory and intervention. Many of the crisis dichotomies and typologies imply a strong time dimension, and one model is explicitly developed around temporal progression (Shneidman 1973). Life cycle sequences, stage theories, anticipation/preparation for loss, suddenness of stressor, period of disequilibrium, transition period, elimination of waiting lists, and planned short-term treatment are just a few of the concepts and processes affected by one's view of time. The traditional model adopts a linear view of time, especially in regard to crises, coping, and intervention.

Differential Use of Staff

The crisis model has come to include a large variety of practices and programs with important implications for the use of differentially trained helpers. Despite this range, crisis intervention continues to be used primarily as a method of mental health treatment, either offered directly as a therapy by clinicians or provided by other than mental health professionals and paraprofessionals with mental health supervision and consultation (Bard and Berkowitz 1967, Langsley and Yarvis 1975, Rabkin 1977). Some theorists have suggested that staff assignments and levels of training should correspond to the severity of trauma or level of psychopathology (Baldwin, 1978, Jacobson et al. 1968). Others disagree (Bloom 1977, Shneidman 1973), and several self-help crisis programs appear to adopt both views (Lieberman and Borman 1979, Silverman 1978). This element of flexibility differentiates the crisis approach from most other areas of mental health activity. A significant task for researchers will be to delineate which helpers are effective with which clients and crises at what given moment.

Work with Self-Help Groups

The numerous purposes and functions of mutual aid organizations have received much attention in the literature (Gartner and Riessman 1977, Killilea 1976, Silverman 1978). The growth of mutual aid groups for coping with crises (Lieberman and Borman 1979) reflects trends associated with the self-help and community mental health movements. Both forces developed in response to the shortcomings of traditional professional services, technological (medical) advances, increasing longevity and survival from trauma, and the disruptive, alienating effects of rapid social change (Silverman 1978). All of this contributed to an increased examination of the role of informal social networks in mitigating stressful life situations.

The traditional model of crisis intervention appears to have incorporated self-help groups largely as a treatment methodology requiring professional leadership, supervision, or consultation. Where professional sponsorship is not part of the helping service, clinicians and self-helpers may develop a relationship marked by competition, mistrust, and hostility (Silverman 1978).

Availability to Effectiveness Research

In addition to all of the problems that make evaluating the outcome of psychotherapy so complex, one additional difficulty exists when examining the effectiveness of crisis intervention services—namely, the necessity of defining a crisis . . . Relevant life events must be unambiguously definable as either crises or noncrises. The success of studies of attempts to intervene or influence the outcome of such life experiences will be partially dependent on the adequacy of this fundamental definition (Bloom 1977:167).

This difficulty in defining the state of crisis is further compounded by tendencies to refer to the stressor event *and* the response to the event as the "crisis," even though the major formulations clearly separate them (Golan 1978, Hill 1949). Other crisis concepts, such as the "vulnerable state," are usually difficult to operationalize. Despite this, several researchers have attempted to describe the effectiveness of a particular crisis service or approach. Specific studies have concluded that brief intervention at the time of crisis is no more helpful than longer treatment at a later point (Polak et al. 1975), and that crisis therapy does not seem to produce improved coping mechanisms later in life (Gottschalk et al. 1975).

Effectiveness research has all but avoided the issue of deterioration or iatrogenic consequences of crisis intervention. In the absence of empirical data, Mechanic's caveat would seem to have programmatic and clinical value:

If we could successfully identify family crises early, it is not at all clear that it would be advantageous for individuals or society to pursue a policy of placing these problems is a psychiatric or mental health perspective. The act of defining a person's behavior as indicative of a psychiatric condition may undermine his limited self-confidence and efforts at continuing to cope in work and family life, and it may encourage a stance of dependency which leads to further disability and the acceptance of illness (Mechanic 1969:75–76).

Crisis Intervention in the Eco-Systems Perspective

The use of a different perspective with the crisis intervention model of practice results not in an implantation, but in a fundamental shift in thinking and orientation. This can best be illustrated in a "redoing" of the framework for analysis that was just applied to the model itself.

Ideological Biases

According to Umana et al. (1980), a systemic approach to crisis intervention emphasizes the social context in which the individual and the crisis event come together. This emphasis reflects two general assumptions: the perception of the stresssful event depends on the social context, and the resolution of the crisis depends on the availability of social support.

The significance of the social environment in this crisis formulation stands in marked contrast to the psychodynamic person-focus of the traditional model. However, any deemphasis of the personal and familial contribution to both the production and resolution of the crisis situation would reflect a misunderstanding of the transactional nature of an eco-systems approach, for such a perspective is concerned with the interconnectedness of the salient variables of person and environment. In effect, it demands that crisis theorists need equal appreciation of endocrine and cognitive systems, as well as social networks, cultures, and societies.

Values

An eco-systems approach to crisis intervention draws many of its assumptions from GST. These include:

1. The key variable is whether an effective support system is provided to the individual or group experiencing the crisis.
2. Interaction between the personality of the individual in crisis and the crisis stimulus occurs in a social context.
3. Return of the individual to a homeostatic state may involve correcting ineffective or detrimental patterns of relating within his social system.
4. The focus of intervention should be on changing those current patterns of interaction that are maintaining the crisis.
5. Assessment of etiology is not relevant to crisis resolution.
6. Insight and awareness are not causal in producing change in current patterns of interaction (Umana et al. 1980:84).

The impact of systemic thinking on crisis intervention can be seen in values and beliefs which favor a less simplistic, deterministic, and more complex view of crises and intervention. In place of the problematic concept of the crisis state, one would focus on the meaning attached to stressful life events and the perception of social support as key elements of the crisis situation. Such a formulation allows for variation in distress and coping behavior due to ethnic, religious, and class differences, yielding a more sensitive and individualistic clinical approach.

The concept of coping is a second area affected by eco-systems ideas. The literature regarding adaptation tends to depict man as reactive and individualistic, and coping as largely an intrapsychic process (Coelho, Hamburg, and Adams 1974). Eco-systems beliefs would expand this position, as Mechanic suggests:

Man's ability to cope with the environment depends on the efficacy of the solutions that his culture provides, and the skills he develops are dependent on the adequacy of the preparatory institutions to which he has been exposed (Mechanic 1974:33).

A significant literature also suggests that contrary to the psychodynamic approach, coping may well depend on the nature of actual and perceived social support available.

Another implication of this view is that various stressful life events may be inherently more or less "copable," in light of the subjective meaning attached to such events, the cultural preparation available, and so on. Coping and adaptation would thus be measured in relation to the severity of the blow.

A final observation regarding this issue is that the actual coping behavior of the individual or family need not follow a deterministic, linear path. Again, Mechanic notes:

> It is incorrect to assume that successful adaptation requires an accurate perception of reality. . . . Many misperceptions of reality aid coping and mastery, energize involvement and participation in life endeavors, and alleviate pain and discomfort that would detract the person from successful efforts at mastery. Reality, of course, is a social construction, and to the extent that perspectives are shared and socially reinforced, they may facilitate adaptation irrespective of their objective truth. It is well known that if men define situations as real, they are real in the consequences (Mechanic 1974:38).

In terms of intervention, an eco-systems crisis model would alter the clinician's role, expand the range of helpers, and alert the practitioner to the possibility of negative feedback or the iatrogenic consequences of providing service. These will be discussed later.

Knowledge Base

An eco-systems perspective of crisis theory draws its knowledge base from many of the same sources as the extant model, with a greater emphasis on systemic concepts and social science data than the traditional psychodynamic model. The effects of the physical and social environment are important sources of practice data, with social networks emerging as probably the most significant clinical construct (American Psychiatric Association Task Force Report 1979, Lee 1979, Mitchell and Trickett 1980, Swenson 1979, Unger and Powell 1980).

A seriously underutilized source of data in both the traditional and eco-systems approach is the body of knowledge known as stress research. Two reasons for this are apparent: stress data remain difficult to translate into clinical strategies, and the biochemical and neurological aspects of stress may exceed the professional training of nonmedical practitioners. Yet, stress theory holds the potential for "demedicalizing" the traditional crisis model, and for providing an eco-systems approach with a problem definition and unit of attention more familiar than concepts such as interface and transition.

Unit of Attention

As in the traditional formulation, the coping tasks serve as the unit of attention in an eco-systems crisis model. However, unlike the simple ranking of psychological and social tasks which some crisis literature has offered, task as a systemic and transactional construct serves to unify and integrate ecological variables and systems levels. Tasks which inhere in the stressful life event, interact with the individual's competence and coping style (multidetermined via biological through social structure variables), all in the context of one's social network. Thus, the existence, definition, and performance of these tasks extend well beyond the psychosocial efforts of the individual or family.

Problem Definition

In an eco-systems perspective, the case problem is defined as an imbalance or "lack of fit" between the needs and coping resources of the person and the impinging demands of the stressful life event and its physical and social environment. This adaptive balance varies directly with the performance of the coping tasks, the unit of attention.

Yet, when systems theorists locate problems at the interface, or at the transaction between person and environment, it is not always clear how to use such schemas in direct practice (Hellenbrand 1978). A more useful approach both practically and theoretically would be to view crisis situations as evidence of stress (distress), assessing the quality and quantity in terms of intensity, frequency, duration, and so forth. This conception of stress as the manifestation of the "lack of fit" derives from the observation that "disease can occur through factors which disturb the balance between the ubiquitous disease agent and the host that is harboring or exposed to them" (Cassel 1974:473). Psychosocial stressors which disturb this homeostatic balance and represent a lack of fit would include, to name just a few: (1) migration, (2) residential mobility, (3) inadequate role preparation, and (4) status inconsistency and role conflict.

Social workers have long been familiar with these kinds of stresses, but have apparently lacked a conceptual framework connecting stress theory to clinical interventions. An eco-systems oriented crisis model may well provide such an opportunity.

Congruent and Explicit Interventions

The systemic perspective yields a significantly different model of crisis practice. Because systems phenomena promote an intrinsically more complex view of human behavior, the crisis model adopts a stance lacking the certitude and determinism of the traditional approach. As Voltaire observed, "therapeutics is the pouring of drugs, of which one knows nothing, into a patient of whom one knows less." This is a wholly appropriate humility when the helping professions adopt systems concepts.

A second philosophical idea derives from the above, that is, the need to search out, prevent, and mitigate the iatrogenic potential of any form of intervention. For centuries, physicians have begun their education with the inculcation of *primum non nocere* (first do no harm), and it has now been repeatedly documented that a variety of social work and mental health methods (perhaps all human services) entail the risk of deterioration as a result of professional activity (Fischer 1976, Gaylin et al. 1978, Gurman and Kniskern, 1978, Stuart 1973). Actually, Hollis comments on this as it concerns the dual casework goals of increasing or maintaining the client's competence and self-worth:

> This requires that the worker avoid procedures that will threaten the client's sense of his own worth or his own competence, and that he communicates an attitude of support, sustainment, and basic respect (Hollis 1972:301).

Nonetheless, the traditional crisis model has not stressed enough the possible negative effects of intervention, especially with vulnerable populations.

Crisis intervention in an eco-systems perspective is rooted in the coping tasks and processes of the particular stressful life situation. Just as the eco-systems assessment evaluates the range of actors and forces impairing or promoting task achievement, systemic intervention surveys the variety of methods and services which can prevent or remedy problematic responses to stress.

The how of this model requires an understanding of the potential impact of all extant and possible professional activities in relation to the specific coping tasks and processes. Family interviews, homemakers, tranquilizers, medical treatment, debt counseling, legal advice, and a myriad of other services are orchestrated by the practitioner, whose roles may range from therapist to advocate to broker to educator. Thus, the choice of method is not predetermined, but is selected by considering the goodness of fit between the particular task and the specific strategy for a given person or family.

The location of systemic interventions ranges from the intrapsychic to the societal, from preventive to rehabilitative. Such flexibility is based on the concept of equifinality, though this principle is regarded as one of the most difficult concepts to translate into direct practice (Freeman 1977), since all levels and tasks cannot be addressed at once. A hierarchy of interventions, those most effective and parsimonious, must await empirical validation; however, current social work ideologies can help to inform these practice decisions. Therefore, strategies should endeavor to promote coping first within the natural network of family, kin, friends, and neighborhood, and secondarily via the artificial network of professional providers. This health-oriented approach reflects the self-help strengths of individuals, families, and groups, and recognizes the limitations, even disadvantages, of "altruism under professional auspices" (Timms and Timms 1977).

The dilemma of equifinality can also be addressed by drawing on well-known classifications of needs and motivations and casework typologies (Hollis 1972, Perlman 1968). One only has to keep in mind that these are restricted to intervention with the individual or family (not the transactional whole), and that interventions move from provision of material resources and information on a cognitive, conscious level to a focus on patterns of behavior, and to an exploration of the consequences and etiologies of those patterns. These interventions suggest the assumption of decreasing levels of client competence, and the sequential paradigm is paralleled by a typology of emotional crises progressing from *Class* 1 disposition/information/referral issues to Class 6 life-threatening/deteriorative/psychiatric emergencies (Baldwin 1978).

Use of the Professional Relationship

The eco-systems approach to crisis intervention extends the linear model by not relegating the professional relationship to one point of entry and one type of helper in crisis management. The therapeutic turf, so to speak, is shared by a variety of actors, activities, and forces. This broader ecological range accommodates the therapist role, but equal attention is given to the practice roles of educator, broker, and facilitator. The latter is vital in both engaging and as enhancing existing social networks, and in creating new networks to promote coping (Swenson 1979).

Desired Outcomes

The eco-systems orientation to the crisis model clearly upholds adaptation within and among various systems levels as the desired outcome, with task achievement as the central focus. Outcome in systemic terms occurs when optimal exchanges of energy between each subsystem and its environment takes one of two forms: assimilation or accommodation.

In the former, the person attempts to fit the new experience into old schemas, whereas in the latter, the person's old schema is modified around the event or situation (Anderson and Carter 1974). Since different stressors may signal or be more compatible with either type of adaptation, an adaptive outcome is again an issue of achieving a dynamic balance, and clinically this probably represents a combination of minimal emotional distress and socially competent, satisfying role functioning.

Uses of Time

Germain's discussion of a linear vs. systemic concept of time has bearing on the development of a crisis formulation:

> As another face of determinism, linear time suggests that what has been governs the sequences of what is, and what will be. Thus, linear time is apt to conceal the elements of freedom, creativity, and innovation within human beings. By contrast, transactional time in the ecological perspective is concerned with cycles and the spiraling accumulations of recurring patterns and processes. It focuses on the manifest and latent functions of what is going on, rather than on the division into effects neatly preceded by causes. . . . In transactional time, change is directed less toward the historical roots of motivation and more toward present transactions that continue the past in current relations with all elements of the complex environment (Germain 1976:423).

The practice consequences of adopting either approach are numerous and wide-ranging, and clinicians may find it helpful to clarify their beliefs and methods in relation to this crucial dimension. The "when" or timing of interventions in a crisis model using the eco-systems perspective reflects the diversity, complexity, and relativity of biological, psychological, cultural, and social time as an ecological variable (Germain 1976). Linear assumptions concerning the temporal limits of the crisis period require that contact be established "in time," during the four-to-six-week period of disequilibrium if the coping outcome is to be positive. In contrast, systems theorists adopt a less restrictive view of coping in that interventions may be "on time," or timely, at a number of points in the process of adaptation.

The construct of the transition state, an extended period of time following a stressful life situation during which new role behaviors are learned, increases the points of entry for therapeutic services (Golan 1980, Weiss 1976). A systemic view of time also affects the clinician's view of the client's personal readiness to confront the trauma and stark reality of many crisis events. Traditional crisis theorists seem willing to acknowledge the need for denial and distortion of painful situations, but at some point a time limit defining the normalcy of the response is imposed. In ecological terms, however, such responses are measured according to the adaptive value provided.

Differential Use of Staff

The eco-systems perspective views the professional helper as one among many actors with a potential influence on the outcome following a stressor event. The focus is on the coping tasks and processes inherent in the situation rather than on predetermined strategies and tactics of crisis services. This is a crucial distinction, since the traditional crisis approach assumes the need for clinical intervention and thereby risks overlooking the natural adaptive qualities in individuals, families, and social networks. Even when the resources of those systems are recognized, they are understood and utilized as psychotherapeutic agents or extensions of the clinician (Guerney 1969).

The eco-systems-oriented practitioner is vitally interested in therapeutic forces such as "natural helpers," neighborhood and community organizations, and mutual aid groups, recognizing that the utilization of such resources is likely to precede and obviate the need for professional services (not merely complement them), and that their impact on task achievement may be distinctive and more effective in certain situations. This view was adopted by the President's Commission on Mental Health (1979), which regarded this ideology as "one of the most significant frontiers in mental health at all levels of care" (Commission 1979:15).

Similar to the perspective regarding professional interventions, it is necessary to understand the benefits and risks of this full cast of helping agents, in relation to specific tasks. This provides an essential organizing framework by which to evaluate the appropriateness of hot-line personnel, rape service volunteers, widow-to-widow helpers, and bereaved parent contacts, to name a few.

Work with Self-Help Groups

An eco-systems perspective includes the professional use of self-help activities, but offers a broader, more encompassing approach to helping, in general. Thus, self-help organizations are seen as rooted in the natural helping forces of individuals, families, and communities. A major implication for practitioners is the opportunity to observe and co-opt these strategies, when appropriate. In a system of care givers, the credentialed therapist and the lay helper can be mutually reinforcing and complementary rather than isolated from each other in self-serving groups. An adaptive, cooperative relationship of this kind emphasizes the commonality of objectives and the diversity of formal and experiential preparation.

Availability to Effectiveness Research

Effectiveness research regarding eco-systems-oriented practice poses a number of dilemmas:

> The systems model has not as yet developed a reliable system of classifying interaction that is relevant either to notions of improved functioning or to discriminating dysfunctional family interaction patterns from functional or adequate patterns (Umana et al. 1980:164).

Measuring the effectiveness of eco-systems crisis practice is compounded by all the research difficulties concerning systems theory (Umana et al. 1980). The methodological problems center on the need to measure process and interaction rather than to sample traits or environmental forces at a given moment, and then to generalize over time or across situations. This process orientation is echoed by Austin:

> A second source of current difficulty to apply science on a prescriptive basis to the practice of social work is the alternative nature of social work interventions; that is, that the outcomes of social work are co-produced (Austin 1977:61).

An eco-systems orientation can address some of the research difficulties, but not all of them. Moreover, systems concepts are notoriously difficult to put into operation. Nonetheless, a more reasonable crisis model can begin by focusing on the concept of stress, not the crisis state, as the central process. Consistent with an eco-systems perspective, Lazarus et al. view stress as "a *relational* concept that refers to transactions between person and environment, which are characterized by harm-loss, threat, or challenge." (1980:106).

Stress research has tended to focus on three levels of analysis: physiological, psychological, and social stress. These levels are, to a degree, independent, and refer to different conditions and mechanisms which cannot be reduced to a single common denominator:

> The methodological implication of this, and of the fact that each level plays a crucial part in understanding the relationship of stress to adaptation, is that the most thorough research must be designed to assess all three concurrently. Only then will the interrelationships be properly evaluated and understood (Lazarus et al. 1980:107).

Since the essence of adaptation is change, research regarding the relationship between stress and adaptational outcome should, by design, enable us to assess flux and change as well as stability.

To illustrate the difference, a linear crisis model might use personality scales, which include coping traits or styles, to predict how a person will actually cope in a specific situation (such predictability has generally been poor). The eco-systems orientation would push one to focus on how the individual copes with a variety of stressors, in effect, measuring the coping process rather than a trait. We could then observe coping changes based on the nature of the encounter and on the overall stability of the coping patterns for a given person or family. Given this framework, naturalistic field studies would appear to be more useful than surveys and other quantitative approaches.

Similar to process, outcome in an eco-systems perspective would require special technology, as illustrated by a recent attempt to develop an instrument to measure person-environment fit (Coulton 1979), and by an ecological study of depression (Wetzel and Redmond 1980).

Ultimately, the crisis practice model will need to identify the coping tasks for particular stressful life situations, and then to specify which interventions, provided by what kind of helper, for what kinds of clients, at what given time, will result in what kinds of outcomes.

SIDS Bereavement and the Eco-Systems Perspective

The sudden infant death syndrome (SIDS), also known as crib death or cot death, is the sudden and unexpected death of an apparently healthy baby whose death remains unexplained after a complete postmortem examination. SIDS is the leading cause of death in infancy. The incidence is 2–3 per 1,000 live births, and in the United States nearly 8,000 such deaths occur yearly. Clinical, epidemologic, and theoretical aspects have been reviewed extensively (Valdes-Dapena 1980).

A substantial anecdotal literature depicts SIDS bereavement as particularly severe, with suicide attempts, psychiatric hospitalizations, and serious depressions occurring among previously well-functioning persons (Cain 1979, Smialek 1978, Cornwell et al. 1977, Krein 1979). The limited empirical research confirms the intensity of the grief response but does not support the conclusion that long-term negative consequences follow SIDS bereavement for the majority of families (DeFrain and Ernst 1978, Lowman 1979, Rubin 1981).

While the variables which account for high vs. low risk of dysfunctional outcome have not yet been delineated, there is some evidence that the actuality and/or perception of social support plays a vital stress-buffering role. This factor plus the coping style of the individual or family (a composite of psychosocial resources and competencies) would seem to determine the amount of stress which develops, as well as the manner in which it is managed—in traditional terms, "whether or not the client is in a state of crisis."

A modification of Hill's paradigm (figure 6.2) illustrates the effect of ecological and systems thinking on crisis practice:

FIGURE 6.2

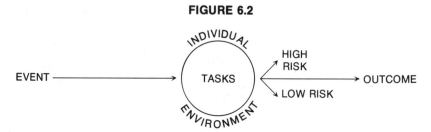

Crib death as a stressful life event may be inherently less copable than other forms of bereavement. The intensity of the mother-child bond, and the uniqueness and irreplaceability of each individual in Western society, preconditions bereavement to be a life-shattering experience (Volkart and Michael 1957). Moreover, the sudden, unexplained death of an infant violates life cycle expectations, allows no opportunity for anticipatory grief, and is perceived as painfully unjust in a technologically advanced society. Yet, it is the particular meaning attached to the event (and to the infant) which further determines the stressfulness of the event, as well as the coping response. To understand the stressor, both must be considered (Dohrenwend and Dohrenwend 1980).

Numerous characteristics of the person and environment influence stressfulness, task performance, and coping. These include general factors such as family structure, stage in life cycle, nature of social network, adaptive style, past or current impaired functioning, concurrent or cumulative life stresses. SIDS-related factors would include: the idiosyncratic meaning attached to the infant and his death (name, age, sex, appearance) as well as familial, cultural, class, and religious influences. Also significant are the handling of the SIDS situation by emergency personnel, the nature of support provided by the social network, and previous experience with bereavement. It is these general and specific stressors which determine the degree of risk for each person and family.

Three essential coping tasks of SIDS bereavement are:

1. Attribution—the cognitive process of attributing an internal vs. external locus of control; a key issue affecting self-blame in the absence of a known cause of death

2. Maintainance of role performance—including the "sick" role and the mourning role as well as the roles of parent, spouse, friend, worker, and so on.

3. Regulation of stress—this broadest category ranges from internally distressing thoughts and memories to insensitive handling of the crisis event by professional helpers. In connection with this task, some have postulated the existence of a "trauma membrane" serving as a stress regulator (Lindy et al. 1981:475).

It is important to note that all three tasks result from the interaction of person and environment. Thus, religious dictates may mix with one's cognitive style to affect the nature of attribution; role performance depends on the expectations, sanctions, and supports of the individual within his social network; and sources and control of stress are multilevel and transactional.

The eco-systems perspective does not assume that intense grief is a universal response to bereavement (Albon 1971, Miller and Schoenfeld 1967, Rosenblatt et al. 1976, Yamamoto et al. 1969). The clinician is thereby alerted to the wide, nonpathological variation among the bereaved. Also, stage concepts of grieving are considered problematic and therefore cautiously applied in direct practice (Bugen 1977, Kastenbaum 1975).

In addition, the previously applied time parameters concerning grief have been challenged:

> First, it reveals our realization that Lindemann's early conceptualization of bereavement as a typical life crisis was an oversimplification. . . . We have learned that the forces of bereavement and adjustment operate over a much longer period of time that is more appropriately labeled "a period of life transition" than a "life crisis". . . . The second main theoretical lesson has been an increased un-

derstanding of the normality and benign predictive significance of many of the strange individual reactions (Caplan 1974:vii–viii).

Thus, grief and mourning in this crisis model are not calibrated or categorized, but rather are approached as multidetermined adaptive responses.

Intervention moves philosophically from an emphasis on self-coping within one's existing social network to linkage with existing services and resources, to the development (by providers) of artificial support networks (parent groups), responsive medical examiner policies, and well-trained emergency personnel.

In actual practice, the clinician surveys the ecological range of actors and activities which potentially affect task achievement, and then with the person or family, orchestrates these forces toward therapeutic ends. A husband blaming his wife for the infant's death may be struggling with attribution, and a talk with an admired clergyman or attendance at a parents' meeting may address the problem. Similarly, to regulate the stress of postbereavement insomnia, a single working mother may need short-term psychotherapy, a mild sedative, or advocacy with her employer to enable her to retain her job.

Overall, an eco-systems crisis model would approach SIDS as a stressful life event, with the degree of stressfulness determined by societal and ideological factors as background to the subjective perception of the event, itself a product of person (cognitive) and environment (cultural, network) interaction. At the point of assessment, the quality and quantity of stress, further specified in terms of the capability of task performance, should permit some predictive statement regarding the risk of dysfunctional outcome. Lastly, within this model, professional intervention, with its inherent risks and liabilities, is but one therapeutic force to support task achievement.

Case Illustration

The D. family consisted of Robert, age 28, New York City fireman for the past seven years; Judy, age 26, his wife, and their two children, Debbie, 3 years old and Andrew, 3 months of age.

Andrew was discovered cold, discolored, and not breathing by his mother one morning. She called police, who arrived with a team of paramedics, who immediately began cardiopulmonary resuscitation as they prepared to transport the baby to the nearest hospital. During the wait outside the emergency room, Mrs. D. allowed the patrolman to call her husband and mother. Shortly, the attending physician made the pronouncement of death, suggesting that the cause was probably SIDS, and that an autopsy would be performed to rule out any known disease or condition. By the time the other family members had arrived, a hospital social worker and chaplain were with Mrs. D. in a private room, and she and her husband were accompanied by a staff nurse to hold their son one last time.

When the medical examiner ruled the next day that the cause of death was, in fact, due to SIDS, an SIDS Project counselor phoned the family to provide this information, to assess the risk of a problematic bereavement, and to begin engaging the family as indicated. Neither parent reported an extreme or life-threatening grief reaction, and a significant social network was available and helping with the funeral arrangements. The counselor forwarded SIDS literature and offered a family meeting which Mrs. D. readily agreed to, while her husband questioned the value of any talking.

During the interview, held several days after the funeral, the counselor helped the parents review the tragic events and then reexplained SIDS with particular emphasis on its lack of predictability or preventability. The parents were not blaming each other, and the sensitive responses of police, paramedics, and hospital staff confirmed the parents' lack of culpability (the training of these professionals representing primary prevention, and a strategy to foster task achievement).

However, an attribution problem was emerging, with the maternal grandmother frequently shaking her head and remarking that the baby was always "overdressed." This was a source of real distress for Mrs. D. and threatened to undermine her external attribution and her regulation of additional stress. The dysfunctional effects for the grandmother were equally apparent. The D.'s noted that the mother could be influenced only by the family priest, and with the couple's permission, the counselor forwarded literature and a letter of introduction to him, and then followed up with a phone call, offering to serve as consultant to the priest in his involvement with the family.

Current and past stresses in other areas—health, money, legal, work, and interpersonal—were explored, and there was some discussion of how Andrew's death might affect his older sister.

The couple was also helped to anticipate common features of the grief process, as a way of minimizing fear and distress over unusual thoughts, feelings, and behavior. The benign predictive significance of hallucinations during the early grief period, as well as fears of death and extreme reactions to seeing other infants were noted as examples. Also, the couple was advised of the frequently reported differences between husbands and wives in their expression of grief.

The D's indicated that their social network was active and was perceived as caring, with many friends and relatives offering condolences and help with small tasks such as babysitting, car repair, and so on.

At the end of the session, the couple was invited to attend the monthly parents' meeting, and they agreed to have a public health nurse visit their home.

The nurse visited three weeks later and found significant reduction in the acute grief reaction. However, in her report, Mr. D. was described as being somewhat "dazed and lethargic," frequently expressing fatalistic and negativistic thoughts and feelings. This kind of learned helplessness may be temporarily adaptive, but given Mr. D.'s dangerous occupation, it posed reason for concern. The SIDS counselor arranged to meet with Mr. D. and learned during the interview that a number of near accidents had already occurred. With Mr. D.'s agreement, the counselor got in touch with the fire chief, who assigned Mr. D. to nonhazardous duty, thereby minimizing stress but allowing adequate role performance to continue.

Four months after the loss, the D.'s made contact with the SIDS counselor to announce that Mrs. D. was pregnant and that they wanted information about the subsequent risk of SIDS, neonatal evaluations, and monitoring devices. The counselor was guided by his awareness of the significance of the replacement child (Cain and Cain 1964), as well as the evidence that pregnancy subsequent to infant death is associated with a positive bereavement outcome, and may therefore represent an effective coping strategy (Videka 1981).

There was no further contact with the family except for receiving a birth announcement later that year.

Summary/Conclusion

Crisis intervention has long served as one of the arenas where theorists and clinicians of all persuasions have found a common ground. Using the parameters of practice models—ideology to staffing—this chapter has attempted to examine the clinical consequences of adopting a linear vs. a systems perspective regarding stressful life events, coping, and professional intervention.

The traditional crisis formulation offers a deterministic, prescriptive approach to crises and treatment, providing practitioners with a set of concepts and guidelines ready for application. For the most part, the psychodynamically based approach emphasizes the clinician as a major therapeutic force, and psychotherapy sessions as the primary modality. The widespread conceptual and methodological consistency evident among the helping professions attests to the utility and overall soundness of the model.

Yet, the professional's need for direction and certitude has led to an entropic stance wherein practice assumptions of the model are both untested empirically and unmodified by challenging and contradictory social science findings.

New paradigms emerge under such conditions, and ecological and systems concepts yield significant theoretical advances and promising clinical strategies. Eco-systems views the physical and ideological environment—social structure, culture, institutional organization and social network—not as a backdrop to the crisis, distressed individual or family, but rather as a full and equal factor in the nature, amount, and adaptation to stress. It is the lack of fit, of preparation, expec-

tations, and capabilities, within the event-person-environment for-
mula that produces maladaptive stress responses. Tasks become
transactional as they are institutionalized by the culture, inhere in
the event, and are perceived and enacted by the individual or family.
Ecological and systems variables yield a crisis model which ranges
from the physiologic to the societal, from primary prevention to rehabilitation. Coping occurs naturally within the context of a familial
support system, and is augmented by the provider network when
that system (itself a focus of intervention) is unresponsive or non-
existent. The clinician assumes a variety of roles, but is perhaps most
effective as the orchestrator of actors and forces supporting the coping tasks.

At the present time, the technology to both employ and evaluate
an eco-systems approach to crisis intervention lags behind the conceptual and theoretical formulation. It is difficult, for example, to
"clinicalize" equifinality when professionals must intervene in a parsimonious and selective manner, and even known techniques such as
social network assessment require marked refinement. In terms of
research, "fit," interface, and transaction remain difficult to operationalize empirically, an entropic risk in and of itself.

These challenges of epistemology, model development, and clinical intervention present social work with the opportunity not only to
retool our own rationale and methods, but to provide leadership in
the crisis intervention field.

REFERENCES

Albon, Joan. 1976. "Bereavement in the Samoan Community." *Brit-
ish Journal of Medical Psychology* (November).

Aguilera, Donna and J. Messick. 1970. *Crisis Intervention: Theory and
Methodology.* St. Louis: Mosby.

Anderson, Ralph and I. Carter. 1974. *Human Behavior in the Social
Environment.* Chicago: Aldine.

American Psychiatric Association. 1979. *Relating Environment to Mental Health and Illness: The Ecopsychiatric Data Base.* Task Force Report No. 16. Washington, D.C.: American Psychiatric Association.

Austin, David. 1979. "Identifying Research Priorities in Social Work." In Aaron Rubin and Aaron Rosenblatt, ed., *Sourcebook on Research Utilization*. New York: Council on Social Work Education.

Baldwin, Bruce. 1978. "A Paridigm for the Classification of Emotional Crises." *American Journal of Orthopsychiatry* (July).

Bard, Morton and B. Berkowitz. 1967. "Training Police as Specialists in Family Crisis Intervention." *Community Mental Health Journal* (Winter).

Bartlett, Harriet. 1970. *The Common Base of Social Work Practice*. Washington, D.C.: NASW.

Bloom, Bernard. 1963. "Definitional Aspects of the Crisis Concept." *Journal of Consulting Psychology* (December).

—— 1977. *Community Mental Health: A General Introduction*. Monterey, Calif.: Brooks Cole.

Bonnefil, Margaret and G. Jacobson. 1979. "Family Crisis Intervention." *Clinical Social Work Journal* (Fall).

Bugen, Larry. 1977. "Human Grief: A Model for Prediction and Intervention." *American Journal of Orthopsychiatry* (April).

Burgess, Ann and B. Baldwin. 1981. *Crisis Intervention: Theory and Practice*. Englewood Cliffs, N.J.: Prentice-Hall.

Burr, Wesley. 1973. *Theory Constructs and the Sociology of the Family*. New York: John Wiley.

Butcher, James and G. Maudal. 1976. "Crisis Intervention." In I. Wiener, ed., *Clinical Methods in Psychology*. New York: John Wiley.

Cain, Albert. 1979. "The Impact of Sudden Infant Death Syndrome on Families." In S. Weinstein, ed., *Mental Health Issues in Grief Counseling*. Washington, D.C. Department of Health, Education Welfare.

Cain, Albert and B. Cain. 1964. "On Replacing a Child." *Journal of the American Academy of Child Psychiatry* (Winter).

Caplan, Gerald. 1974. "Introduction." In I. Glick et al., *The First Year of Bereavement*. New York: John Wiley.

Cassel, John. 1974. "Psychosocial Processes and 'Stress': Theoretical Formulations." *International Journal of Health Services* (Summer).

Coelho, George, D. Hamburg, and J. Adams, eds. 1974. *Coping and Adaptation*. New York: Basic Books.

Cornwell, Joanne et al. 1977. "Family Response to the Loss of a Child by Sudden Infant Death Syndrome." *Medical Journal of Australia* (April).

Coulton, Claudia. 1979. "A Study of Person-Environment Fit Among the Chronically Ill." *Social Work in Health Care* (Fall).

DeFrain, John and L. Ernst. 1978. "Psychological Effects of Sudden Infant Death Syndrome on Surviving Family Members." *Journal of Family Practice* (May).

Dohrenwend, Bruce and B. Dohrenwend. 1980. "What Is a Stressful Life Event?" In H. Selye, ed., *Selye's Guide to Stress Research.* New York: Van Nostrand.

Erickson, Gerald. 1975. "The Concept of Personal Network in Clinical Practice." *Family Process* (Spring).

Fischer, Joel. 1976. *The Effectiveness of Social Casework.* Springfield, Ill.: Charles Thomas.

—— 1978. *Effective Casework Practice: An Eclectic Approach.* New York: McGraw-Hill.

Freeman, David. 1977. "The Family Systems Practice Model: Underlying Assumptions." *Family Therapy* (Fall).

Gartner, Alan and F. Riessman. 1977. *Self-Help in the Human Services.* San Francisco: Jossey-Bass.

Gaylin, Willard et al. 1978. *Doing Good: The Limits of Benevolence.* New York: Pantheon Books.

Germain, Carel B. 1976. "Time: An Ecological Variable in Social Work Practice." *Social Casework* (July).

Golan, Naomi. 1974. "Crisis Theory." In Francis J. Turner, ed., *Social Work Treatment.* New York: Free Press.

—— 1978. *Treatment in Crisis Situations.* New York: Free Press.

—— 1980. "Intervention at Times of Transition: Sources and Forms of Help." *Social Casework* (May).

Gottschalk, Louis et al. 1975. "A Study of Prediction and Outcome in a Mental Health Crisis Clinic." *American Journal of Psychiatry* (February).

Guerney, Bernard. 1969. *Psychotherapeutic Agents: New Roles for Nonprofessionals, Parents, and Teachers.* New York: Holt, Rinehart and Winston.

Gurman, Alan and D. Kniskern. 1978. "Deterioration in Marital and

Family Therapy: Empirical, Clinical, and Conceptual Issues." *Family Process* (March).

Hellenbrand, Shirley. 1978. "Integration Takes Time." *Social Service Review* (September).

Hill, Reuben. 1949. *Families Under Stress.* New York: Harper and Row.

Hollis, Florence. 1972. *Casework: A Psychosocial Therapy.* New York: Random House.

Jacobson, Gerald et al. 1968. "Generic and Individual Approaches to Crisis Intervention." *American Journal of Public Health* (February).

Kaplan, David and E. Mason. 1960. "Maternal Reactions to Premature Birth Viewed as an Acute Emotional Disorder." *American Journal of Orthopsychiatry* (July).

Kastenbaum, Robert. 1975. "Is Death a Life Crisis?" In N. Datan and L. Ginsberg, eds., *Life-Span Developmental Psychology: Normative Life Crises.* New York: Academic Press.

Killilea, Marie. 1976. "Mutual Help Organizations: Interpretations in the Literature." In G. Caplan and M. Killilea, eds., *Support Systems and Mutual Help.* New York: Grune and Stratton.

Krein, Nicole. 1979. "Sudden Infant Death Syndrome: Acute Loss and Grief Reactions." *Clinical Pediatrics* (July).

Kuhn, Thomas. 1970. *The Structure of Scientific Revolutions.* 2d. ed. Chicago: University of Chicago Press.

Langsley, Donald and R. Yarvis. 1975. "Evaluation of Crisis Intervention." In Jules Masserman, ed., *Current Psychiatric Therapies 1974.* New York: Grune and Stratton.

Lazarus, Richard S. et al. 1980. "Psychological Stress and Adaptation: Some Unresolved Issues." In Hans Selye, ed., *Selye's Guide to Stress Research.* New York: Van Nostrand.

Lee, Gary. 1979. "The Effects of Social Networks on the Family." In Wesley Burr et al., eds., *Contemporary Theories About the Family.* New York: Free Press.

Lewis, Marc et al. 1979. "The Course and Duration of Crisis." *Journal of Consulting and Clinical Psychology* (January).

Lieberman, Morton and L. Borman. 1979. *Self-Help Groups for Coping with Crisis.* San Francisco: Jossey-Bass.

Lindemann, Erich. 1944. "Symptomatology and Management of Acute Grief." *American Journal of Psychiatry* (September).

Lindy, Jacob, M. Grace, and B. Green. 1981. "Survivors: Outreach to a Reluctant Population." *American Journal of Orthopsychiatry* (July).

Lowman, Joseph. 1979. "Grief Intervention and Sudden Infant Death Syndrome." *American Journal of Psychology* (June).

Lukton, Rosemary. 1974. "Crisis Theory: Review and Critique." *Social Service Review* (September).

McCubbin, Hamilton et al. 1980. "Family Stress and Coping: A Decade Review." *Journal of Marriage and the Family* (November).

Mechanic, David. 1969. *Mental Health and Social Policy.* Englewood Cliffs, N.J.: Prentice-Hall.

—— 1974. "Social Structure and Personal Adaptation: Some Neglected Dimensions." In George Coelho, D. Hamburg, and J. Adams, eds., *Coping and Adaptation.* New York: Basic Books.

Miller, Sheldon and L. Schoenfeld. 1967. "Grief and the Navajo: Psychodynamics and Culture." *International Journal of Social Psychiatry* (Fall/Winter).

Mitchell, Roger E. and Edison J. Trickett. 1980. "Task Force Report: Social Networks as Mediators of Social Support." *Community Mental Health Journal* (Spring).

Morley, Wilbur. 1980. "Crisis Intervention with Adults." in Gerald Jacobson, ed., *Crisis Intervention in the 1980's.* San Francisco: Jossey-Bass.

Nelsen, Judith C. 1980. "Support: A Necessary Condition for Changes." *Social Work* (September).

Panzer, Barry. 1978. "Readers' Comments: Crisis Intervention." *Social Casework.* (November).

Parad, Howard and L. Parad. 1968. "A Study of Crisis-Oriented Planned Short-Term Treatment." *Social Casework* (June and July).

Perlman, Helen Harris. 1968. *Persona: Social Role and Personality.* Chicago: University of Chicago Press

Polak, Paul et al. 1975. "Prediction in Mental Health: A Controlled Study." *American Journal of Psychiatry* (February).

Porter, Robert. 1966. "Crisis Intervention and Social Work Models." *Community Mental Health Journal* (Spring).

The President's Commission on Mental Health. 1979. *Report to the*

President. Washington, D.C.: Department of Health, Education and Welfare.

Rabkin, Richard. 1977. *Strategic Psychotherapy.* New York: Basic Books.

Rapoport, Lydia. 1967. "Crisis-Oriented Short-Term Casework." *Social Service Review* (March).

—— 1970. "Crisis Intervention as a Mode of Brief Treatment." In Robert W. Roberts and R. Nee, eds., *Theories of Social Casework.* Chicago: University of Chicago Press.

Rapoport, Rhona. 1963. "Normal Crises, Family Structure, and Mental Health." *Family Process* (January).

Reid, William J. and Ann W. Shyne. 1969. *Brief and Extended Casework.* New York: Columbia University Press.

Rosenblatt, Paul et al. 1976. *Grief and Mourning in Cross-Cultural Perspective.* Human Relations Area Files Press.

Rubin, Simon. 1981. "A Two-Track Model of Bereavement." *American Journal of Orthopsychiatry* (January).

Rueveni, Uri. 1979. *Networking Families in Crisis.* New York: Human Sciences Press.

Schneidman, Edwin. 1973. "Crisis Intervention: Some Thoughts and Perspectives." In G. Specter and W. Clairborn, eds., *Crisis Intervention.* New York: Behavioral Publications.

Selby, Lola. 1979. "Support Revisited." *Social Service Review* (December).

Silverman, Phyllis. 1978. *Mutual Aid Groups.* Washington, D.C.: Department of Health, Education, and Welfare.

Siporin, Max. 1975. *Introduction to Social Work Practice.* New York: Macmillan.

Smialek, Zoe. 1978. "Observations on Immediate Reactions of Families to Sudden Infant Death." *Pediatrics* (August).

Smith, Larry. 1978. "A Review of Crisis Intervention Theory." *Social Casework* (July).

Speck, Ross. and C. Attneave. 1973. *Family Networks.* New York: Vintage Books.

Stuart, Richard B. 1973. *Trick or Treatment: How and When Psychotherapy Fails.* Champaign, Ill.: Research Press.

Swenson, Carol. 1979. "Social Networks, Mutual Aid and the Life Model." In Carel B. Germain, ed., *Social Work Practice: People and*

Environments—An Ecological Perspective. New York: Columbia University Press.

Timms, Noel and R. Timms. 1977. *Perspectives in Social Work.* London: Routledge and Kegan Paul.

Umana, Roseann F. et al. 1980. *Crisis in the Family.* New York: Gardner Press.

Unger, Donald. and D. Powell. 1980. "Supporting Families Under Stress: The Role of Social Networks." *Family Relations* (October).

Valdes-Dapena, Marie. 1980. "Sudden Infant Death Syndrome: A Review of the Medical Literature, 1974–79." *Pediatrics* (October).

Videka, Lynn. 1981. "Coping with the Death of a Child." Paper presented at American Orthopsychiatric Association Meeting, New York.

Volkart, Edmund and S. Michael. 1957. "Bereavement and Mental Health." In A. Leighton, J. Clausen, and R. Wilson, eds., *Explorations in Social Psychiatry.* New York: Basic Books.

Weiss, Robert. 1976. "Transition States and Other Stressful Situations." In G. Caplan and M. Killilea, eds., *Support Systems and Mutual Help.* New York: Grune and Stratton.

Wetzel, Janice Wood and F. Redmond. 1980. "A Person-Environment Study of Depression." *Social Service Review* (September).

Wikler, Lynn. 1981. "Chronic Sorrow Revisited." *American Journal of Orthopsychiatry* (January).

Yamamoto, Joe et al. 1969. "Mourning in Japan." *American Journal of Psychiatry* (June).

PART THREE

INTRODUCTION

Carol H. Meyer

The two final essays reach toward the future as they consider implications of the analysis that has gone before. The essay on clinical application of the eco-systems perspective, using an eclectic approach, suggests a way that most clinicians probably practice anyway; one seldom sees cases treated with practice models applied in their pure form. The use of the eco-systems perspective, however, introduces a new element that seems to be effective in the two cases discussed.

The concluding essay offers me an opportunity to have the last word, and to ponder future directions for clinical social work practice.

VII

CLINICAL APPLICATION OF THE ECO-SYSTEMS PERSPECTIVE: AN ECLECTIC APPROACH

Rosemary Grieve

Eco-systemic epistemology is concerned with the network or simultaneous events and circular interactions that compose an ecological reality. Bateson states that "if you want to understand some phenomenon or appearance, you must consider that phenomenon within the context of all completed circuits which are relevant to it" (Bateson 1971:244). For the therapist the relevant "completed circuits" are the networks of completely intertwined human relationships within which the symptoms have a function.

An eco-systemic approach to diagnosis and treatment affords a structural way to organize and conceptualize complexity. Since it is not a method of intervention but a perspective—a way of looking at phenomena within a framework—interventions must be drawn from other sources. This perspective allows for the assessment of the clinical situation, the identification of tasks that need to be done, and the determination of the most appropriate approach to these tasks. Practice models are used differentially, dependent on the needs of the case. Within the eco-systems approach use of many different practice models are possible.

In eco-systemic thinking there is no hierarchy of interventions since all parts of a system are responsive to change in any one part. The concept of equifinality, indicating that the same goal can be reached by a number of alternative means, implies that the therapist can choose from a myriad of possible interventions. The therapist's task is to determine which parts of the system are more accessible to change and thereby establish priorities for intervention.

In the two cases described in this paper many different treatment approaches and sites for intervention were possible. Those employed were arrived at by considered choices about the receptivity of the various components of the case at any given time in treatment. The family's or client's responses to interventions always determine the subsequent treatment directions.

Two tools aid in organizing the complex eco-system of which the client is a part. The *genogram* visually represents the intergenerational family data and the *eco-map* presents the family or individual in the life space, picturing the nurturing or conflict-laden connections between the family and the world. Both tools aid in characterizing problematic conditions as transactional and as a function of many variables. The following cases were known to an outpatient psychiatric clinic of a community general hospital.

Case Illustration—the Lewis Family

Bruce and Sally Lewis are 37 and 35 years old respectively. They were married fifteen years ago when Mrs. Lewis was pregnant with their older child, Laura, now 14 years old. David, their son, is 6 years old. Mr. Lewis is a food salesman and has recently purchased his own business, a franchised sandwich shop. Mrs. Lewis does not work outside the home, but is being encouraged by her husband to handle the accounts for the new business.

The family sought treatment because of their concern about Laura's "rebellious, resistant behavior" and frequent arguments with her mother. Mr. and Mrs. Lewis dated the problem to three years ago when they noticed Laura "talking back," being argumentative with her mother, appearing bored, and being overprotective and intrusive with her brother. There seemed to be no apparent precipitant for the behavioral change. Mr. Lewis complained that he felt like an arbiter in the family, constantly settling fights between his wife and daughter.

In the initial family session a pattern emerged of a strong alliance between Mr. Lewis and the children, serving effectively to exclude Mrs. Lewis. Mr. Lewis often spoke for Laura, defending her behavior to his wife. Mrs. Lewis acknowledged that she expected a lot from her daughter and tended to nag her. Mr. and Mrs. Lewis presented their marital relationship as solid, but their interaction was characterized by Mrs. Lewis' passivity and emotional vulnerability and a protective, paternalistic stance by Mr. Lewis. Mrs. Lewis seemed to operate as the emotional barometer in the family, with Mr. Lewis trying to moderate or control this. By the end of the first session there had been a subtle shift from the family's presentation of Laura as the identified patient, identifying Mrs. Lewis as "too nervous" and having gastrointestinal problems when stressed.

The genogram (figure 7.1) visually presents family history details briefly described here. Mr. Lewis was an only child in a single-parent family. His father had died from leukemia when Mr. Lewis was an infant. His mother never remarried, and Mr. Lewis maintains a close relationship with her. Mrs. Lewis has three younger brothers. She had a close relationship with her father, but frequently had conflicts with her mother who was always critical of her, particularly during adolescence. The parallels to the Lewis family's current problems are striking. Mrs. Lewis states that she married to escape her family.

Laura seemed to be an intelligent, strikingly attractive fourteen-year-old who had had no significant developmental problems. David appeared to be a well-developed and adjusted six-year-old. During his first year he was plagued by medical problems. He had two surgeries for hernia, further surgery to correct webbed fingers, and a diagnosed heart murmur. Both Mr. and Mrs. Lewis worry about David's health.

At the end of the first session it was clear that a number

Figure 7.1

THE LEWIS FAMILY–GENOGRAM

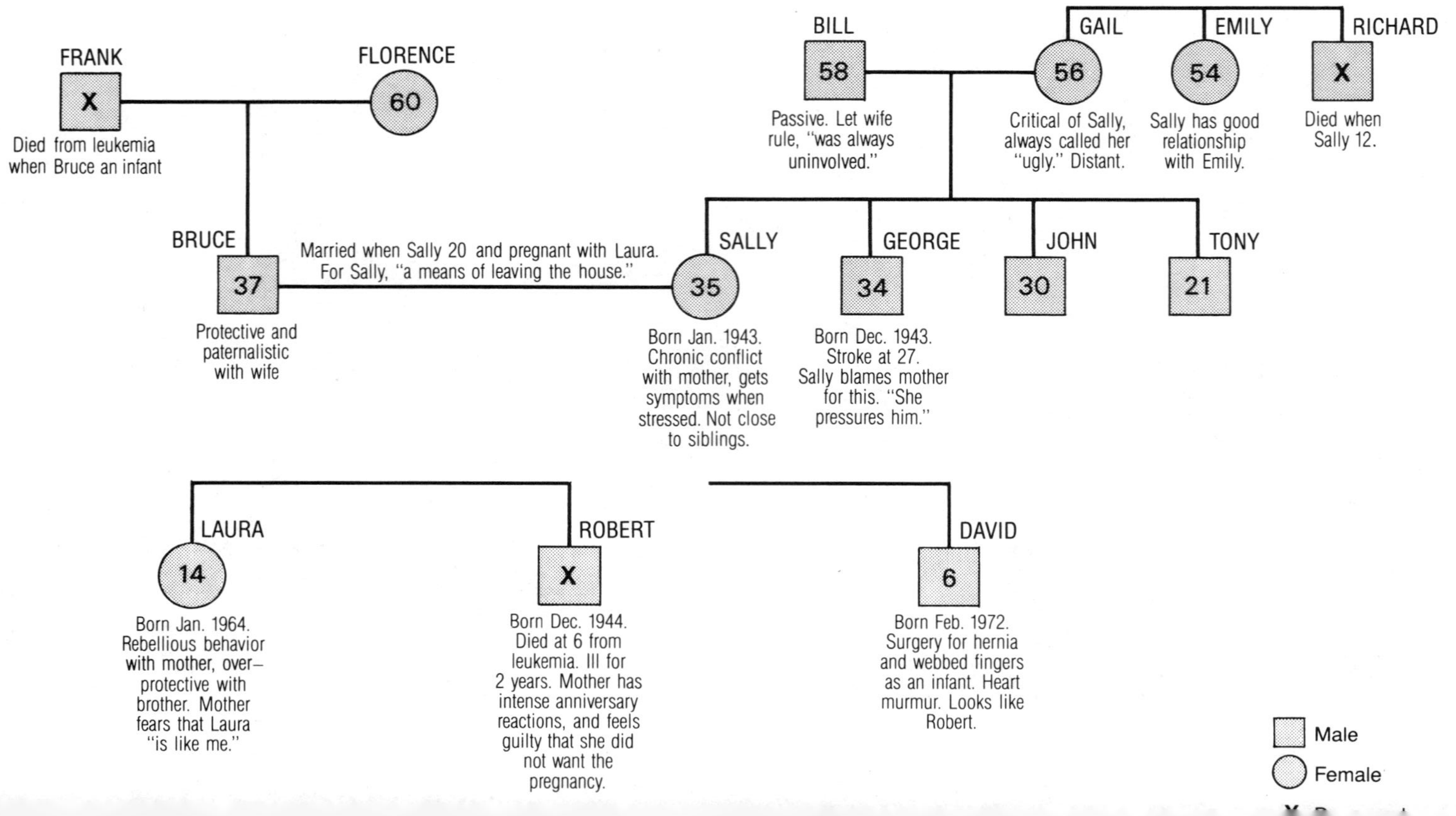

FRANK
Died from leukemia when Bruce an infant

FLORENCE
60

BRUCE
37
Protective and paternalistic with wife

Married when Sally 20 and pregnant with Laura. For Sally, "a means of leaving the house."

SALLY
35
Born Jan. 1943. Chronic conflict with mother, gets symptoms when stressed. Not close to siblings.

LAURA
14
Born Jan. 1964. Rebellious behavior with mother, over–protective with brother. Mother fears that Laura "is like me."

ROBERT
X
Born Dec. 1944. Died at 6 from leukemia. Ill for 2 years. Mother has intense anniversary reactions, and feels guilty that she did not want the pregnancy.

DAVID
6
Born Feb. 1972. Surgery for hernia and webbed fingers as an infant. Heart murmur. Looks like Robert.

BILL
58
Passive. Let wife rule, "was always uninvolved."

GAIL
56
Critical of Sally, always called her "ugly." Distant.

EMILY
54
Sally has good relationship with Emily.

RICHARD
X
Died when Sally 12.

GEORGE
34
Born Dec. 1943. Stroke at 27. Sally blames mother for this. "She pressures him."

JOHN
30

TONY
21

☐ Male   ○ Female

THE LEWIS-FAMILY ECO-MAP

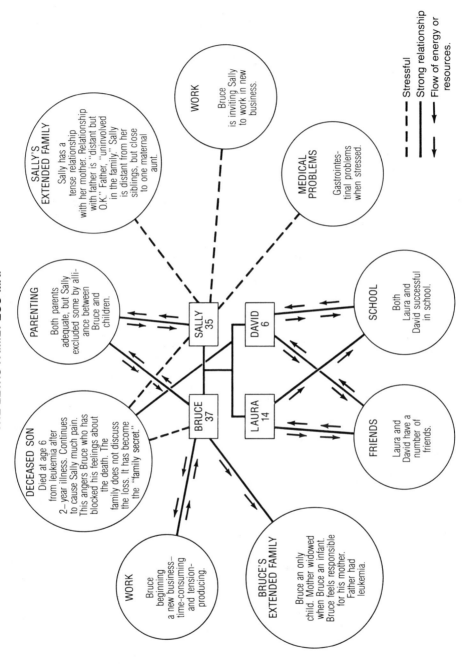

SALLY'S EXTENDED FAMILY
Sally has a tense relationship with her mother. Relationship with father is "distant but O.K." Father, "uninvolved in the family." Sally is distant from her siblings, but close to one maternal aunt.

WORK
Bruce is inviting Sally to work in new business.

MEDICAL PROBLEMS
Gastrointestinal problems when stressed.

PARENTING
Both parents adequate, but Sally excluded some by alliance between Bruce and children.

DECEASED SON
Died at age 6 from leukemia after 2-year illness. Continues to cause Sally much pain. This angers Bruce who has blocked his feelings about the death. The family does not discuss the loss. It has become the "family secret."

SALLY 35

BRUCE 37

DAVID 6

LAURA 14

SCHOOL
Both Laura and David successful in school.

FRIENDS
Laura and David have a number of friends.

WORK
Bruce beginning a new business—time-consuming and tension-producing.

BRUCE'S EXTENDED FAMILY
Bruce an only child. Mother widowed when Bruce an infant. Bruce feels responsible for his mother. Father had leukemia.

- - - - Stressful
——— Strong relationship
——→ Flow of energy or resources.

of problems were stressing the family system and its homeostasis (see figure 7.2). The most obvious were: the family
having to accommodate to the developmental phase of
Laura's adolescence and her demands for more autonomy;
the mirroring of Mrs. Lewis' ongoing conflict with her own
mother; the stress of the family purchasing a new business
and Mrs. Lewis feeling pressure to work; the implicit marital tension, with Mr. Lewis attempting to suppress his wife's
emotional upset and her passive acceptance of this; and
Laura's overprotective stance with her brother being a behavioral expression of her parents' concern for him. Although the various problems noted suggested a number of
possible interventions, it seemed that the problems were insufficient to account for the intensity of the family's concern. Thus it was decided to continue family meetings to
investigate whether the presenting problems were camou-
flaging other major difficulties. Since the family was expressing most concern about an interactional problem, they
were receptive to family treatment.

The family "secret" emerged in the second session. It
crystalized that the family had failed to complete the tasks
associated with an earlier developmental phase. Members of
the family system had been unable to solve certain problems
generated by this phase to enable continued growth and development.

The "secret" was the death of Robert, the couple's second
child, from leukemia, when Laura was six years old. Robert
was ten months younger than Laura (the same age span as
Mrs. Lewis and her next sibling) and was neither planned
for nor wanted by Mrs. Lewis. When he was three years old
he became ill with leukemia, and there ensued a two-and-a-
half-year period of frequent hospitalizations, of Mrs. Lewis'
absorption in her son's illness, and her emotional isolation
from Laura and Mr. Lewis. Mr. Lewis assumed much of
Laura's care while his wife stayed at the hospital with Robert. During this period Mrs. Lewis felt deserted by her husband and her extended family. She believed her son's illness was punishment for not wanting the pregnancy. She
also privately blamed her husband for the genetic transmis-
sion of the disease. The marital relationship suffered. Mrs.

Lewis was angry with her husband for his emotional distance from her, his capacity to continue functioning seemingly unscathed, and his preoccupation with Laura. Mr. Lewis was angry with his wife for her emotional lability, her apparent inability to function as other than a caretaker for Robert, and for her neglect of him and Laura.

When their son died Mr. and Mrs. Lewis spoke little of their feelings of sorrow, guilt, helplessness, and anger. The family entered a conspiracy of silence in which Robert's death and its repercussions were not discussed. Cain, Fast, and Erickson (1964) note the desperate need in such families to "avoid the open assessment of blame, for each parent was struggling with his own self-accusations."

After Robert's death Mrs. Lewis tried to become pregnant. The couple knew that they wanted a replacement for Robert, but were fearful of producing another afflicted child. When David was born two years later, they did not share their mutual horror of his medical problems, or their feelings associated with the resemblance David bore to Robert. Late in treatment the couple was able to acknowledge the fear that David would not survive beyond the age of six. This fear was behaviorally expressed by Laura, who became increasingly intrusive with David and angry with her mother when David was three years old—Robert's age when he became ill.

After the "secret" was revealed, several family sessions focused on a detailed review of the loss of Robert. Krell and Rabkin (1979) note the painful but potentially solidifying effects of allowing a family to grieve together. Mrs. Lewis was the primary person expressing feelings with Mr. Lewis being relatively distanced. He expressed concern and some anger that each year his wife seemed to have a more intense anniversary reaction (both at the time of Robert's birth and of his death). Laura was reticent during these sessions but was clearly attentive to the interactions. David expressed curiosity—much of the material was new for him. During each family session either the marital or the sibling subsystem met alone for a short time to facilitate establishing clear boundaries around each of these two functional subsystems. The goal was to counteract the triangulation between Mr.

Lewis and the children that excluded Mrs. Lewis. Bowen's (1966, 1976) concept of triangulation is helpful in dealing with the complexity of family systems.

After four family sessions, Laura was no longer symptomatic. Her parents described her behavior as cooperative, pleasant, and more appropriate with David. There was evidence of improved communication in the family. Mrs. Lewis, however, was experiencing much anxiety and gastrointestinal distress. This phenomenon of changing symptom site is common when working eco-systemically. Symptoms are so inextricably a part of the fabric of the family's relationships that the site and nature of symptom manifestation may shift from one person to another. Symptom relief or significant change in one part of the system may trigger symptom expression or change in another site. Speck and Attneave (1973) refer to this phenomenon as "the ripple effect." This demands a flexible therapist who is prepared to consider multiple intervention alternatives and to determine during the course of treatment which factions of the system are more accessible to change at any given time.

With the alleviation of Laura's symptoms and the manifestation of Mrs. Lewis' problems, the treatment moved to the marital unit. Mrs. Lewis was preoccupied with the forthcoming anniversary of Robert's death—three weeks hence. Thus, marital sessions focused on Robert's illness and death and the impact of this on the marriage. The couple accepted the task of visiting Robert's grave on the anniversary. Mrs. Lewis had never seen Robert's grave and felt tense and overwhelmed in anticipation of this. The couple completed the task of the ritual ending, and when they returned to treatment reported an improvement in Mrs. Lewis' symptoms. She did not have gastric upset, did not feel depressed or nervous, was spending more time with Laura, and had tentatively begun to learn the accounting process for her husband's business. The couple did not want to continue marital work, but Mrs. Lewis expressed an interest in some individual work to help her improve her self-esteem.

Mrs. Lewis continued in treatment for twelve individual sessions, during which she concentrated on understanding her relationship with her family of origin. Her attempts to develop closer ties with her mother were abortive, but she gained some distance from this and began to view her mother's behavior as often reactive to her husband's passive uninvolvement. As Mrs. Lewis became more differentiated from her family of origin, she concentrated on improving her relationship with her husband and children. For some time, Mr. Lewis resisted his wife's increased independence, but Mrs. Lewis persisted in her efforts to negotiate issues with him. She became more sensitive to, and appreciative of, her husband's vulnerability and his characteristic mode of handling this by denial and distancing.

Contact was made with the family three months after the termination of Mrs. Lewis' treatment. They reported no major problems and were particularly pleased that the anniversary of Robert's birthday on December 23, had not adversely affected their Christmas celebrations.

Case Interpretation

The Lewis family illustrates the salient concepts emphasized in this book. The eco-systems perspective allowed for knowledge and assessment of family members, their relatives, history, current events, strengths, and problems in the case. Having established the "habit" of assessment, noting that new information, changes in the family, and the influence of the clinician continually shaped the status and dynamics of the case, the clinician maintained an open interventive system geared to adaptation of the family members' requirements and desires.

In systems terms, reciprocity indicates that intervention in any area of the family's life space would effect a change in their perceptions, affect, and behavior. Thus, baring the family "secret," doing their mourning, visiting Robert's grave, expressing past hurts, coming to terms with parental distance, understanding the children's developmental tasks, becoming aware of acting-out of family problems, exerting cognitive mastery of family patterns, Mrs. Lewis' learning accounting, and establishing more appropriate marital and parental boundaries—all of these things happened. Sometimes they were simultaneous occurrences, sometimes sequential; most of the time they were planned; and often enough they were serendipitous consequences of other events. As always occurs in a system, change in one part reverberates in another part; the challenge to clinical certainty lies in the fact that it is not always possible to predict or control the direction or pace of the changes because they often occur simultaneously and move in multiple directions.

The genogram and the eco-map are examples of how much a clinician should know to serve as the basis of professional judgments, *and* how little the clinician may have to do in actual interventions. The Lewis family discussion indicates how carefully the clinician observed the principles of salience and parsimony.

It should be noted that the clinician believed in unconscious motivation, as her running interpretations made clear. Yet, she stayed with the family's current functioning, using her understanding of unconscious processes to contribute to her judgments, but not to become the focus of her interventions. This use of knowledge in balance with actual interventions in an excellent example of salience and parsimony.

The genogram is a factual, uninterpreted picture of the family history, while the eco-map is a factual ecological picture of the family's current life and stresses. The pictorialization of the eco-systems perspective in these historical and present-oriented forms makes it possible for the clinician to make an assessment based upon a comprehensive understanding of the case at hand. The data so presented and the consequent understanding are the basis for interventive choices. A clinician using any model of practice can partialize and choose with the client among the pressing issues in the case on which to work.

The concept of equifinality is well demonstrated by the clinician's flexibility in addressing different units of attention: the family, the marital pair, and Mrs. Lewis alone, or, if the case had moved to another point, the children together or alone. Interventive focus shifted from current concerns to past fixations; from relationships to tasks to be accomplished. Choices of entry points were not predetermined, but were guided by the family's concerns and readiness. Different beginnings, with interventions following different timing and sequence, could result in similar outcomes as long as the balance of systemic dynamics is observed and used to inform the interventions.

The practice models are recognizably psychosocial and problem-solving, with some use of crisis intervention and a touch of behavioral task accomplishment—all used consciously within the eco-systems framework. C.H.M.

Case Illustration—the Johnson Family

Rocky Johnson, 25 years old, is married to Susan, 24, and has a 3-year-old son, John. Rocky works the evening shift as a machinist on a milling machine, a dangerous job requiring a high degree of concentration.

Rocky went to the outpatient psychiatric clinic in a community hospital, complaining that he felt "lousy" and cried uncontrollably at times. He mentioned having the following symptoms: decreased energy, decreased appetite, with a fifteen-pound weight loss in one month; restless sleep; increased irritability; auditory hallucinations—he heard the name "Ricky" being called and a male voice begging for help (it later emerged that Rocky's father always called him "Ricky")—a feeling of impending doom; and decreased concentration, particularly at work. He had left work precipitously three days previously and had not returned or called to explain his absence.

Rocky seemed younger than his stated age, having at times a childlike, naïve quality. His affect was depressed, he appeared suspicious, jumpy, and tense and exhibited both speech and psychomotor retardation. There was no apparent thought disorder, despite the auditory and visual hallucinations. He was preoccupied with thoughts of his father's death.

In understanding the history and complexity of Rocky's problems it is useful to refer to Rocky's family genogram (figure 7.3) and eco-map (figure 7.4) which visually represent the impact on Rocky of his family and other pertinent influences in his life.

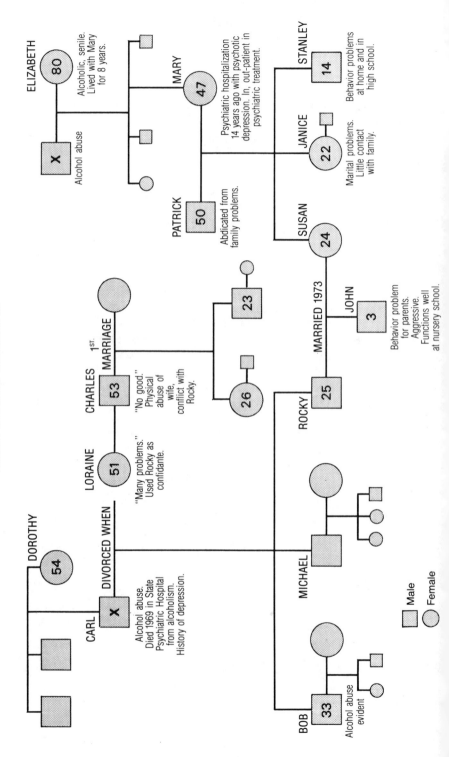

Figure 7.3
ROCKY'S FAMILY GENOGRAM

ROCKY JOHNSON ECO-MAP

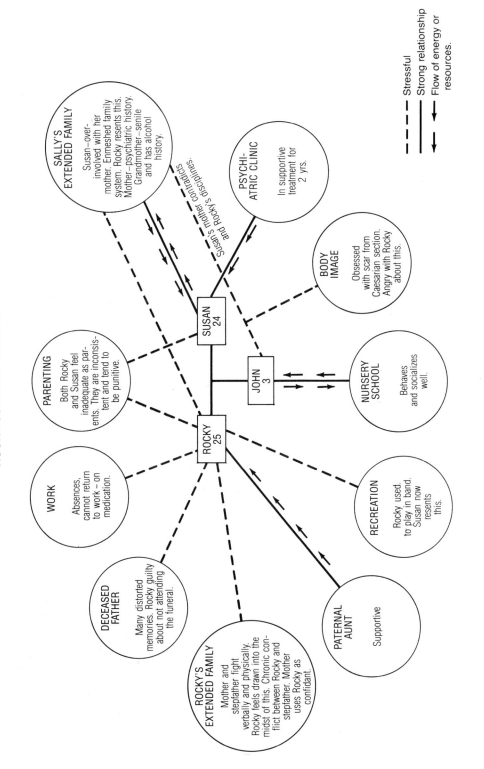

Rocky dated his problems to 1969 and described a gradual accumulation of tension since then. He was unable to identify any reason for this particular date, but later it was clarified that Rocky's father died in a state psychiatric hospital from alcoholism in 1969. Rocky was under the misconception that his father had died in 1962.

Rocky focused on several major areas of distress:

1. He and his wife were having marital tension and problems in parenting John, who was behaviorally quite aggressive. Susan's mother's inconsistent treatment of John compounded Rocky and Susan's efforts to control their son.

2. Rocky felt overinvolved with his wife's family. Susan spent every day from 9:30 A.M. to 7:00 P.M. at her mother's house with her mother and maternal grandmother. Rocky usually accompanied her there until he left for work at 2:00 P.M. Susan's rationale for spending time with her mother was that her mother was lonely and under extreme stress from her own mother who was alcoholic and senile. Susan feared her mother might become psychiatrically ill again, as she was when Susan was ten years old.

3. Rocky's mother and stepfather had a violent, physically abusive relationship from which Rocky had difficulty distancing. His mother tended to use him as a confidant and support.

4. Rocky was preoccupied with memories of his father and his father's death. Rocky was particularly concerned that he had failed to attend his father's funeral.

Diagnostically, Rocky presented as depressed with some psychotic symptoms. There was a question of an organic impairment that was not substantiated by psychological testing. A descriptive evaluation of Rocky at the time of initial contact was that he was experiencing an unresolved grief reaction to the death of his father, and was responding with depression and anxiety to extreme situational stress from various relationships and events in his life (marital, parental, his own parents, parents-in-law, work). The eco-map clearly represents the impingement of the numerous stresses on Rocky.

The immediate treatment concern with Rocky was to avert the need for a psychiatric hospitalization by providing some immediate symptom relief. Intensive individual contact was implemented (three times a week with the social worker and once a week with the psychiatrist). The social worker was also readily available by telephone.

Rocky was placed on Etrafon by the psychiatrist with the goal of decreasing his psychotic symptoms and alleviating his depression. In individual sessions the initial goal was to defuse Rocky's panic to allow him to focus on specific aspects of his situation. Rocky's major concern was the auditory hallucinations which he identified as messages from his father. It became clear that Rocky had a dearth of information about his father, who always had been painted by Rocky's mother as an alcoholic ogre totally disinterested in his children. Rocky's hallucinations provided him with a means of retaining or holding on to his father.

A genogram was done with Rocky to identify possible supports or information sources in the extended family. His paternal Aunt Dorothy was the only person who seemed likely to have some valid information about Rocky's father. Rocky agreed to visit her with the task of talking about his father. Rocky spent five hours with his aunt and returned to therapy armed with much information about his father. Rocky reported feeling a sense of relief, a decrease in tension, and a diminishing of the auditory hallucinations. It is postulated that Rocky was able to grieve for the loss of his father and relinquish the fantasies about him by talking with his aunt and gaining a realistic view of his father.

As Rocky's preoccupation with his father decreased he became more aware of more current stresses. The focus in treatment moved to the marital system since this was presented by Rocky as the most pressing. For some time, marital sessions were interspersed with less frequent individual sessions. As Rocky and Susan began working on their relationship the repercussions were felt in the extended family. Susan's mother made frequent phone calls to the social worker about Rocky's behavior in particular. These were viewed primarily as efforts to triangulate the therapist in an attempt to maintain the homeostasis of the larger family system. The phone calls were used advantageously with Susan, Rocky and Susan's mother, however, to reinforce the clarification of the varied family subsystem boundaries in the larger extended family system. The contacts with Rocky's mother-in-law clearly demonstrate the concept of component parts of a system being related and the movement of any one of those parts necessarily meaning a change for the other parts. The axiom of eco-systemic theory is that all parts within a system simultaneously act on one another.

After several weeks individual sessions were discontinued. Marital sessions continued with a gradual introduction by the couple of parenting issues. Rocky and Susan were concerned about their adequacy as parents and their difficulties in setting limits for their son. His behavior tended to be erratic, aggressive, and rebellious. A behavior modification program was worked out with the couple and was implemented with some noticeably positive effects. As the couple began to feel more competent in handling their son, Susan's self-esteem improved and she was able to establish some rules with her mother about when and how she could take a parenting role with John. Susan's mother was angry about this, but Susan remained relatively consistent in her demands.

The treatment process met an obstacle when Rocky was ready to resume work. His machine shop would not allow him to work if he were taking medication. This posed a problem, since it was important that Rocky return to work to support his family, to provide some structure to his time, and to bolster his self-esteem, but it was also imperative that he not immediately stop his medication. The role of the therapist then moved to that of labor negotiator. The clinic psychiatrist phoned both the shop physician and the shop steward in an effort to negotiate Rocky's return to work. The shop's concern was that Rocky might not be able to concentrate sufficiently to opeate a milling machine. The clinic negotiated with the shop to have Rocky return in a different capacity. He was to work on a less dangerous machine, such as a lathe or grinding machine, with the plan that he would return to his former job when his medication was discontinued.

It was at this juncture that Rocky and Susan decided to terminate treatment. They felt there were no further pressing problems warranting attention. Rocky's presenting symptoms had diminished, and the couple had done some significant work on their marital and parental relationships. Their son's behavior was less stressful for them, and they were experiencing a sense of mastery and competence in their parenting.

In looking at the genogram and eco-map it could be predictable that Rocky and Susan will be highly susceptible to future crises and stress from any one of life's events. For any permanent decrease in stress it will be important that both Rocky and Susan extricate themselves from their present overinvolvement with their families of origin. This would have been the direction for further treatment, but a treatment defined as necessary by the therapist and not by the clients risks value conflict, damage, and risk of driving the family away, thereby eliminating the possibility of future contacts. It is anticipated that Rocky and Susan might reenter treatment when new conflicts or struggles threaten the family's present equilibrium.

In the eco-systemic approach to assessment and treatment planning the clinician views a mass of information from a broad perspective and then uses the evaluation of the various systems and their interactions to determine the most efficient and productive routes for intervention. The eco-systemic perspective allows for many intervention alternatives. It is not wedded to particular practice models, but uses them expeditiously to facilitate change. Flexibility and a conceptual organization of complexity are the key factors in this perspective.

Case Interpretation

Rocky's case is different from the Lewis family, for the problems are not confined to family relationships. The clinician follows the problems wherever they go, including toward Rocky's aunt to learn about his father and to help Rocky abreact his mourning for him, and toward Rocky's workplace to negotiate a necessary job change. In this case not only do goals change as Rocky gets better, but also practice models change so as to suit new events and problems.

The closing of Rocky's case seemed to the clinician to reflect unfinished business, as clinical practice usually does. Yet, she understood that it is hardly realistic to expect cure in psychosocial situations, but rather improved adaptations. This case illustrates a fairly typical precipitant ending with the expectation that the case would begin again at a time of later stress. Perhaps, but the ending of the case is not the ending of Rocky's life. Intervention was brought to bear at a time of serious dysfunction; the clinician moved into Rocky's life space and then moved out, leaving Rocky better able to handle things as a consequence of important changes in his own construction of the past, in his wife's redoing of her relationship with her mother, and their ability to turn their attention to their son. The ultimate "systems message" in relationship to the question of cure or "goodness of fit" lies in the small but powerful change effected at the workplace—the opportunity for Rocky to work at a different machine while he is on psychotropic drugs. Rocky's ability to go back to work will reverberate in all aspects of his life, in his income, his self-esteem, his family relationships, and his work relationships—a vastly improved outcome reflective of a rather modest but appropriate and timely environmental intervention. (C.H.M.)

REFERENCES

Bateson, Gregory, 1970–1971. "A Systems Approac: Part II." *International Journal of Psychiatry*.

Bowen Murray. 1966. "The Use of Family Theory in Clinical Practice." *Comprehensive Psychiatry* (October).

—— 1976. "Theory in the Practice of Psychotherapy." In Philip Guerin, ed., *Family Therapy: Theory and Practice*. New York: Gardner Press.

Cain, Albert, Irene Fast, and Mary Erickson. 1964. "Children's Disturbed Reactions to the Death of a Sibling." *American Journal of Orthopsychiatry* (July).

Krell, Robert and Leslie Rabkin. 1979. "The Effects of Sibling Death on the Surviving Child: A Family Perspective." *Family Process* (December).

Speck, Ross and Carolyn Attneave. 1973. *Family Networks.* New York: Pantheon Books.

VIII

BEGINNING AGAIN

Carol H. Meyer

'Tis ten to one this play can never please All that are here. . .
Shakespeare, *King Henry VIII,* Epilogue

In eco-systemic terms things do not really end; they recycle and they seem to be different as a consequence of having been affected by other things. Having begun this book with a discussion of casework, we have seen that the imposition of the eco-systems perspective has changed it. The use of the perspective in the foregoing articles has demonstrated that any model of practice can be selected for use in social work cases, but that they seldom can be used alone. The eco-systems perspective draws attention to life events, relationships, and environmental factors that impinge upon individuals, and no single practice approach can prescribe interventions that are applicable to so many dimensions in even a single case.

What have we learned from this exercise? What new problems and issues derive from our presentation? Where do we go from here?

The Practice Models

All the models discussed in this book draw upon a range of theories about personality and growth and development of individuals. Yet all the models use the social work screen of purposes, values, and knowledge; none derives directly from the particular personality theory used. None of the models we selected has developed environmental interventions to the degree that it has identified interventions with individuals, although all the approaches provide for environmental interventions. All the models seem to maintain their integrity when the perspective is applied; that is, it is possible to recognize the model in use even though the perspective draws attention to factors in the case that require interventions drawn from other theoretical sources. Remembering that the four practice approaches used here were intended to be only illustrative of the repertoire in social work, the reader might want to engage other models that address such environmental concerns as organizational problems, self-help networks, uses of space and time, and development of resources. The eco-systems perspective would inevitably draw attention to the need for interventions applied to these concerns as they impinge upon the client.

How to Select Among Models

The analytic framework used in this book was intended to be helpful in the social work clinician's choice of practice models to use at particular times, with particular cases. Are the clinician's ideological and value commitments syntonic with those explicated in one or another model? Does the staff situation require a clinical model that would allow for differential use of various levels of staff? Does the client seem to be sufficiently verbal to engage in a clinical encounter requiring thoughtful reflection, or is that client more apt to be responsive to work based upon defining behavioral tasks? Is the clinician familiar with the knowledge base upon which the practice model is based? Can he or she learn a new approach through continuing education or through reading? Is the clinician interested in evaluation of his or her practice? Does that particular model make it possible to define outcomes and evaluate effectiveness? Does the issue of time impose upon the clinician the use of a short-term versus a long-term model? Does the model allow for environmental interventions of a particular type? The analytic framework used to explicate the practice models should help the eclectic clinical practitioner to decide which models to use, when, and under what conditions. The eco-systems perspective is proposed as the unifying conceptualization to make coherent and cohesive the application of any or all of the models chosen.

Two aspects of the framework that are most important as differentiating components among models are the unit of attention and problem definition. Some models can be applied easily to individuals, families, and groups, while others cannot. Which model should be used in a specific case is one of the questions the clinician must ask in the selection process. As for problem definition, this often is the key to the usefulness of the model, for the interventive methods rely upon the way problems are defined. Barring value commitments to particular ways of defining problems, the clinician usually selects a practice model that suits his or her view or problems, which often depends upon the way he or she was trained to view problems. The use of the eco-systems perspective as a persuasive assessment instrument should allow for a more open system of thought about problem definition.

Overlap Among Models

When all is said and done, is there much difference among the clinical practice models? Despite the different profiles of each model that use of the analytic framework demonstrates, are case outcomes expected to be that different? This is hard to answer without empirical investigation; certainly the current empirical models such as Fischer's (1978) and Reid and Epstein's (1972) begin and end with different, certifiable inputs and outcomes. Despite some observable likenesses among clinical approaches, it behooves the professional practitioner to be conscious of the theoretical model he or she chooses to apply. Without this awareness, clinical practice would rely upon hit-or-miss or intuitive practice, which would finally turn out to be characteristic of the idiosyncratic predilictions of individual social workers, and not of a professionally defined practice. The matter of choice of models is discussed more fully in my chapter in the *Handbook of Clinical Social Work* (1983). Here we are more concerned with the influence of the eco-systems perspective upon all clinical practice approaches.

Circles and Lines in the Case Illustrations

Thinking about a case in a linear way means that progression is expected in certain directions; for example, that an identified cause will lead to a specific effect, and that intervention will lead to a different, more desirable effect. Linear thinking can control our view of "outside" causes and of serendipitous effects, so that we do not account for what appears to be extraneous, and we do not accredit as therapeutic that which happens unaccountably. That line of thinking pushes us forward, but in fairly constricted ways.

When we shift to thinking about cases in circles, as in an eco-map, different ideas come to us. First, we recognize that the individual in the center of the circle (his ecology) is bearing the impact of multiple events, and thus we are freed of the constraint to seek out singular causation for the person's condition or complaint. Second, we become acutely aware that there are multiple points of intervention available within the circle, some of which we can manage, and some of which manage themselves because they respond to reciprocal events.

The use of circles, or an eco-systems perspective, places inordinant pressure upon the clinician to be cognizant of the complexities in cases, some of which he or she will grapple with while others will be left to reciprocate when something else changes. The perspective is where the assessment of the total case takes place; it is where the clinician faces the truth of social work practice, that despite full awareness of the problems in a case, some things are unsolvable. There is an ethical issue involved here: it is one thing to find that something is unsolvable through the efforts of the clinician—like institutional racism or poverty—and it is quite another thing to avoid recognizing, and thus to deny, the impact of these problems at the outset because they are unsolvable by the clinician.

The proper assessment must be made, then the clinician must partialize and choose among interventions and even engage in advocacy in situations beyond the practitioner's clinical capacities. Here we confront the epistemological problem of clinical social work that has plagued the field for years. Does one define problems in accordance with the methodology available, or does one define them as they appear in reality and then determine what to do, what to pay attention to, what to parcel out to others, or what to give up on because of unaccountable factors such as lack of resources, lack of time, the imperviousness of social institutions, the recalcitrance of clients, lack of skill, or lack of supports? The choice is always tinged with value commitments, but, at least it should be made deliberately, after comprehension of the real situation. To do otherwise would be comparable to the actions of a doctor who, unable to cure cancer, or not "liking" the disease or the afflicted person, avoids seeing the disease and its symptoms in the diagnostic workup, and offers instead to treat the patient for a preferable ailment.

In order to be effective and "correct," clinical social work assessment has to confront case situations boldly as they are, and equally boldly to affirm what can and cannot be done. The use of the eco-systems perspective may serve to push the clinician to "see all," to avoid denial of the client's reality, and to develop inventive repertoires for doing a range of things to make things better.

What Future for Clinical Social Work Practice?

What shall clinical social work be *because* it is social work? (Ewalt).

According to the purposes of social work, the required transactional focus on person-in-environment defines the way social workers perform, be it in clinical or nonclinical practice. The eco-systems perspective can be used as an assessment tool so as to determine what is needed, and clinical practice models can be used to determine the how-to's of practice interventions themselves. Among the psychosocial, problem-solving, behavioral, crisis-oriented, generalist, and empirically based approaches to clinical (or direct) social work practice, there is a wide choice available for interventions. Furthermore, in the interventive repertoire of every clinician there are always strategies and techniques invented on the spot, bearing no reference to existing practice models.

The interest in developing practice theory, either through the device of drawing "complete" models or of empirical testing, appears to be ongoing, but it should not be overlooked that varied as they are, forward-looking in orientation as they are in regard to person-in-environment focus, and broad-ranging, clinical social work intervention models are essentially still methods-and-skills models. While one can never say there are enough of them, because each generation of theoreticians and practitioners undoubtedly will continue to think of new ways to work, all the traditional and current models continue to emphasize processes of practice. The closest that practice models come to addressing substantive psychosocial problems is in Siporin's "Situational Assessment and Intervention" (1972) and *The Life Model* (Germain and Gitterman 1980) although in its present stage of development The Life Model has general definitions of problems, such as transactional life events, environmental obstacles, and interpersonal obstacles. Crisis intervention theory also relies upon identifiable crises for the specific task thrust up by the crisis event, such as fire, earthquake, rape, accidents, sudden death. In these models, efforts have been made to relate practice processes to specific problem definition, an approach that we consider to be the necessary next phase of theory development in clinical social work practice.

Returning to Bartlett (1970), who wrote of tasks generated by the case situation as a different way of developing practice theory, social workers might be ready to move to the next level as Bartlett proposed. What will it mean to the clinician, this suggestion that attention now be paid to the *context* of practice? Methods and skills as developed in the practice models discussed in this book, in addition to the dozen or so other current practice models in use, may be sufficient for this generation of practitioners. The use of the eco-systems perspective has had multiple effects. First, it has broadened our view of case situations. Second, it has indicated that use of diverse practice models is possible and probably necessary in the typical clinical social worker's repertoire. Third, it has made us recognize that in our departure from reliance upon methods and skills as the primary lens for viewing person-in-situation, we have discovered how little we know about the multiple transactions occurring in the client's field. In other words, just as the use of the perspective raises new questions for the clinician, so it has for the profession. What do we *do* now that we see more in the case situations? How do we learn to define the transactions and problems our new lens has allowed us to see?

The Rationale for Contextual Knowledge

William Gordon and Margaret Schutz (1977), Harriet Bartlett (1970), and a host of others have raised again and again in the last three decades the issue that the profession ought to turn its attention to the "what" as well as to the "how" of practice. Through the interests of social work research David Fanshel and Eugene Shinn (1978) and others have sought to interest clinicians in developing knowledge of situations as well as of effectiveness of practice skills. Social workers in social policy, like Alfred J. Kahn (1965) and Robert Morris (1977) among others, have worked to relate substantive policy issues to the practitioner so as to raise consciousness of the content as well of the processes of practice. There has been no lack of professional attention to this matter of developing interest in contextual knowledge building. We return to this issue now in political terms, in hopes that where prior efforts have failed to engage practitioners, perhaps an analysis of threats to professional survival will succeed.

Social work is both a profession and a social institution, and so it continues to exist at the behest of its public. Through funding and moral support, social work's public makes the final determination as to its survival. Whether the funding be through government programs, voluntary agencies, or third-party payments, it always represents some kind of consensus about the purpose of social work practice. The public must know what social workers do, and that interpretation has not been an uncomplicated one, as most social workers are aware (Meyer 1981). Interpretation has not been eased in the modern world of interdisciplinary practice, where psychologists, psychiatrists, nurse practitioners, and the vast undefined world of mental health and human service workers converge in the life space of clients and patients.

Social workers have taken a long time but have finally achieved some consensus about the special purposes and values that describe social work, but it is likely that social work practice methodology and the personality theories used in social work are not very dissimilar from methodology and personality theory used by all other disciplines. It is not enough to define social work practice through its special purposes and values; it also has to be able to demonstrate particular knowledge that is necessary to this society but is not addressed by any other discipline. Without this achievement, only the discipline having the greatest prestige or the lowest cost will survive in the next decades of public scrutiny and economic constraint.

In building block fashion, social work has developed agreed-upon purposes, a set of values and ethics, a repertoire of useful practice models, and a professional membership of more than ninety thousand people. It is only left to decide what is addressed that is unique and necessary to the society.

When it was thought that clinical practice was synonymous with psychotherapy, professional issues were clearer. The context of practice was the individual, and knowledge derived solely from psychological sources which explained individual psychic structure and behavior. The passage of time, the changing society, and the broadening of practice purposes made inevitable the shift in the scope of the knowledge base. For clinical social work practice, what is that knowledge to be? What are its boundaries? What is its uniqueness? What can be done that is both effective and yet incremental, so that we do not have to reinvent social work practice? What is a possible next step?

Clinical Practice Rooted in the Social Work Context

"We suspect that much of the knowledge that determines practice today originates in the context of practice" (Rein and White 1981:34). Rein and White suggest that real and evocative knowledge is not to be found in the general social sciences but rather in the immediate, institutional context of practice itself, that this knowledge "is not timeless nor spaceless, nor personless," (1981:37) rather, that it is precisely defined by specific events, places, and individuals. The task of clinical practice, then, is to connect practice methodology to the specific institutional setting in which the practitioner is located, and/or to the specific problems being addressed. The practice models can be applied differentially across time and space and people, but they are inadequate by themselves to define unique professional practice. As we have mentioned, they might even be generic across disciplines, making the further case that a social work context is necessary to promote professional uniqueness.

The institutional context for social work practice could well be the fields of practice conceptualization that is currently being considered within the profession. The field of practice idea is a response to knowledge overload and the need for boundaries, expertness, and a sense of professional competence. But it also reflects "social workness" more than any other feature of the profession; it expresses what social workers do and have always done, what they are expert in, and what makes them unique. A field of practice is not only defined by the settings in which social workers practice, it is a conceptualization of an arena, a context for practice. It includes the particular clients seen, the special problems that are presented, the special resources that are used, the related policies that are brought to bear on those fields, and the particular kinds of funding that are applicable. Field of practice, as a concept, also suggests particular staffing arrangements both within the profession and with other disciplines. It is a broad concept that includes more than a single agency and less than the world of social welfare. It is the context of practice which evokes the professional tasks that have to be done, and practice methodology then becomes the servant and not the master of practice (Meyer 1979).

The fields of practice currently in use are family and children's services, health and mental health, corrections, schools, and services for the aging. Social change will introduce new fields just as it might change the shape of existing fields. The clinical social worker, the individualizing social work agent, using an eco-systems perspective in a field of practice and drawing upon the repertoire of methods, skills, and practice models, will find unique purpose in what he or she does. The boundaries of knowledge contain everything there is to know about the field in which he or she practices, about people, organizations, policies, and problems; the central, unique concerns in each field. The use of the eco-systems perspective makes possible this contextual view of social work fields. Following are examples from two fields of practice: family and children's services and health and mental health.

Clinical Social Work Practice in Family and Children's Services

As always, when viewing phenomena contextually, we call upon cognitive skills to look at things in multiple dimensions and forms. Circles depict such phenomena most easily. Figure 8.1 pictures this field of practice, indicating how the clinical practitioner can intervene at almost any place, calling upon the concepts of equifinality and reciprocity to allow for this freedom from predetermined beginnings.

The perspective allows us to see the whole field, the boundaries of which are often set by institutional tradition or funding. The practitioner can intervene in any part of the picture through the use of appropriate practice models to practice prevention, placement, protection, treatment, or advocacy as the case situation demands. Attention to psychosocial dysfunction as always is the governing purpose, and in this picture one can imagine multiple interfaces where dysfunction might occur. The implementation of a field of practice orientation clearly requires knowledge of the services involved, the families and children, and their impinging relationships and institutions, the way social policies define needs and services, and the tremendously complicated staffing arrangements throughout the service structure.

What defines such a practice as clinical is that the practitioner individualizes each case and does what is needed to improve the lot of the client, whether through improving coping, enhancing mastery, providing safety, or enabling love to be expressed. It is clinical be-

Figure 8.1

FAMILY AND CHILDREN'S FIELD OF PRACTICE

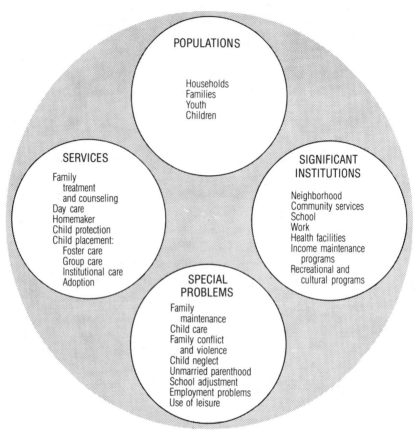

cause the practitioner either through his or her own practice, through delegation to others, or sharing the work in a team, engages in direct, "hands-on" practice. And it is clinical practice because it is intended to be helpful to the client.

Clinical Social Work Practice in Health and Mental Health

In this field, the principles of construction and clinical practice are exactly the same (see figure 8.2), only the context is different.

Figure 8.2

HEALTH AND MENTAL HEALTH FIELD OF PRACTICE

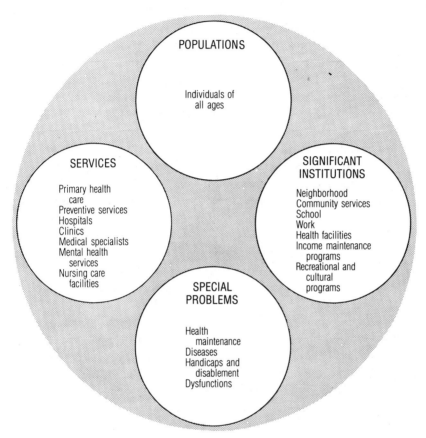

POPULATIONS

Individuals of
all ages

SERVICES

Primary health
   care
Preventive services
Hospitals
Clinics
Medical specialists
Mental health
   services
Nursing care
   facilities

SIGNIFICANT
INSTITUTIONS

Neighborhood
Community services
School
Work
Health facilities
Income maintenance
   programs
Recreational and
   cultural
   programs

SPECIAL
PROBLEMS

Health
   maintenance
Diseases
Handicaps and
   disablement
Dysfunctions

As in family and children's services (and all other fields of practice), the clinical social worker identifies through the assessment of those areas where there is "dislocation" or "lack of fit" or psychosocial dysfunction. What changes among fields is the nature of services and problems; they are the context and the special knowledge base of the field of practice. What stays the same for the clinical practitioner across fields are professional purposes and values and the practice repertoire to be used differentially where appropriate.

The Uses of the Professional Relationship

We have gone beyond limited definitions of clinical practice to offer purposes in addition to psychotherapy where the client-worker relationship is central to the work, where client change is expected to grow from the relationship, and where environmental factors in a case could be viewed as extraneous. We have, in fact, gone far beyond the definition of a social work case as an individual client. We have come to the point where we define clinical practice as individualizing the client and his situation in keeping with the accepted social work purpose of addressing person-in-environment. Thus, we must reexamine the use of the professional relationship since we have shifted our perceptions so radically.

In the eco-systems perspective where fields of practice define the tasks of the social work clinician, the professional relationship must be carefully tended, for it has to be used in accordance with the client's needs and readiness (as always), but also it has to be used in different time frames—short-term, long-term, and perhaps episodically. Furthermore, as more actors will appear in this formulation, the professional relationship will have to shift in its functions and purposes. As Siporin (1972), Hartman (1980), and others have said, among other roles, the clinician must be supporter, liaison, advocate, therapist, limit-setter, adviser, group leader, consultant, resource person, coach, and choreographer. This exceedingly long list of practice roles reflects more or less what social work practitioners always have been doing, but perhaps without a clear theoretical or conceptual basis for carrying out those roles. The eco-systems perspective, drawing in multiple variables as the unit of attention in any case, really requires this larger repertoire of practice roles. Relationship then, is multilayered, multidimensional, and multidirectional. Lest the clinician panic that so many horses must be held in tow at any one time, reassurance lies in the fact that the clinician always has cognitive control of the case situation and can manipulate the reins of the horses by exercising professional judgment.

The Issue of Staffing

To the extent that social work can successfully move beyond its self-definition as a counseling profession, which after all is a methodological definition, it will be possible to consider work-load issues in a rational manner. Naturally, the clinician who views him or herself only as a counselor with responsibilities for interviewing a client one-to-one will only be able to carry a work load equal to the number of counseling hours available. This is the traditional view of clinical practice, and it helps to explain why environmental tasks are often avoided. Time limitations alone inhibit the counselor-clinician from doing more than the interview hour allows. But we have described the clinician differently here; we have said that a *social work* clinician uses counseling as only one of many roles in practice, that a *social work* case includes the client's unique impinging environment, and that interventions can take place in many places and show reciprocal effects that ripple through the case.

Given this conception of the social work case and the roles of the clinical practitioner, it is more possible to consider work load as the truly complex issue that it is. In our framework, allocation of professional tasks cannot be considered as numbers of counseling hours—not when counseling must share time and space with school visits, organizational advocacy, family treatment sessions, adolescent group meetings, community networking, provision of services, and so on. We have attempted here to offer a reconceptualization of the clinical social work role, so that we can begin to rethink the uses of professional social work staff.

A medical analogy would be clarifying at this juncture. Hospital medicine is surely more broadly conceived than a doctor's office hours. Hospitals contain vast numbers of staff required for the hospitals to function. Even given that the primary purpose of a hospital is surgery or medical treatment of a disease, the surgeon's role can only be carried out along with the roles and functions of administrators, nurses, social workers, dieticians, lab technicians, maintenance workers, ambulance drivers, aides of all kind, and, of course, patients. The hospital is the "house" of medicine and is shaped by purposes of the medical profession, but it cannot be said that doctors do all that is necessary to be done in a hospital. As medical specialization and expertness have increased, increasing numbers of tasks that were once thought of as only doctors' procedures have been assumed by other disciplines, and there is now a well-accepted total reliance upon the workings of all staff in the hospital for medicine to carry out its purposes.

Analogously, it could be said that social work's "hospital" or domain is the fields of practice. Social work purposes, duly defined in each field, can be supported through a rational use of multiple staff. Interdisciplinary work in all fields is common by now, as is the use of varied social work levels of graduate and undergraduate professional staff. For example, in family and children's services, homemakers, foster parents, residential cottage parents, case aides, professional social work practitioners, supervisors, administrators, client groups, and so on must work in some kind of coordination for the enterprise to function at all. The problem in social work seems to be that as long as the practitioner defines his or her job as "counseling," the clinical work has to be carried out only by the most skilled psychotherapeutic staff, the clinical social worker. But, as we have taken great pains to indicate, social work cases are seldom that narrowly defined, and thus the field of practice is open to an array of interventions, many of which can be best carried out collaboratively, by associative staff.

Social workers are aware that the competition for jobs and status between social worker with the degree of BSW and social workers who have the MSW has become quite tense; naturally so, if practitioners (on either level) understand cases as requiring "counseling" as the primary or singular intervention. But if we perceive the case eco-systemically, and if we make proper assessments of the psychosocial dynamics in the case, inevitably we note tasks that must be done that call upon many other roles in addition to counseling. Competition is not the issue here, but rather conceptualization of the case leading to a rational allocation of staff in accordance with their educational preparation and skill levels. The smooth-working interweaving of staff roles and functions in a field of practice can be worked out in ways that hospitals have done. There will, of course, be ongoing competitive tensions in all organizations and within all fields, but there is usually an agreed-upon set of rules about who does what job. Dieticians do not do neurosurgery, and nurses do not do maintenance work.

It is beyond the scope of this paper to discuss the ways in which staff might be appropriately classified and utilized. In fact, in keeping with our view that clinical practice must be institutionally specific in order to be rational, each field of practice must make its own rules. For example, a team approach in child welfare could make good sense, while in health a more hierarchical arrangement of professionals and aides might (or might not) be more functional. In corrections, salience might be given to the clinician's advocacy with judges, while in a particular school, greater professional attention might be addressed to parents' groups, with less well-trained staff given responsibility to work with a good teacher. Whatever staffing arrangements are made, as well they must be in this modern organizationally and socially complex society, the cornerstone of professional activity must remain the assessment. For without a sound understanding of what a case is about and what is needed, all else is aimless work.

REFERENCES

Bartlett, Harriet M. 1970. *The Common Base of Social Work Practice.* New York: NASW.

Ewalt, Patricia. 1982. Book Review: Florence Lieberman, *Social Work with Children, Social Work* (March).

Fanshel, David and Eugene B. Shinn. 1978. *Children in Foster Care: A Longitudinal Investigation.* New York: Columbia University Press.

Fischer, Joel. 1978. *Effective Casework Practice: An Eclectic Approach.* New York: McGraw-Hill.

Germain, Carel B. and Alex Gitterman. 1980. *The Life Model of Social Work Practice.* New York: Columbia University Press.

Gordon, William E. and Margaret L. Schutz. 1977. "A Natural Basis for Social Work Specialization." *Social Work* (September).

Hartman, Ann. 1980. "Competencies in Clinical Social Work." In

Patricia Ewalt, ed., *Toward a Clinical Definition of Social Work*. New York: NASW.

Kahn, Alfred J. 1965. "New Policies and Service Models: The Next Phase." *American Journal of Orthopsychiatry*. (July).

Meyer, Carol H. 1979. "What Directions for Direct Practice?" *Social Work* (July).

—— 1981. "Social Work Purpose: Status by Choice or Coercion." *Social Work* (January).

—— 1983. "A Framework for Clinical Practice Models." In Aaron Rosenblatt and Diana Waldfogel, eds., *The Handbook of Clinical Social Work*. San Francisco: Jossey-Bass.

Morris, Robert. 1977. "Caring for versus caring about People." *Social Work* (September).

Reid, William J. and Laura Epstein. 1972. *Task-Centered Casework*. New York: Columbia University Press.

Rein, Martin and Sheldon White. 1981. "Knowledge for Practice." *Social Service Review* (March).

Siporin, Max. 1972. "Situational Assessment and Intervention." *Social Casework* (February).

CONCLUSION

Carol H. Meyer

This book provides a context for clinical social work practice through the application of an eco-systems framework. As has been said throughout, the four practice approaches discussed are used illustratively, only to show that an eclectic clinical practice is not only possible but desirable within such a framework. After reading, the clinician may want to test out use of his or her selected model from whatever source, to see what happens in practice when case phenomena are viewed eco-systemically.

As the concluding paper notes with some emphasis, development of the context of clinical social work practice may turn out to be crucial to the future credibility of the social work profession. Refined and advanced models of interventive processes nothwithstanding, social workers will be known by what they are expert in, what they *do* specifically. The specificity we refer to is institutional, having to do with psychosocial problems that are particularly responsive to social work interventions, relevant policies, organizational and service structures, staffing patterns, and the specific knowledge base to support this institutional context.

The practice approaches we have cited, and most others that are in use in social work, are practical because they can be applied generally, across fields of practice and types of problems, and with individuals, families, and groups. Some are more widely applicable than others, but all lay nonspecific claim to practice problems. For example, there is no schizophrenic, alcoholic, unmarried mother or child abuse practice model—and it would be regressive were we to try to shape one. The practice approaches in use are adaptable to many problems across the board.

As the Milford Conference long ago made clear, practice is specific to a case, and it seems that the way to become adept in specifics is to know the institutional context within which practice models are applied. "Everything there is to know" about the type of problems just mentioned and their associated fields of practice will specify clinical practice, leaving it to the practice models to be applicable almost anywhere. It is the specificity of context that will differentiate social work clinical practitioners from clinicians in other disciplines. Every profession is known by *what* it can do, but existing practice models can only—and should only—suggest *how* to do it. The public is not really interested in *how* doctors operate, *how* engineers build bridges, or *how* architects design houses; these "how" questions, important as they are, mainly concern internal communications within the professions. Naturally, students of practice and new graduates are always preoccupied with methodology and skills while they are learning their craft. But the professional objectives, focus of attention, special expertise in knowledge and skill with certain kinds of problems are more likely to interest the public and funding sources.

That is the reason I conclude this book about clinical practice with a view toward future investigation into contexts and institutional specificity. One form this can take is research into substantive matters, such as why some unmarried mothers relinquish their babies and others do not. Currently, we seem to be more concerned in our practice research with *how* we work with unmarried mothers toward the decision about their babies. Another form it can take is to move the practitioner in the direction of prevention where one has to learn to recognize social phenomena occurring in their preclinical phases.

Methodology has ruled social work since 1917, and now that we know how to perform, we can learn to use that methodology in context. That is why we have taken pains (and risks) to clarify the ecosystems perspective; for we believe it offers a context within which practice models can be made specific. The task ahead appears to be a conceptual one.

Author Index

Subject Index

The Columbia University School of Social Work publication series, Social Work and Social Issues, is concerned with the implications of social work practice and social welfare policy for solving problems. Each volume is an independent work. The series is intended to contribute to the knowledge base of social work education, to facilitate communication with related disciplines, and to serve as background for public policy discussion. Books in the series are:

Shirley Jenkins, editor. *Social Security in International Perspective.* 1969.

George Brager and Harry Specht. *Community Organizing.* 1973.

Alfred J. Kahn, editor. *Shaping the New Social Work.* 1973.

Shirley Jenkins and Elaine Norman. *Beyond Placement.* 1975.

Deborah Shapiro. *Agencies and Foster Children.* 1975.

David Fanshel and Eugene B. Shinn. *Children in Foster Care.* 1978.

Carol Meyer, editor. *Clinical Social Work in the Eco-Systems Perspective.* 1983.